Contributors include

Tanya Aldred
Mike Atherton
Philippe Auclair
Marcus Berkmann
Rahul Bhattacharya
Lawrence Booth
Stephen Brenkley
Daniel Brettig
Dylan Cleaver
Jonathan Coates
Paul Coupar
Peter Della Penna
Richard Edwards
Matthew Engel
Peter English
Alan Gibson
Richard Gillis
Nagraj Gollapudi
Gideon Haigh
Duncan Hamilton
Alan Hill
Richard Hobson
Nick Hoult
Rabeed Imam
Steve James
Emma John
Patrick Kidd
Will Luke
Neil Manthorp
Vic Marks
Robin Martin-Jenkins
Andrew McGlashan
Leo McKinstry
Andrew Miller
Kevin Mitchell
Fazeer Mohammed
Sidharth Monga
Alex Moorblack
Gavin Mortimer
Andy Nash
Paul Newman
Mark Nicholas
Julian Norridge
Sam Peters
Sam Pilger
Sarah Potter
Dileep Premachandran
Siddarth Ravindran
Peter Roebuck
Christian Ryan
Osman Samiuddin
Rob Smyth
Andy Stockhausen
Ivo Tennant
Sharda Ugra
Telford Vice
Mark Wallace
John Woodcock

CRICKET 2010

The story of the year as told by *The Wisden Cricketer*

Staff
Editor
Edward Craig

Sub-editor
Jeremy Alexander

Designer
Zamir Walimohamed

Pre-press production
James Bunce

Photography
Patrick Eagar
Getty Images

Where to find us
Editorial, advertising and
administration
The Wisden Cricketer, 2nd Floor,
123 Buckingham Palace Road,
London SW1W 9SL
tel 020 7705 4911
email twc@wisdencricketer.com

From the pages of
the**wisden**
cricketer

The best of times, the worst of times

WELCOME to *The Wisden Cricketer*'s inaugural annual *Cricket 2010*, a digested record of the magazine's content over the last 12 months.

It has been a year of success for the England team – they have won the World Twenty20 in the Caribbean, defeated Pakistan and Bangladesh in Test series and have moved calmly into a post-Flintoff era. The magazine interviewed all the leading characters: KP, Andrew Strauss, Graeme Swann, Eoin Morgan and Flintoff himself.

But it has also been a year of fixture confusion and congestion; the curse of match-fixing re-emerged; Pakistan mixed on-field brilliance with off-field ineptitude; Lalit Modi – the energy behind the IPL – found himself under investigation from the law; and the first signs of Twenty20 fatigue began to show.

In among such boardroom battling there have been some great matches and series – Morne Morkel and Dale Steyn provided an authentic, quick, opening bowling partnership for South Africa; Virender Sehwag took his helicopter-style stroke-play to new levels; the Australians, short on the class players of the last decade, still managed to produce skilful and polished performers.

And the happiest story of the year has been Afghanistan's emergence – a country in need of hope finding it in cricket, as their national side fought its way through various world leagues and divisions to qualify for the World Twenty20.

Closer to home the team of the season ended trophy-less – Somerset came second in each of the three domestic competitions. And there were a few farewells: David Shepherd and Alec Bedser, giant characters in the rich tapestry of the sport who gave so much. *TWC* celebrated their lives in the magazine and remembers them again here.

Cricket 2010 will stir memories of all that has taken place in the past 12 months and, as it is taken from the pages of the magazine, it is also an excellent read. Enjoy.

Edward Craig
Editor, *Cricket 2010* & deputy editor, *The Wisden Cricketer*

If you have enjoyed *Cricket 2010* and do not already subscribe to *The Wisden Cricketer*, visit www.wisdencricketer.com to subscribe. The magazine is published monthly and a year's subscription costs £39.99.

Contents

A year in an instant

It's been 12 months of great games and depressing off-field goings-on. It was never dull. By **Edward Craig**

September 2009

England suffer a severe and instant Ashes hangover with a 6-1 thrashing in a one-day series against Australia **p16**. Andrew Flintoff retires from Test cricket announcing he's available for hire to any Twenty20 side in any part of the world, or to any brand in fact, who needs a simple lad from Preston who's moved to Dubai for tax reasons **p14**. All this pending recovery from more knee surgery… Ireland give England a fright in a one-dayer. Durham wrap up their second successive County Championship, continuing to supply England with a stream of world-class quick bowlers. The Champions Trophy in South Africa and England expects its usual diet of under-performing players and misfiring tactics. Much to everyone's surprise, England light up the tournament with aggressive batting and some huge hitting. It's still a bit hit-and-miss and they lose to Australia in the semi-finals – but there are clear signs of a one-day corner being turned **p16**. And they do better than hosts South Africa who fail to qualify for the knock-out stages, blaming it on Andrew Strauss not allowing Graeme Smith a runner when he's a bit tired. Stuart Broad pulls a buttock muscle and England get attacked by locusts.

October

Australia smash New Zealand in the Champions Trophy final with Shane Watson scoring his second hundred in a row. Then Peter Siddle embarks on his 324th flight to his 3,563th hotel room in 16 months when he flies to represent Victoria in the Champions League – the inaugural, international, club Twenty20 competition in India **p40**. Siddle ended his travels flying home injured and missed eight months' cricket. But players seemed to have stopped moaning about the schedule with so many million-dollar tournaments to play in. The Champions League, not to be confused with the Champions Trophy, sees Trinidad & Tobago put a smile on everyone's face, Somerset and Sussex look out of their depth, New South Wales being slick and, well, Australian. Brett Lee wins the final – with his batting.

November

India and Australia slug out another one-day series in India. England steal a draw in Twenty20s against South Africa, winning by a Duckworth/Lewis-ed one run in the first game, then failing to make as many as South Africa's first wicket in the second. They continue a one-day renaissance winning a five-match series 2-1 (two abandoned due to rain), despite conceding a record total against South Africa (354) in the game they lose. Paul Collingwood's batting and James Anderson's bowling clinch the series **p17**. Unwatched, New Zealand play Pakistan in the series of the year – quick bowlers and exciting young batsman light up the southern summer **p69**.

December

Sehwag defies statistics, common sense, reality and gravity to pile up 293 against Sri Lanka at Mumbai in 254 balls **p74**. It's an innings of an era – short and loud. India become the No.1 ranked Test side in the world after their 2-0 series win. England then continue to fluctuate in form turning an easy draw into a near defeat at Centurion in the first Test against South Africa **p18**, with Graham Onions hanging on, then deliver a knock-out performance at Durban thanks to Broad and Graeme Swann **p19**. Chris Gayle defies Australia, Sehwag-style, for a bit – but West Indies go down 2-0 **p64**. Meanwhile the Test series of the year finishes as New Zealand draw 1-1 with Pakistan – no one notices.

The year that was: clockwise from top left Andrew Flintoff poses for the cameras; Sachin Tendulkar stops the presses; Eoin Morgan redefines batting; Dale Steyn destroys England; IPL cheerleaders in action; Kevin Pietersen beats the world; Virender Sehwag blasts past Sri Lanka and batting records

January 2010

England continue their trend of getting hammered in Test matches without actually losing **p20** – this time it's Cape Town and Onions again defying yorkers and bouncers. Onions is rewarded for his efforts with a P45, dropped for the decider at Jo'burg, and ultimately finishes the year under the surgeon's knife with a nine-month lay-off. England lose a wicket from the first ball in this last Test and, moaning about a third umpire, get what they deserve from the excellent Morne Morkel and Dale Steyn **p21**. Shahid Afridi bites the ball in a one-day series against Australia and is done for ball tampering. "I was trying to smell it and see how it was feeling," he explains.

February

Strauss decides that Bangladesh is a tour too far – too easy and too difficult – so hands over the captaincy to Alastair Cook **p24**. Australia continue merrily to destroy any opposition on their home soil, West Indies in limited-overs games this time. Sachin Tendulkar scales cricket's Everest, scoring the first one-day double hundred. India play South Africa at Gwalior and he passes the mark from his last ball as India make 401. Indian fans then break the internet **p76**. New Zealand and Australia rack up 428 in a tied T20 match (that's 214 each…). Black Caps win it in the 'super over'. India and South Africa play an entertaining two-Test series in which Hashim Amla refuses to get out and both sides win a match by an innings **p78**. Afghanistan qualify for the World T20 in the year's most heart-warming story **p52**.

March

Cook breathes a sigh of relief when he flies out of Bangladesh after leading England to victory in every game – the three ODIs and two Tests. But it's not easy as England finally take notice of a new world-star in Tamim Iqbal, who drew comparison with Brian Lara. Eoin Morgan guides England to a one-day victory with a hundred of such intensity he doesn't even realise he's passed three figures. KP struggles against left-arm spin. Again. The IPL kicks off – Essex's Graham Napier gets used to warming the Mumbai Indians' bench and Dimitri Mascarenhas turns his ankle for the Rajasthan Royals. He would miss the entire first-class season **p48**. Collingwood finds time to win games for Delhi **p26**.

April

The IPL continues and seems to have no end, no beginning – just one constant morass of noise, DLF maximums, dancing girls and screaming commentators **p58**. Eventually the league is cut in half, where the top four teams play in a knock-out stage – rendering league positions nearly pointless. Chennai win. In the background Pakistan's ex-captain Shoaib Malik tries to marry Sania Mirza, the Indian tennis star, until another Indian woman claims to have already married Malik – by phone. After a quick divorce Malik's nuptials are allowed to continue. Durham kick off the domestic season with a match against MCC – as is tradition – in Abu Dhabi under floodlights using a pink ball – which is not. The Championship also begins – four rounds completed before the end of April in enough sun for the ECB to avoid instant reproach. But the full horror of the fixture list begins to come to light **p94**. News from the IPL that Lalit Modi may appear to be too good to be true **p132**…

May

As journeymen county cricketers shiver Collingwood's England enjoy Caribbean hospitality and success at the World T20 **p28**. Apart from a Duckworth/Lewis defeat against West Indies in Guyana, England look the form team and defeat a fading Australia in the final. The Mike-Hussey powered Aussies had found their way into the final past Pakistan, scoring 34 in the last 12 balls. KP is man of the tournament, Craig Kieswetter and Michael Lumb take many of the plaudits. Morgan **p36** forces his way into the first Test side against Bangladesh. Steven Finn, Middlesex's pet giraffe who made his debut in Bangladesh, enjoys a dream home debut with nine wickets and suddenly England have post-Harmison options. Notts lead the Championship but not by much **p97**.

June

Tamim Iqbal lights up the two Tests against England with dashing hundreds **p25** but that's all Bangladesh can offer as their batting crumbles twice. They didn't get beaten as badly as their last visit back in 2005 is the only, limp defence. County cricket switches into Twenty20 mode – after the first game, Marcus Trescothick **p92** says: "One down, 15 to go." This is a summer of fixtures chaos and density that will confuse and frustrate fans and players **p104**. To everyone's surprise Australia arrive to play a one-day series against England. To everyone's delight they comfortably lose the first three games (and the series). Then their class bites back – 3-2 is the final scoreline **p29**. Back in India Lalit Modi's world appears to collapse around him **p58**.

July

Not since 1912 has England hosted neutral Test cricket and, despite two wonderful matches where ball dominates bat, no one really turns up to watch. Mohammad Amir and Mohammad Asif bowl spectacularly throughout. In the first game the captain, Shahid Afridi, provides the maddest and best moment making 31 off 15 balls as part of a backs-to-the-wall Pakistan recovery. He quits the captaincy and Test cricket after the game. Salman Butt takes over and to make the home-neutrals feel a bit better, Australia are rolled for 88 at Headingley and lose **p83**. England Under-19 captain Azeem Rafiq blows hot and blue on Twitter, earning him a ban and a fine, and Muttiah Muralitharan takes his 800th Test wicket with his last ball at Galle against India **p114**.

August

Somerset lose the Twenty20 final to Hampshire **p106**, they did enough to win it, then didn't know the laws about running out runners. It's all a bit farcical and sums up the entire competition. It's taken till the start of August but England's flagship summer series kicks off with a strong display at Trent Bridge – Morgan scores a first

Test hundred, otherwise England's batting looks brittle but the ball swings for Anderson, Amir and Asif – 2010 is the year the bowler gets his revenge **p32**. In the second Test Pakistan's batting looks even worse – they win the toss, bat and are 37 for 6 at lunch – a mysterious decision **p33**. They are all out for 72 and lose the game comfortably, Anderson remains unplayable (he took 11 wickets in the first Test). Matt Prior and Jonathan Trott are the only England bowlers showing form. Strauss **p12** struggles. Mohammad Yousuf is recruited out of retirement for the third game at The Oval, immediately providing calm and a true test for England's bowlers – but it's really the batsmen who fail, although Cook does enough to save his immediate Test future **p34**. So England lead 2-1 heading to the final Test at Lord's, fall to 102 for 7 before Trott and Broad play innings that no one will ever forget **p35** … until they bought the *News of the World* that Sunday. The spot-fixing allegations cast a shadow over the whole series. England complete a routine victory in a fractured atmosphere – Asif, Butt and the player of the series, Mohammad Amir, who has warmed a cold late summer, are implicated. That Sunday everything changed **p110**.

And finally …

All county competitions end the same way – with Somerset coming second **p106**. It's a nail-biting end to the Championship with Nottinghamshire stealing the final bonus point they need in the final session of the final game to break Somerset hearts. Somerset retain their Championship-less history. Two days later Ian Bell's class relegates Somerset to their third runners-up spot in the final of the CB40. In the background a bad-tempered one-day series between England and Pakistan is played with spot-fixing allegations flying around and detracting from a fantastic, on-field, contest.

Edward Craig is deputy editor of *The Wisden Cricketer*

Highs and lows: clockwise from top left Tamim Iqbal hits out; James Anderson swings it both ways; Andre Adams wins Notts the Championship; Alastair Cook celebrates his Oval hundred with Jonathan Trott; Ricky Ponting's Australia lose to England; Shahid Afridi loses it at Lord's

HAVE YOU BEEN NOBBLED BY A BETTING SYNDICATE OR ARE YOU JUST HOPELESS?

ENGLAND'S

YEAR

It was, Paul Collingwood said, the time of his life. "I'm living the dream," he told us after lifting the World Twenty20 in Barbados in May, England's first global title.

The upturn in England's limited-overs fortunes was one of the great stories of an impressive year. Yet none of this seemed possible back in late summer 2009 when England received the harshest of post-Ashes reality checks, losing 6-1 to Australia in the one-dayers that followed the Tests. When they got revenge in mid-summer 2010 with a 3-2 series victory talk turned to the possibility of England having a tilt at the World Cup.

An unexpected appearance in the Champions Trophy semi-final – losing again to Australia – was followed by an equally improbable series win in South Africa, a result that whetted the appetite for the subsequent four-Test series.

That England, pulverised by the pace of Dale Steyn and Morne Morkel, clung on grimly in two Tests did not undermine the quality of a 1-1 draw against a leading Test nation.

There was concern, though, about Kevin Pietersen, who was off colour in South Africa and, despite fleeting glimpses of his best through the year, including a man-of-the-tournament performance in the World Twenty20, he finished the summer out of the one-day side and uncertain of himself.

Graeme Swann defied the presumptions that orthodox finger-spin was dead, taking seven Test five-wicket hauls in a 10-month period that yielded 65 wickets at 23, including 22 in four summer Tests against Pakistan.

Back-to-back Test series victories over Bangladesh proved little other than to offer Alastair Cook some captaincy practice and to announce the arrivals of Steve Finn and Eoin Morgan, who took immediate advantage of an injury to Ian Bell by scoring his maiden Test hundred in only his third Test at Trent Bridge against Pakistan.

Despite the batsmen's travails against Pakistan's stellar new-ball attack and the match-fixing scandal that tainted the end of the series, the post-Flintoff mood around England cricket was of an emerging team in rude health relishing, rather than dreading, their upcoming tour down under. ◪

John Stern is the editor of *The Wisden Cricketer*

Contents

England stars: Newman's June cartoon celebrates the team's diversity ...

Victors at last: England **left** celebrate winning their first global event – the World T20 – with captain Paul Collingwood holding the trophy

Taking the lead

Andrew Strauss thought he would never play for England again, let alone captain them. In a post-Ashes glow in October 2009, he spoke to **Sam Pilger**

Strauss's career stats *at August 31, 2010*

	M	R	HS	AVGE	SR	100s	50s
Tests	77	5777	177	**43.11**	50.13	18	21
ODIs	108	3375	154	**34.09**	78.83	4	22
T20Is	4	73	33	**18.25**	114.06	0	0

It was at the start of 2008, in a sparse and basic hotel room in the New Zealand country town of Palmerston North, a place John Cleese had once said anyone not brave enough to commit suicide should visit, that Andrew Strauss believes he has never felt lower.

After being cast aside by England his plan to resurrect his Test career by playing cricket on the other side of the world (for Northern Districts) had not been working. He was utterly miserable, struggling to sleep and questioning whether he even wanted to play for England again.

"I had been out of form for a long time and kept thinking, 'What am I doing this for?' I was away from my family and nothing was happening, I was banging my head against a wall," he reflects.

"I really began questioning my motivation and thinking, 'Should I bother to try to get back into the England team?' because I wasn't sure I actually missed playing for England and I was preparing myself to never play for them again.

"The catalyst for everything was actually the belief that it wasn't going to happen, I had almost given up, I told myself to give myself a break and enjoy what I expected to be my last innings for England [at Napier against New Zealand. Strauss made 173]. I let go of all the pressure and it then became so much clearer, the power of thinking positively about yourself, and from that moment everything began to change for me."

Only 17 months after suffering the overwhelming loneliness and self-doubt Strauss found himself at The Oval lifting the Ashes, as captain, leading scorer and man of the series, bathed in sunshine and surrounded by his admiring team-mates.

"As I went up to pick up the urn I remember thinking to myself, 'Can you believe it? Here I am, this has actually happened.' You dare to dream but here I was reaching forward for it."

Since that innings at Napier Strauss has been reborn as a batsman and scored more Test runs (1,769) and more centuries (seven) than anyone in the world.

Strauss's story is England's story; together they made the same journey from despair to redemption and managed to triumph in a seemingly impossible short period of time.

England's Ashes success was born in Strauss' own deeply personal experience, which he used as a model to inspire his players, an ostensibly ordinary group, to find something within, to play above themselves and overcome the then leading Test side in the world.

At the start of 2009 amid the smouldering wreckage of Kevin Pietersen's failed coup attempt over Peter Moores, Strauss had to step over the bodies and tidy up the mess. "I knew it was bad but I didn't know it was that intense. There was an undercurrent [between Kevin and Peter], you could sense something. When there are cracks in the relationship at the top between captain and coach it feeds down to the rest of the team.

"I still maintain he did what he thought was right for England. It wasn't about him. It was his genuine belief that things needed to change. I never held it

66 I was thinking: 'Should I bother to try to get back into the England team?' 99

against Kevin for trying to change things but it wasn't pleasant to be around."

Unable to exorcise this bad feeling immediately, the Strauss era would get off to a horrible start by losing to West Indies by an innings and 23 runs at Kingston, after being bowled out for 51 in their second innings. It left Strauss "disconsolate and depressed".

It was at a team meeting after this humiliation when Strauss believes his captaincy properly began. "It was the first time that the players opened up and really spoke about how they were feeling, their insecurities and what they felt about their team-mates. Andy Flower did an amazing job. I feel that was the breakthrough and after that moment things went far better.

"As a captain I was concerned going into the Ashes, it was a step into the unknown for me. I had always been incredibly impressed with how Michael Vaughan had been in 2005, the poise he had shown. I was hopeful I could do something similar but I didn't really know, so it came as a nice surprise."

Throughout the summer Strauss led by example, scoring 474 runs, over 200 more than England's second-highest scorer, Matt Prior, and overall managed that rare trick even Vaughan could not pull off of improving as a batsman with the captaincy. "As much as you can, look after your own game; that helps everything."

So far Strauss's success as a leader has been rooted in his ability to radiate a calm authority to his players: "I have always believed for players to respond you need to do three things: lead by example, don't ask anything you wouldn't do yourself, and be honest. If you exhibit those simple traits, people will want to help you succeed.

"Looking back, I might have been bolder at times, and even before the Ashes I wouldn't have declared like that in Antigua again. I know now you have to be more bold if you want to take wickets."

Strauss has banished the fraught, self-doubting figure of New Zealand and grown into a captain of substance. "I have far better mechanisms to deal with everything," he says. He talks about an inner calm and a sense of tranquillity in his life and, especially when he bats, refusing to allow problems to affect him. "Now I replace negative thoughts with positive ones. I know it isn't rocket science but, if you feel things getting on top of you, the idea is to think about anything that makes you happy, like family, your golf swing, your bank balance ... "

He stops and smiles before adding, "I suppose after this summer I now have the best thing of all in the memory bank if I ever need to use it in the future: winning the Ashes." *The Wisden Cricketer, December 2009*

Sam Pilger is a freelance sports writer

Job done: clobbered but happy with the urn

"Would I ever turn down

The three chapters

Flintoff's best Test cricket was a tasty treat in the middle of a slightly stale sandwich

	RUNS	AVGE	100s	WKTS	AVGE	5WI	S/R
First 29 Tests (Jul '98-Dec '03)	1209	25.72	2	52	45.55	0	94.7
Next 33 Tests (Jan '04-Jun '06)	1918	39.95	3	134	25.80	2	50.8
Last 17 Tests (Jul '06-Aug '09)	718	27.61	0	40	39.57	1	80.2
Career (79 Tests)	3845	31.77	5	226	32.78	3	66.1

Table from Cricinfo.com

As Andrew Flintoff looked ahead to life as the first freelance cricketer, he told **Sam Pilger** it was only playing for England that kept him going and why bungee-jumping is not for him

When the captains walked out for the toss at Centurion Park on the morning of the first South Africa-England Test they were not watched from the balcony by England's talismanic allrounder. Instead Andrew Flintoff expected to be more than 4,000 miles away in Dubai, watching on a television fixed to a gym wall.

"I'm really not looking forward to that precise moment, that's going to be horrible," Flintoff says with a grimace. "Until then I can be in denial, I can avoid it, but when that happens I think the penny will finally drop and I will know a big part of my life has gone forever."

The day after England won the Ashes Flintoff had a knee operation. Two weeks

of sitting down with his leg in a machine for eight hours a day followed. "That gave me the time to reflect on my Test career and I tried to come to terms with the fact that I'm not going to do it ever again. I couldn't accept it and the truth is that even now I don't think it has sunk in," he says. "I can't get used to talking about my Test career in the past tense."

Nearly four months after Flintoff brought his Test career to a premature end at The Oval aged 31 he is a strange mixture of emotions, regularly veering between sadness and excitement.

For all the bravado and bold talk about new beginnings, he speaks about no longer being a Test player in a mournful tone, as if it were a bereavement. "If I had my way, I would still be in the Test side,"

he says. "I would go to South Africa and then to Australia next year but sadly that isn't an option for me."

Yet at the same time there is also a real excitement about the immediate future and knowing that the burden of Test cricket and the punishment it inflicted on his body has been lifted. "I only have a few years left in cricket and I want to make the most of them," he says. "I want to do things that excite me and this new life does that."

It was the persistent injuries that persuaded Flintoff to end his Test career. Did he ever consider giving his body a complete rest and retiring from all forms of the game? "No, not unless the surgeon had told me there was nothing he could do for me. I was determined to carry on playing. There is always a chance I might never play again. I'll be honest, there is that element of doubt at the back of my mind but, if I thought like that, I wouldn't bother going to the gym. The surgeon says the chances of playing again are good."

If the surgeon is correct, Flintoff expects to begin his new role as a freelance one-day and Twenty20 specialist next spring. "I want to play for England and Lancashire, I've got my contract with Chennai and now I have the opportunity to play around the world as well," he says. "I'm keen to play in Australia. When I'm fit again I would love to play in their Big Bash Twenty20 competition."

So can Flintoff completely rule out, if fit and selected, that he would ever turn down playing for England? "Would I heck, no. I would never turn down England ... If I didn't think I was going to play for England again, I would not have had this latest operation, no way. It is all about playing for England.

"I don't think other players will follow what I've done. There is a real misconception at the moment, people go on about the riches involved in Twenty20 cricket but you earn your reputation playing Test cricket."

The decision to go freelance provides him with time to devote to the business that is simply being Andrew Flintoff; there will be more days for sponsors, more opportunities to boost off-field earnings which, according to *Forbes,* have already made him the fifth wealthiest cricketer in the world with annual earnings of £2.5m. "I have seen cricketers come to the end of their careers and they have got nothing to do but now I can explore other areas for later in my life," says Flintoff.

What this actually means remains vague. He talks about "TV work" and business ventures and his agent, Andrew Chandler, said one reason for turning down an England contract was so he could take part in a television show where he would do a bungee-jump, though Flintoff denies this: "Nah, I can't imagine me bungee-jumping, can you? That stuff is further down the line, I'm not going to play cricket forever and there have been opportunities to do lots of other things."

The public have always been drawn to Flintoff's down-to-earth personality as much as his on-field heroics. He plays up the wide-eyed 'big lad from Preston' caricature but is smarter than that.

In recent years he has not, of course, exercised this smartness when it comes to alcohol. There was the infamous drunken pedalo incident at the World Cup in the Caribbean in 2007 that saw him banned for a game and stripped of the one-day vice-captaincy. And before that on the 2006-07 tour of Australia Flintoff had turned up to an England training session smelling of alcohol. He admits to turning to drink as "a release" to deal with the self-doubt and relentless embarrassment as he captained England to a 5-0 defeat in the Ashes.

He has acknowledged this drinking might have had an adverse impact on England sides but denies he is an alcoholic. But now, with his Test retirement and his career winding down, could drinking become a greater problem? "No, it wouldn't happen again," he says quickly. "I'm a different person, I have a different perspective on the game now, I'm enjoying it now. Before, it all built up so much and the pressure got to me.

"The best thing about this stage of my career is I have never felt better mentally. I'm playing on now just to enjoy it. I have had my low moments and lost some enjoyment but, with the injuries I've had, I know it can't get any worse, the fear of failure has gone ... I feel brilliant."

Does this mean Flintoff could even recapture his best form? "I'm not sure I have even played my best yet, so now I am having this break I think I have got the chance to get better as a player. I am not going to just get by. I genuinely think I can now play my best ever cricket."

Flintoff could not have stage-managed a better Test exit at The Oval; holding the Ashes and saluted by a full house. He now plans a similarly impressive encore when he retires fully. "The best way to finish now would be to win the 2011 World Cup, and then the one in 2015. That would be pretty good. Why not?" he laughs. ∎

The Wisden Cricketer, January 2010

Sam Pilger is a freelance sports writer

Farewell Fred: Flintoff at The Oval, 2009

Losing the will to watch

England were hopeless and thumped but did anyone care? By Richard Hobson

MIDWAY through the NatWest Series an online poll conducted by *The Guardian* asked readers whether anyone cared about these one-day games. Seventy-one percent said no, a figure that would surely have risen as England's fortunes slipped in the opposite direction.

From the day before the first contest, when Owais 'bite yer legs' Shah crocked Joe Denly with a knee-high tackle during a game of football, to the penultimate match at Trent Bridge, a team which had achieved its summer objective of winning the Ashes lurched from one setback to the next.

As early as the second game Cricinfo used the phrase "groundhog day" to describe defeat and Andrew Strauss

began to struggle for fresh words after each successive loss. "The batsmen at some stage will come right," said the captain, in Micawber-esque mood at 4-0 down. Wisely he did not add the words "in this series". They grew used to heavy defeat in India last winter when the early return home after terrorist attacks in Mumbai spared them a 7-0 whitewash. But at least then they could cite unfamiliar conditions and the sheer brilliance of Yuvraj Singh, Virender Sehwag and Mahendra Singh Dhoni. Australia, in contrast, were flattered.

England lacked equivalents of Brett Lee and Mitchell Johnson to take wickets. Lee's fast swinging yorkers at Lord's were nothing less than awesome.

Shah was a disappointment. In the absence of Kevin Pietersen and Andrew Flintoff he should have viewed himself as the senior batsman rather than a marginal choice. But he caused as many problems as he solved with nervous running, a sympton of low confidence.

Ashes-winning captain and England's leading run-scorer in the series, poor Strauss must have wondered why he deserved the booing that followed him on to the podium at 6-0 down. Strauss described it as "a bit of a horror show". Only a bit?

The Wisden Cricketer, November 2009

Richard Hobson is deputy cricket correspondent of *The Times*

Scores

1st ODI Sept 4, T Oval
♀ **Aus 260-5** in 50 ov;
†**Eng 256-8** in 50 ov. Aus won by 4 runs.

2nd ODI Sept 6, Lord's
Aus 249-8 in 50 ov; †**Eng 210** in 46.1 ov. Aus won by 39 runs.

3rd ODI Sept 9, R Bowl
♀ †**Eng 228-9** in 50 ov;
Aus 230-4 in 48.3 ov. Aus won by 6 wkts.

4th ODI Sept 12, Lord's
†**Eng 220** in 46.3 ov; **Aus 221-3** in 43.4 ov. Aus won by 7 wkts.

5th ODI Sept 15, T Bge
♀ †**Eng 299** in 50 ov;
Aus 302-6 in 48.2 ov. Aus won by 4 wkts.

6th ODI Sept 17, T Bge
♀ †**Aus 296-8** in 50 ov;
Eng 185 in 41 ov. Aus won by 111 runs.

7th ODI Sept 20, C-le-St
Aus 176 in 45.5 ov; †**Eng 177-6** in 40 ov. **Eng won by 4 wkts.**

Aus won series 6-1

Normal service resumed

The Champions Trophy was full of surprises, then Australia won. Telford Vice writes

Friday September 25
Another nation in another hemisphere starts to forget "6-1" as England beat Sri Lanka on another environmentally liberated Wanderers pitch. Everything goes right for England, from the toss to James Anderson, Graham Onions and Stuart Broad to Owais Shah, Paul Collingwood and Eoin Morgan knocking off the target of 213.

Sunday September 27
South Africa lose to revitalised England. The locals make way too much of Andrew Strauss refusing the cramping centurion Graeme Smith a runner.

Wednesday Sept 30
The semi-finals are decided: England v

Australia at Centurion, and New Zealand v Pakistan at The Wanderers. India are denied a place in the final four by a scrambled bye off the last ball to get Australia over the line against Pakistan.

Friday October 2
England's batting was bog standard when it had the chance to be grand on a pitch that was gagging for it. There was no panic from the Australians in the field and at the crease, where Ricky Ponting and Shane Watson score unbeaten hundreds to put Australia in the final.

Monday October 5
The final. Can't I have dinner with my mother-in-law instead? It's hard knowing the Aussies are going to win another

trophy and it becomes even harder to know this when Vettori pulls out with a hamstring problem. All goes to plan as Australia hardly break sweat and win.

The Wisden Cricketer, December 2009

Telford Vice is a freelance cricket writer

Blazer of glory: Australia victorious

Scores

1st semi-final Oct 2 Centurion ♀ †**Eng 257** in 47.4 ov (TT Bresnan 80, LJ Wright 48; PM Siddle 3-55); **Aus 258-1** in 41.5 ov (SR Watson 136*, RT Ponting 111*). **Aus won by 9 wkts.** *MoM: Watson 8.4-1-35-2; 132b, 10x4, 7x6.*

2nd semi-final Oct 3 Jo'burg ♀ †**Pak 233-9** in 50 ov (Umar Akmal 55, Mohammad Yousuf 45; IG Butler 4-44; DL Vettori 3-43); **NZ 234-5** in 47.5 ov (GD Elliott 75*, Vettori 41). **NZ won by 5 wkts.** *MoM: Vettori 10-2-43-3; 42b, 3x4.*

Final Oct 5 Centurion ♀ †**NZ 200-9** in 50 ov (MJ Guptill 40; NM Hauritz 3-37); **Aus 206-4** in 45.2 ov (Watson 105*, CL White 62; KD Mills 3-27). **Aus won by 4 wkts.** *MoM: Watson 129b, 10x4, 4x6.*

Australia won Champions Trophy
Man of tournament: Ricky Ponting (A)

SOUTH AFRICA v ENGLAND two Twenty20 matches and five ODIs

Terrific win, honestly

Never mind wash-outs, England showed stand-out logic, says **Richard Hobson**

ENGLAND had spent so long trying to convince themselves and everyone else that they were really a good one-day side in the face of poor results that they did not seem to know how to take a genuinely exciting success. Andrew Strauss looked as if he wanted to scream from the rafters. But honesty and pragmatism had the better of him.

No side bar Australia (twice) had previously beaten South Africa in a bilateral series on their home soil and that two of the five games were washed out could not detract from England's win this time. It left Strauss's side fifth in the ICC one-day rankings, two places behind their opponents.

South Africa batted first in all three games, so England were not tested in setting a total. They bowled well at Centurion and Port Elizabeth but were slain at Cape Town where South Africa posted the highest total, 354 for 6, in one-day games between the sides. England could not answer that.

But their self-styled team without stars had a better balance and Paul Collingwood overtook Alec Stewart's mark of 170 ODI appearances in style at Centurion with a hundred, two wickets and a screaming catch. Even with time to fill through the rain breaks the absence of Andrew Flintoff was barely mentioned.

Strikingly positive
There is still no Gayle, Sehwag or Gilchrist to attack the new ball but the top five overall was as versatile and positive as anything England have fielded in memory. Strauss is taking a lead, Collingwood has shown that old dogs can master new tricks if they work hard enough and Eoin Morgan, described by James Anderson as a genius, has a stroke for every occasion.

Whether or not Strauss would be in the side but for the captaincy is

irrelevant. He and Andy Flower must continue to work together across the two main formats. His one-day average now (32.06) is as close as makes no difference to the figure when he was dropped in 2007 (31.98).

But he is a more effective player, hitting straighter more cleanly and more often. As he put it himself, shots that once seemed risky are not all that risky after all. It is just having the confidence to play them.

Butt of the bowling
The hunt for that elusive mystery bowler is over. Strauss admitted that he is just not there. So forget the rubber-fingered spinner with a googly or a doosra, or the snarling man with blinding pace who snaps poles in mid-innings. England reverted to the tried and not always trusted method of taking wickets by creating pressure through economy.

66 The absence of Flintoff was barely mentioned 99

Top man: Collingwood at Centurion

This may be bad news for Adil Rashid, relegated after conceding four sixes in his one Twenty20 over and then 27 runs from three overs in the first 50-over contest. It is better for his Yorkshire team-mate Tim Bresnan, whose spell at Port Elizabeth earned wickets for Anderson at the other end.

Bresnan will be a litmus test of where England go from here. He lacks the cutting edge to turn a moderate side into a good one but, with more dynamic players around him, his supporting role can add value. If Bresnan is still around by the World Cup, England will be either serious contenders or struggling.

Simulation benefits
England set great stall by 'middle' practices, different stages of matches simulated on a full-size playing area. They worked on powerplay and tip-and-run scenarios, for example. In one case a regular fall of wickets prompted an onlooker to suggest they were reproducing a World Cup 2007 scenario.

They were popular – which is important – and tested batting, bowling and fielding at the same time. Flower noted that squad members playing among themselves created pressure because nobody wanted to look a fool to peers. With four days between Sunday and Friday matches, a day so filled proved a day well spent.

There was much talk about improved fielding. Owais Shah's rather laboured work cost him his place after the Champions Trophy. But England (like South Africa) did not execute a single run-out in the series and dropped as many as five catches at Centurion. The fielding coach, Richard Halsall, still has work to do. *The Wisden Cricketer, January 2010*

Richard Hobson is deputy cricket correspondent of *The Times*

Scores

1st T20I Nov 13, Jo'burg ♀ ⚬ **Eng 202-6** in 20 ov (EJG Morgan 85*, PD Collingwood 57, IJL Trott 33); †**SA 127-3** in 13 ov (LL Bosman 58, GC Smith 41). **Eng won by 1 run D/L method.** *MoM: Morgan 45b, 7x4, 5x6.*

2nd T20I Nov 15, Centurion †**SA 241-6** in 20 ov (Bosman 94, Smith 88); **Eng 157-8** in 20 ov (Trott 51). **SA won by 84 runs.** *MoM: Bosman 45b, 5x4, 9x6.*

Series drawn 1-1

1st ODI Nov 20, Jo'burg ♀ ⚬ **Match abandoned without a ball bowled.**

2nd ODI Nov 22, Centurion **SA 250-9** in 50 ov (AN Petersen 64, HH Amla 57, JP Duminy 41; JM Anderson 3-60); †**Eng 252-3** in 46 ov (PD Collingwood 105*, IJL Trott 87). **Eng won by 7 wkts.** *MoM: Collingwood 6-0-25-2; 110b, 7x4, 2x6.*

3rd ODI Nov 27, Cape Town ♀ †**SA 354-6** in 50 ov (AB de Villiers 121, Amla 86, GC Smith 54, Petersen 51; SCJ Broad 4-71); **Eng 242** in 41.3 ov (Collingwood 86, KP Pietersen 45; WD Parnell 5-48). **SA won by 112 runs.** *MoM: de Villiers below 85b, 14x4.*

4th ODI Nov 29, Port Elizabeth †**SA 119** in 36.5 ov (Petersen 51; Anderson 5-23); **Eng 121-3** in 31.2 ov (Trott 52*). **Eng won by 7 wkts.** *MoM: Anderson 10-3-23-5.*

5th ODI Dec 4, Durban ♀ ⚬ **Match abandoned without a ball bowled.**

England won the series 2-1

Man of the series: Paul Collingwood

The history repeating boys

THE ONLY thing missing was Monty Panesar. Other than him – and he was only 30 miles away in Johannesburg playing for the Highveld Lions – all the ingredients from England's unlikely rearguard action at Cardiff in the first Ashes Test last July were present in 'Great Escape: the sequel.'

England's nail-biting survival at Centurion in the first Test of their South African series was a carbon-copy of Cardiff, with the last-wicket pair required to hold on for dear life. Here Graham Onions and Paul Collingwood survived 19 balls where Panesar and Jimmy Anderson held firm for 69 in Wales.

Where the two gripping finales differed was in the lead-up. England were expected to lose to Australia as seven wickets were down at tea. This time they looked to be cruising to a draw until, 10 minutes after tea, Kevin Pietersen became their fourth second-innings victim after a comical run-out that ended a fine stand of 145 with Jonathan Trott.

Top spinner: Swann celebrates

Tale of the toss

Nasser Hussain has never been allowed to forget Brisbane 2002-03, when he inserted Australia in the first Test of the Ashes and paid a heavy price. And Ricky Ponting will forever be haunted by his arrogance in putting England into bat at Edgbaston in 2005 despite having just lost his star fast bowler Glenn McGrath.

Andrew Strauss only narrowly avoided joining those two in the tossing hall of infamy when his decision to insert South Africa backfired because of his bowlers' failure to make the most of a greenish first-day pitch.

In truth it was a 50-50 call. The day before the match the surface was very green and very wet, the result of rain that had fallen on the highveld for weeks, and the statistics told England that the majority who win the toss at Centurion bowl first, usually with productive results.

The reality was that the sun that returned on day one and lasted throughout the match quickly dried out the pitch and negated any tangible benefits in Strauss continuing his pleasing habit of winning tosses.

Far more pertinent was England's decision to go in with four bowlers instead of the five that won them the Ashes – admittedly with a certain A Flintoff to balance the side both times. England's conservatism, however, was widely criticised before the match.

Spin is the king

The last thing anyone expected was that the two frontline spinners involved – England's Graeme Swann and South Africa's Paul Harris – would play such a dominant first-innings role on such a seamer friendly surface. There was even talk, at nets before the game, that the hosts might entrust spin to JP Duminy, in a country where slow bowlers have rarely prospered, and go in with an all-seam attack. If the late recurrence of injury to Dale Steyn put paid to that, then South

Africa will be truly grateful as Harris, ranked ninth in the world, again surpassed expectations with 5 for 123.

That was not before Swann, culminating a highly productive first year of Test cricket with a man-of-the-match performance, had taken five wickets of his own as South Africa crawled along to 418 off 153.2 overs. Strauss was partially let off by South Africa scoring at 2.72 an over rather than a more modern rate.

The final word

Thanks to Swann England's deficit was only 62. But that was extended to 363 by the time of Smith's declaration on the fourth evening due to a century from Hashim Amla and the refusal of the pitch to misbehave unless you had a new ball.

With Pietersen and Trott batting comfortably and stylishly on the final afternoon, there seemed little danger until the second new ball was taken. The impressive debutant Friedel de Wet – a clone of Steyn apart from a skip in his run-up – ended Trott's five-hour vigil with a brute and five wickets tumbled for 23 runs in 14.2 overs as South Africa moved dramatically towards victory.

That they did not achieve it was down to the reliability and temperament of Collingwood, repeating his Cardiff resistance, and Onions. The decisive moment in the denouement came when Smith inexplicably took off de Wet for the final over and threw the ball to Makhaya Ntini, a highly significant cricketer making his 100th Test appearance but South Africa's least impressive bowler throughout. Only a fourth-ball grubber came anywhere near to troubling Onions, who had been sentenced to face the final over by a naïve piece of running from Collingwood in the penultimate over.

The Wisden Cricketer, February 2010

Paul Newman is cricket correspondent of the *Daily Mail*

Scores

1st Test Dec 16-20, Centurion **SA 418** (JH Kallis 120, JP Duminy 56; GP Swann 5-110) **and 301-7 dec** (HH Amla 100, AB de Villiers 64, MV Boucher 63*; JM Anderson 4-73); **†Eng 356** (Swann 85, PD Collingwood 50; PL Harris 5-123) **and 228-9** (KP Pietersen 81, IJL Trott 69; F de Wet 4-55). **Match drawn.** MoM: Swann 85 and 72.2-13-201-5

Headlines

Day One
Daily Mail

HAS HE TOSSED IT ASIDE?

Day Two
The Guardian

Strauss steadies England after Ntini's storm blows itself out

Day Three
Daily Telegraph

Swashbuckling Swann gives England glimmer of hope

Day Four
Sunday Times

ENGLAND FIGHT FOR SURVIVAL

Day Five
The Guardian

England tumble in late chaos but save their skin with Onions

Second-innings sweep: Amla on his way to 100

SOUTH AFRICA v ENGLAND 2nd Test Durban by **Andrew McGlashan**

From one extreme to the other

ENGLAND rarely produced a dull year during the Noughties but 2009 was extraordinary even by their standards. It started with the dual demise of captain and coach, quickly included a collapse for 51 all out, transformed into regaining the Ashes and was closed out with only their fourth overseas victory in four years.

They had hung on at Centurion for a draw that should have been comfortable and South Africa had not been shy at pointing out weaknesses. However, Andrew Strauss and Andy Flower remained calm and in the manner that has become their trademark backed their team steadfastly. They were rewarded with a performance that became ever more clinical and a fourth-afternoon bowling display from Graeme Swann and Stuart Broad which secured victory in the blink of an eye.

Steady does it
Yet before England's bowlers had ignited their charge the Test moved along on a slow burn. Both sides continued to feel each other out and South Africa's first-innings 343 was enough to be unsure which way the match would go. It could have been more but Swann removed the obdurate Jacques Kallis and Graeme Smith contrived to be run out. Dale Steyn stole South Africa some momentum with a breezy 47 but the compliment was repaid at once by Strauss who produced more than a passing resemblance to Virender Sehwag during a 49-ball half century.

Strauss had gone before the end of the second day, beaten by the impressive Morne Morkel, but somehow an out-of-form Alastair Cook survived. Cook was under intense pressure coming into the match, having scored two Test hundreds in two years and gone eight innings without a fifty. Talk of England captaincy was leading to suggestions that life was a little too cushy.

His response was a century of little glamour but huge guts, his 10th in Tests – two days after his 25th birthday – and the most valuable since his debut hundred at Nagpur in 2006.

Barely a single shot from the innings was memorable but that did not matter a jot to Cook or England. He ground South Africa down on a third day which showed up a home attack that included two bowlers – Steyn and Kallis – still recovering from injury and another, Makhaya Ntini, who was a shadow. Ntini would not see out the series.

Bell's career-saver
Cook had not been the only batsman looking over his shoulder. Ian Bell's horrendous match at Centurion meant another failure would surely have made his place untenable. His record under pressure did not instil confidence but the result was a serene 140 that matched anything he had produced before.

Morkel produced a hostile spell that Bell survived and on the fourth day he ensured the visitors' hold on the game never weakened. Rarely has Bell displayed such emotion in an England shirt than when he skipped down the pitch to Paul Harris and lofted him over mid-on to reach his hundred. The arms went aloft, the helmet came off and he tugged at his badge. All his hundreds have still come behind a three-figure score from someone else but the middle order is where he belongs. "I knew I needed an innings to save my place."

The double act
For nine overs the South Africa openers settled before Swann changed all that to cement his position as England's bowler of the year. With his second ball he removed Ashwell Prince, superbly caught by Bell at silly point, then mimicked Ricky Ponting's dismissal at Edgbaston with a beautifully flighted delivery to beat Hashim Amla's loose drive.

Amla's wicket was not the only moment that rekindled Ashes memories. On the ground where Broad was hit for six sixes by Yuvraj Singh during the 2007 World Twenty20, he found that Oval length again, ripping out Kallis' off stump as he shouldered arms. AB de Villiers did the same, except his pad was in the way, and JP Duminy, trying to leave, hit the ball by mistake but on to his stumps. When Swann claimed Smith, a four-day finish looked possible. South Africa avoided that but lasted little over an hour into the fifth day. Fittingly it was Swann who sealed England's win, trapping Steyn lbw for his 54th wicket of the year – a record for an English spinner. The first ICC rankings of 2010 placed him third, one place ahead of Muttiah Muralitharan. No one would have expected that at the beginning of the year, but England's 2009 defied prediction from first to last.

The Wisden Cricketer, February 2010

Andrew McGlashan is an assistant editor of Cricinfo.com

Scores

2nd Test Dec 26-30, Durban †**SA 343** (GC Smith 75, Kallis 75, de Villiers 50; Swann 4-110) **and 133** (Swann 5-54, SCJ Broad 4-43); **Eng 574-9 dec** (IR Bell 140, AN Cook 118, Collingwood 91, MJ Prior 60, AJ Strauss 54). **Eng won by inns and 98 runs.** *MoM: Swann 60-6-164-9*

Headlines

Day One
The Observer

England topple Kallis and Smith to finish on top

Day Two
The Guardian

Strauss carries the attack to South Africa in England's fearless reply

Day Three
Daily Telegraph

Cook's long vigil of denial edges England in front

Day Four
Daily Telegraph

Broad and Swann sweep England to brink of victory

Day Five
Daily Telegraph

Swann administers fitting last rites in another England transformation

Last chance: Bell cements his place with a 140

Leaving party: Kallis bowled by Broad

Escape Town

ANOTHER cliffhanger, another draw for England when defeat seemed certain. To Cardiff and Centurion can now be added Cape Town. The 'Get Out of Jail Free' cards are certainly totting up. As at Centurion, five days of utterly absorbing Test cricket came down to No.11 Graham Onions and his ability to withstand one final over.

Whereas at Centurion the bowler was Makhaya Ntini, here it was Morne Morkel. But there, Ntini was clearly a spent force; here, Morkel was swift and full of bounce-inducing menace. Onions had come to the wicket to join Graeme Swann with 17 balls remaining. He faced 11 of them. But it is the final six that will linger long in the memory. There were two bouncers which Onions waved by, two yorkers that he somehow dug out, then another bouncer that produced a raucous appeal and an unsuccessful review for a catch behind and then finally a length ball wide of off stump that Onions left and promptly punched the air in delight. England had survived 141 overs for a creditable draw; they were still 1-0 up in the series, with one to play.

The true heroes, though, were Paul Collingwood and Ian Bell, who added 112 but more importantly stayed together for 235 minutes, surviving 57 overs (including six breathtakingly dangerous new-ball overs from Dale Steyn, with Collingwood playing and missing regularly during those 36 balls he had to face) until there were only 13.3 remaining. We knew Collingwood could play such an innings – he is now a world expert – but it was Bell's breakthrough, evidence of mental sturdiness under fire in an epic 78 in almost five hours. That he did not see it through – he was ninth out – was disappointing but only the most mean-minded criticised. He had proved a point and so had England: their policy of playing six specialist batsmen had been roundly condemned. Their No.6, Bell, had dragged them out of the mire.

Ball tampering?

Goodness, what a fuss. Truly this was a storm in a teacup. It all began on the third day when Stuart Broad stopped a ball off his own bowling with his boot. Then he threw the ball to James Anderson, who twisted it in his hands and appeared to pull off a bit of leather. This was picked up by local TV and highlighted significantly. The South African team then took an interest and raised their concerns with match referee Roshan Mahanama. They did not make a formal complaint, though, and there the matter ended in the eyes of the ICC. And quite right, too. It was something of nothing. Broad should not have stood on the ball with his spikes (there was no such uproar when JP Duminy did likewise late in the game), Anderson should have asked the umpire to remove any leather. End of story. But even at the end of the game both sides were still fighting their moral high ground in various press conferences.

Biff bash: Smith makes a hundred

Scrumpy Jacques

That was Jacques Kallis' nickname when with Glamorgan in 1999, due to a sometime thirst for cider. He also had a thirst for runs then and it has not abated. His first-innings century was a masterclass in technique, application and concentration on a tricky pitch after being inserted by England. Late on the first day, from his 173rd ball, he reached his 50th first-class hundred – his 33rd in Tests, his seventh against England, his sixth at Newlands, his second of the series. Some player.

He was 108 not out at the close, but he lasted only one ball on the second morning, an absolute beauty from Onions, precipitating England's taking of the final four home wickets for just 12 runs in 17 balls. Curiously there was a wicket in the first over on all of the first three days. Ashwell Prince had gone on the first day to Anderson and both Swann and Anderson went on the third day to the excellent Morkel, who finished the first innings with five.

Special Smith

But Kallis's was not the innings of the match. That belonged to South African skipper Graeme Smith for his second-innings 183, the 19th of his career and his fifth against England. Smith simply loves important runs; not for him easy pickings in sedate circumstances. His side needed an innings and he responded. The left-hander's battle against Swann was fascinating, chancing his arm immediately to attack the spinner with sweeps and clips against the turn through a vacant midwicket. His positivity rubbed off on the increasingly impressive Hashim Amla (95), with whom he added 230 to take the game away from England.

The Wisden Cricketer, February 2010

Steve James writes for the *Sunday Telegraph*

Scores

3rd Test Jan 3-7, Cape Town **291** (Kallis 108, Boucher 51; Anderson 5-63) **and 447-7 dec** (Smith 183, Amla 95); **†Eng 273** (Prior 76, Cook 65; M Morkel 5-75, DW Steyn 4-74) **and 296-9** (Bell 78, Cook 55). **Match drawn.** *MoM: Smith 391m, 273b, 25x4.*

Headlines

Day One
The Times
Kallis stands tall as bowlers answer the call from Strauss

Day Two
Daily Mail
BELL THROWS IT AWAY

Day Three
The Times
England left hot and bothered by force of double-edged assault

Day Four
The Times
Bold Smith leaves England on the brink

Day Five
The Guardian
Onions sweats the latest great escape

Point the way: Anderson claims Kallis' wicket

SOUTH AFRICA v ENGLAND 4th Test Johannesburg

Battered in the Bullring

SOUTH AFRICA retained the Basil D'Oliveira Trophy that they wrested from England in 2008, with a bristling, brutalising performance that restored natural justice to the overall series scoreline and saved the blushes of the home side's senior personnel.

England had nothing left after clinging on at Cape Town and looked a spent force. On a bouncy but true pitch they lost a wicket to the first ball of the match and never recovered. They panicked and batted as if they had a plane to catch or rather a plane they wanted to catch. Their two innings lasted 90.4 overs, 18.2 fewer than South Africa's single, uncompleted one.

In their last two series England have scored only four hundreds and 29 fifties. Their opponents (Australia and South Africa) have made 13 hundreds but five fewer fifties than England, whose average first-innings score in the last two years is only fifth-best in the world.

The Test finished at lunch on the fourth day but in terms of real playing time the game lasted less than two and a half days. Few Tests are as one-sided as this and it was a deflating end to a tour defined for England by "resilience and character", according to Andrew Strauss, attributes we have come to expect from his alliance with Andy Flower.

South Africa delighted in the drubbing, revising the close finishes at Centurion and Cape Town to suit the mood of the moment. "We could be sitting here having won 3-1," said Graeme Smith. Strauss questioned his players' ability to adapt to match conditions and, when asked how good England were, replied: "We're not good enough at this stage. We've shown resilience and that we're hard to beat but we're not clinical enough and not consistent enough." Honesty is another hallmark of England's current top brass.

Pitch perfect

Mickey Arthur, South Africa's under-pressure coach, predicted a grassy, result pitch. "But it won't be a green mamba," he reassured everyone. Indeed there were no snakes in the pitch but England still found its sting debilitating.

Arthur also reckoned that the wicket would get uneven. The Test did not last long enough for us to find out. This was a good Test pitch, the pace and bounce reminiscent of South African tracks of yesteryear, the sort of wickets on which Transvaal's famous 'Mean Machine' would have terrorised Currie Cup opponents.

The first session, after less than half of which England were 39 for 4, was exhilarating, evoking England's 2 for 4 start to the Wanderers Test of 1999-2000. The session began with one of the great short-leg catches by Hashim Amla to dismiss Strauss off the first ball and ended with Paul Collingwood hooking Jacques Kallis for six with two men on the fence. This enthralling series was offering up oddities until the last.

Protean pace

Bespoke conditions and a new-ball attack coming to the boil proved irresistible. Steyn was returning to full fitness, Morne Morkel to form. They were South Africa's fourth new-ball pairing of the series, having joined forces initially in the second innings at Cape Town following Friedel de Wet's injury. If that was a dress rehearsal, then their exhibition of complementary skills in this Test was a sparkling first night. Fitness permitting, Steyn and Morkel have a potent future, though a Wanderers trampoline is one thing, sweating it out on an Asian duvet another.

England had picked Ryan Sidebottom hoping the ball would swing. It did but Steyn was doing it five miles an hour quicker than Sidebottom and that is the difference between two for plenty and five for not many.

Morkel found a consistency of line rarely seen in his previous 20 Tests and his length was often unplayable. Playing forward was not an option, playing back fraught with danger, too, as Alastair Cook and Jonathan Trott found, leg-before caught on the crease, beaten for pace.

Strauss reckoned that the first spells from Steyn and Morkel were peerless but life could become easier after that. That they were also facing two debutants in Wayne Parnell and Ryan McLaren made their skittish batting all the more frustrating and unprofessional. The left-armer Parnell barely moved the ball off the straight but he did have the speed to make life uncomfortable. He pinned Strauss to have him lbw in the second innings and tempted Kevin Pietersen, who seemed to be overcoming his demons, to chase a wide one on the final morning.

The Wisden Cricketer, March 2010

John Stern is editor of *The Wisden cricketer*

Steyn removal: Ian Bells falls victim

Scores

4th Test Jan 14-17, Johannesburg †**Eng 180** (Collingwood 47; Steyn 5-51) **and 169** (Collingwood 71; Morkel 4-59); **SA 423-7 dec** (Smith 105, Boucher 95, Amla 75, de Villiers 58). **SA won by inns and 74 runs.** MoM: Morkel 27-6-98-7.

Series tied 1-1.

Headlines

Day One
The Guardian

Morkel and Steyn rip England apart as hosts gather momentum

Day Two
Daily Telegraph

Smith cashes in as review system proves unsound

Day Three
The Observer

Fuming England head for defeat

Day Five
Daily Mail

SLAUGHTER AT THE BULLRING

King keeper: Man of the series Mark Boucher celebrates another wicket

In search of his

aura

A poor series in South Africa led to a rare bout of introspection for Kevin Pietersen. But before heading to Bangladesh, he told **Lawrence Booth** he is still top dog

KP's career stats *at August 31, 2010*						
	M	**R**	**HS**	**AVGE**	**100s**	**50s**
Tests	66	5306	226	**47.80**	16	20
ODIs	104	332	116	**42.17**	7	20
T20Is	28	911	79	**37.95**	0	5

It is not until halfway through our interview that the penny drops: Kevin Pietersen is going to be just fine. We are chatting about his plight in South Africa and the obvious pleasure it gave Graeme Smith's men.

"When you know the best batter in the team isn't scoring runs, of course you love it as the opposition," he says. "And I know South Africa were happy, which is fine. It's totally understandable. You play against Australia and Ricky Ponting doesn't get any runs – you are as happy as anything."

You scarcely need to read between the lines: Pietersen still sees himself as England's main man, despite averaging 25 in the four Tests; and the conviction runs so deep it slips out as instinctively as one of his flamingo whips to leg. Despite all he has been through, Pietersen's subconscious is still doing the talking.

It is not long before he is at it again. This time the subject is his position in the batting order. The question: "Doesn't your best player bat at three?" The answer: "Kallis bats four for South Africa, doesn't he? And I bat four for England. What number does Yousuf bat for Pakistan? Four? Ponting's three – but he's the only one. He plays on good wickets, mind you."

Few traits in the England dressing room have provoked so much chin-stroking among the commentariat as the confidence of Kevin Pietersen. Some regard it as a breath of fresh air in a nation that prefers self-deprecation; more than a few see arrogance. But one thing seems in little doubt: if England are to stand a chance of retaining the Ashes this winter, they will need Pietersen at his strutting best. The almost unwitting allusions to his place in the pecking order suggest he may be through the worst of it.

Until now it has not been clear quite how bad 'it' actually was. Pietersen's fallout with Peter Moores took place a little over a year ago but these days feels like ancient history. Moores is not mentioned once by name throughout the interview: more the dodo in the room than the elephant.

But then other things happened. Pietersen was scapegoated for an instantly infamous sweep shot at Cardiff; damaged his Achilles and hobbled through the second Test at Lord's; missed the rest of the Ashes while he fretted over his future; struggled to recover when his post-operative wound became infected; then faded badly in South Africa after beginning with 40 and 81 at Centurion, although he says, with a slow shake of the head, that even in that game "I never felt right ... never felt right".

"The thing is," he says before launching into a characteristic stream of consciousness, "I didn't go into South Africa with any confidence of having runs under my belt. I literally came from lying on the couch for four months and having a tough time in rehab ... And then coming through it with a horrible-looking scar, ending up in South Africa, not playing any cricket and going straight

66 There are no naughty-boy nets with Andy Flower, nothing silly 99

into international cricket against a South African side as good as they are – it was tough work. Lying on a couch and then playing South Africa. It's tough."

This is the side of Pietersen that strays from the narrative penned by others. His defining moments all scream melodrama: the pantomime villain in South Africa, the Ashes-winning 158, the switch-hits, the Roman Empire brutality of his stint on the throne, even the Red Bull run at Centurion. The public sees grand gestures and swagger; humility adds a layer of subtlety that confuses the issue.

Despite the low-key nature of the Tests in Bangladesh, the antennae will inevitably be primed for evidence of a star on the wane. Failure will invite more theories but Pietersen takes armchair punditry in his stride. He is referring to the Sky commentary team when he says: "You realise that those guys are paid to do a job and it's very difficult for them because some days they've got rain around and they've got to deal with the time."

It is tempting to think Pietersen's sanguine observations would not have been possible while he and Moores were in tandem. But his admiration for Flower has grown after a sticky start. "I don't think Flower was very good in the second-in-command position."

And when he outlines Flower's qualities, the criticism of Moores is implicit. "The good thing about Andy Flower is that five years ago he was playing international cricket. He knows what it is. Andy Flower knows when players need a day off, even when we've had the worst game in the world, like the 51 all out in Jamaica. Not naughty-boy nets, not a training session at six in the morning, not something silly after an international. That's why the boys are responding as well as they are."

Of course, the litmus test awaits later in the year when England defend the Ashes. And as part of the side that lost 5-0 in 2006-07 Pietersen is forthright about what is required this time. "We've got to be mentally tougher," he says, identifying a theme that became familiar throughout the Ashes maulings of the 1990s. "We know that we've got to have some counter-punches. And we've got to realise that's what we're going into. For a lot of us last time was our first tour of Australia and we got hammered. It burns big time. Some of us played in all those Tests and it was just demoralising. I've never known a feeling like Adelaide. And at the end of that series you felt like hanging your boots up."

You sense he is almost talking about himself as much as the team. But he prefers to leave the analysis to the commentary box and as long as he does not hesitate too long over the bit which asks "KP: No.1?", England will feel their main man is back. 🅹 *The Wisden Cricketer, March 2010*

Lawrence Booth writes for the *Daily Mail*

Two ton: Pietersen (226) v West Indies at Leeds

The Tiger tussle

Through the first six months of 2010 England played Bangladesh in two Test and two one-day series first in Bangladesh and then at home …

Three ODIs: Finding a finisher

SOMEHOW, England are the only team in world cricket to have avoided the ignominy of a defeat against Bangladesh but they are starting to cut it mighty fine. A 3-0 one-day series victory was the reward for their latest endeavours in Dhaka and Chittagong, a result which put a small feather in Alastair Cook's cap in his first full series as England captain. But had it not been for an innings of impeccable temperament and judgement from Eoin Morgan in the second match at Mirpur it might all have been very different … Not since the days of Neil Fairbrother have England possessed a "finisher" in ODIs, a man who can arrive in any sticky situation and keep the tempo ticking while the pressure starts to mount. Morgan made 110 not out from 104 balls, an innings of such focus that he did not

even notice the moment, four balls from the end of the match, at which he reached his maiden ODI hundred for England. **Andrew Miller**

First Test: Five sets but no thriller

If the Chittagong Test had been a tennis match, it would have been a Tim Henman special: a three-set thumping dragged out over the full five-set distance by that peculiar English inability to kick an opponent who is down. The final scoreline might have read 6-0, 6-1, 5-7, 6-7, 6-2 – a result to showcase the superiority of the victors while at the same time ensuring that the plaudits went to the plucky losers who refused to go down without a fight. **Andrew Miller**

Second Test: Fortune favours the lions

Flat pitches are supposed to dull cricket's soul, yet emotions ran high after a game in which England pulled clear only on the final afternoon. While Alastair Cook was simply relieved to have ticked off the 5-0 Test and one-day whitewash, Bangladesh were left lamenting cricket's law of the jungle: the big beasts seem to have all the luck. And though England would have preferred a smoother ride, the truth was that on a track branded a "road" by Kevin Pietersen there were moments when it was not entirely clear which way the game was heading. Never before had Bangladesh scored more runs in a Test than their 704 here. And with a better deal from the umpires that statistic might even have underpinned their finest cricketing moment. **Lawrence Booth**

The Wisden Cricketer, March and May 2010

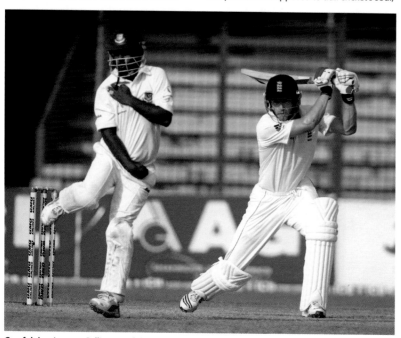

Careful dominance: Collingwood drives during his 145 in the first Test at Chittagong

Nearly man: Pietersen bowled for 99

Nearly nearly man: Shakib stumped for 96

And so to England for the return matches …

First Test: Tame win over wild Tigers
That England beat Bangladesh for the 18th consecutive time was news of the 'dog bites man' sort. Nothing that happened in the first Test at Lord's suggested that man will bite dog any time soon, not, at any rate, in the longer form of the game. In patches the tourists played with skill and aplomb; and for all 363.3 overs that the match lasted they did so with passion. But if their batting at last began to possess the discipline and application (not to mention flair) necessary, their bowling was woefully inadequate. England did what they had to do, although they did not always do it to the standards they would have wished. **Stephen Brenkley**

Second Test: The desperate demolition
It took England just two sessions to bowl Bangladesh out twice. There, sadly, lies the tale of the Old Trafford Test. Bangladesh's batting was the stuff of greenhorns, a display that set new markers for ineptitude and again raised questions about their continued presence at cricket's top table. Test cricket is under enough pressure without such inevitability about an outcome. Bangladesh might point out that this was their first innings defeat since November 2008 but still they have lost 59 out of 68 Tests in nearly a decade. Those are shocking statistics. Supporters will point to progress – they were not hammered as convincingly as they were when here in 2005 but it was almost impossible to detect any such shafts of light amid the gloom and wreckage of Manchester. **Steve James**

Three ODIs: Dominant, desperate, dominant
A veering FTSE index had nothing alongside the near-vertical jerks in fortune through this one-day series. After the sheer drop of a first-ever defeat by opponents they may have taken for granted, England managed to climb back up with a huge win in an unexpected decider. Notwithstanding Andrew Strauss's 154 in that third game at Edgbaston, the best performers for England were all newbies: Ian Bell at Trent Bridge, Jonathan Trott with 94 and 110 and the enthusiastic Ajmal Shahzad (with ball if not in the field) who took five wickets in 14 overs across two games … Strauss said that the three games proved that England have strength in depth and that tournaments are won by squads not teams. That is debatable. But success does require consistency, which remains elusive.
Richard Hobson *The Wisden Cricketer, July and Aug 2010*

Scores

1st ODI Feb 28, Mirpur **Ban 228** in 45.4 ov (Tamim Iqbal 125); †**Eng 229-4** in 46 ov (PD Collingwood 75*). **Eng won by 6 wkts.** MoM: Iqbal below 120b, 13x4, 3x6.

2nd ODI Mar 2, Mirpur **Ban 260-6** in 50 ov (Mushfiqur Rahim 76); †**Eng 261-8** in 48.5 ov (Morgan 110*). **Eng won by 2 wkts.** MoM: Morgan 104b, 8x4, 2x6.

3rd ODI Mar 3, Chittagong **Eng 284-5** in 50 ov (C Kieswetter 107); †**Ban 239-9** in 50 ov (Bresnan 4-28). **Eng won by 45 runs.** MoM: Kieswetter 123b, 9x4, 3x6.

England win the series 3-0

1st Test March 12-16, Chittagong **Eng 599-6 dec** (AN Cook 173, PD Collingwood 145, KP Pietersen 99, IR Bell 84) **and 209-7 dec** (Shakib Al Hasan 4-62); †**Ban 296** (Tamim Iqbal 86, Mushfiqur Rahim 79, Mahmudullah 51; GP Swann 5-90) **and 331** (Junaid Siddique 106, Mushfiqur Rahim 95; Swann 5-127). **England won by 181 runs.** MoM: Swann 78.3-18-217-10

2nd Test March 20-24, Mirpur †**Ban 419** (Tamim Iqbal 85, Mahmudullah 59, Naeem Islam 59*, Shafiul Islam 53; Swann 4-114) **and 285** (Shakib Al Hasan 96, Tamim Iqbal 52; JC Tredwell 4-82); **Eng 496** (Bell 138, TT Bresnan 91, IJL Trott 64, MJ Prior 62; Shakib Al Hasan 4-124) **and 209-1** (Cook 109*, Pietersen 74*). **Eng won by 9 wkts.** MoM: Shakib Al Hasan 96 in 191b, 11x4; 74-27-155-4

1st Test May 27-31, Lord's **Eng 505** (IJL Trott 226, AJ Strauss 83; Shahdat Hossain 5-98) **and 163-2** (Strauss 82); †**Ban 282** (Junaid Siddique 58, Tamim Iqbal 55; JM Anderson 4-78, ST Finn 4-100) **and 382** (Tamim Iqbal 103, Imrul Kayes 75, Junaid Siddique 74; Finn 5-87). **Eng win by 8 wkts.** MoM: Finn 29-11-187-9

2nd Test June 4-6, Old Trafford †**Eng 419** (IR Bell 128, MJ Prior 93, KP Pietersen 64; Shakib Al Hasan 5-121); **Ban 216** (Tamim Iqbal 108; GP Swann 5-76) **and 123** (Finn 5-42). **Eng won by an innings and 80 runs.** MoM: Bell 255b 7x4 1x6

1st ODI July 8, Trent Bridge †**Ban 250-9** in 50 ov (Raqibul Hasan 76); **Eng 251-4** in 45.1 ov (IR Bell 84*). **Eng won by 6 wkts.** MoM: Bell 101b, 6x4.

2nd ODI July 10, Bristol **Ban 236-7** in 50 ov (Imrul Kayes, Jahurul Islam 40); †**Eng 231** in 49.3 ov (IJL Trott 94). **Ban won by 5 runs.** MoM: Mashrafe Mortaza 22r, 25b, 2x4, 1x6; 10-0-42-2.

3rd ODI July 12, Edgbaston **Eng 347-7** in 50 ov (AJ Strauss 154, Trott 110); †**Ban 203** in 45 ov (Bopara 4-38). **Eng won by 144 runs.** MoM: Strauss below 140b, 16x4, 5x6.

England won the series 2-1.

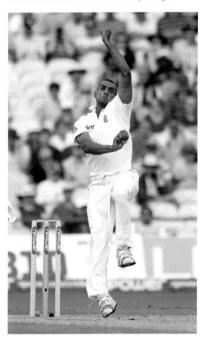

Home debut: Finn bowls Mushfiqur Rahim

Full debut: Ajmal Shahzad in the second Test

The
power,
the
practice,
the
passion

Paul Collingwood became the first England captain to lift a world trophy. In the immediate aftermath he explained just how they did it and what it felt like. Interview by **Edward Craig**

I haven't stopped smiling since I hit that winning run" – England's first World Cup-winning captain, Paul Collingwood, three days after the final against Australia. A week later he is at Downing Street meeting the Prime Minister who, it is said, calls him Colin, then he gets locked out of No.10, that famous door shutting behind him as he stands alone for a photo call. More smiling. Maybe it was when he missed the Test series against Bangladesh, resting an injured shoulder, that something like normality resumed.

Collingwood lived the life of a high-flying, globe-trotting cricketer over the winter, playing in South Africa, Bangladesh, India and the Caribbean. His joy and intensity is unaffected and from the heart. He has had a brilliant winter and he wants to talk about it: "I'm 33 years old and I feel like I am in my mid-20s living the dream. These last eight weeks have been the best times of my life." And it all started with a dropped catch in the desert.

66 I've not enjoyed the game as much as I have in the last two months 99

It was when Collingwood saw the squad selected for the World Twenty20 that he had his first inklings that they had a chance: "I knew the potential was there to win. The power that we'd got at the top of the order was going to be as good as we'd ever had. I was always very confident with the bowlers. Yards [Michael Yardy] came in, you know he's going to do a job. We said we've got a good chance here."

England stumbled upon their explosive openers, Craig Kieswetter and Michael Lumb, earlier in the winter. The pair opened the batting for England Lions in pursuit of England's 157 in a warm-up game in Abu Dhabi, Stuart Broad dropped Kieswetter at mid-off on four and Lumb and Kieswetter bludgeoned 97 for the first wicket. The 1st XI lost to the 2nd XI and

the two players earned themselves spots in the World Twenty20 squad.

Collingwood also spent six weeks before the World T20 in India playing – and impressing – for the IPL side, Delhi Daredevils. He started to look at what was making IPL sides successful: "I have learned from the IPL about left-arm seamers. There were two or three of them in the top five of the averages in terms of wickets taken and economy. There's something about the angle of a left-armer, especially at the death, that right-hand batters don't enjoy. The ball tails away from the batter, it's harder to hit through the leg side for a right-hander. Offcutters go across right-handers." And, much to the surprise of everyone, Ryan Sidebottom played instead of James Anderson.

The winning way
Picking the right players is one thing, getting the best out of them comes down to good management. That was where the coach Andy Flower alongside Collingwood and, yes, Andrew Strauss over the previous 12 months, have made the difference: "A lot of the captain's decisions are made off the pitch. On the field is only 10% of the job. We made sure that every single training session was enjoyable and every player was as confident as he could be."

Then came the attention to detail and practice: the accurate slower balls and slower-ball bouncers, the tactics, plans A, B and C: "And the guys responded to all the pressure situations. The [further] we're getting, we're thinking 'we can win this, we can win this' but not once did anybody take their foot off the pedal."

The England team had a clarity of thought, a simple method for the simplest format, that allowed them to perform at the toughest moments. But Collingwood says there is more to it: "A bowler has only got to bowl 24 balls, a batter has to have a strike-rate of 120 or 130. But there are a lot of skills that people don't give credit for in Twenty20 cricket, the skill of 'how long it takes you to get in on a

pitch'. As a bowler, being told by a captain only two balls before that you are coming on. The decision can be that late because you know as a captain that, if you get the wrong bowler at the wrong time, it can cost you the game."

Indian dreams
Collingwood and man-of-the-tournament Kevin Pietersen both had fruitful times at the Indian Premier League. For other countries this did not always translate into success, as India's failure shows, but it did wonders for England. Michael Lumb's performances (278 runs in 11 matches at a strike-rate of 145 for Rajasthan) gained him confidence, form and cemented his place in the selectors' minds. KP had that sporadic explosive impact for Bangalore (236 runs in seven matches at a strike-rate of 150) but Collingwood profited most: "I learned so much. The confidence you gain as a player simply to be chosen in an IPL team as one of the four overseas players – it's ridiculous. I'm 33, I have played all my life for England and I'm still gaining confidence from a selector of Delhi saying: 'You're in tomorrow.' I'm keeping out Dilshan and AB de Villiers. I'm thinking: 'Have you got that one right?'"

They had got it right – he made three powerful fifties including an unbeaten 75 against Bangalore off 45 balls. He is now a darling of Delhi: "I love the IPL and what it is. I had 65,000 people shouting: 'Collingwood, Collingwood' then 'Sixer, Sixer.' They are normally things you only hear when you're playing against India and bowling at Sehwag or Tendulkar."

Belief that players gained from the IPL and belief from improved form in limited-overs cricket were the biggest difference between this year and last, he admits. Belief born from experience: "The experience of the bowlers, having another year playing on different surfaces, that was a crucial thing. The guys understood their strengths better and had confidence having plans. The emergence of Eoin Morgan's talent has been sensational." ▷

And the final factor? "KP's form, it all kind of came together at the right time." KP's form had become problematic. The one player in the world with the potential to win any game from any position was playing for England – but for much of the winter it was not happening. Then he emerged in the Caribbean with the blistering range of shots that made his name. Pietersen himself puts it down to "a chat with Colly" in Bangladesh. What had Colly done to reawaken the sleeping Kevin? "We've all been through bad times, me more so than others. It's trying to keep things in perspective." Perspective about batting or life? "Batting mostly. Cricket is our lives. You try to remember why you play the game and remember what its fundamentals are. Trying to keep yourself in a good frame of mind is key. This game is one of the hardest sports mentally ever."

Old-fashioned values

Despite everything, there is one thing that is very clear: which does he now prefer, Tests or Twenty20? "Tests. I have been brought up in an environment where Test cricket was the ultimate from a very early age and it's in my blood." He'd prefer an Ashes win to a 50-over World Cup victory and admits that nothing can match the experience of the 2005 Ashes. That said, he has not finished celebrating yet: "Enjoying the success of winning a world cup? It does not get much better than that. Beating Australia in Australia would maybe top that. Hopefully it's just going to be one of those years where everything goes right." 🄹

The Wisden Cricketer, July 2010

Edward Craig is deputy editor of *TWC*

Winning run: the captain leads the team home

The unsurprising surprise

Julian Guyer was one of a handful of English journalists who followed the tournament from start to success. Here is his diary of England's final push for victory

May 13 St Lucia
Heading towards the ground for England's semi-final against Sri Lanka, my eye is caught by a placard for the 'International Pony Club'. Sadly this institution appears to have fallen into a state of some disrepair since the 2007 World Cup and its condition puts me in mind of an old exam question: "The Holy Roman Empire was neither Holy nor Roman nor an Empire: Discuss." Fortunately we arrive soon afterwards at the beguiling Beausejour Stadium. The press-box, although under cover of a stand, is in the open air and it is not long before a drummer in front of us is thumping out a rhythm that will last for the rest of the day. As for the match itself, this is surprisingly straightforward. England's bowlers take a grip on the game from the start and don't let go before Kevin Pietersen – showing no ill-effects from his transatlantic travels to be at the birth of his first child – makes an unbeaten 42, ending the game with a six and a four off successive Lasith Malinga deliveries.

May 14 St Lucia
Pakistan, both on the field and off it, are a source of endless fascination. Here the Akmal brothers, in their contrasting styles, show Australia's quicks can be mastered and the impressive Mohammad Amir then dismisses their openers. When Cameron White is out, Australia are 139 for 6 in the 17th over chasing 192 to win. Like most people who have to finish a report immediately at the end of the match, the bulk of my article is now written, with some space for an introduction. Well, thanks to Mike Hussey, the introduction expands somewhat. Hussey's innings of 60 not out off 24 balls seems no more credible than a finishing sequence of six, six, four, six. The general orthodoxy of his shot-making almost obscures the run-rate. "This game of cricket just keeps amazing me every day," Hussey says afterwards. He is not alone.

May 16 Barbados – the final
England triumph with such ease that one wonders why it has taken them so long to win a one-day tournament. The snide answer is that they have at last found the right South Africans but that is harsh for it is a very English group of bowlers who spark a collapse that leaves Australia on 8 for 3. Ryan Sidebottom bounds in with the energy of a colt and with the nous of a seasoned pro. Now his selection seems obvious but, as historians say, what was in the past was once in the future. The selectors deserve praise.

Michael Clarke bats like a man who has not made many runs lately and his running between the wickets recalls the line about Denis Compton's first call being merely a "basis for negotiation". That Clarke is then involved in the run-out of David Warner is, on reflection, no surprise. Afterwards Clarke, without prompting, admits his own place is under threat. "There's no doubt the selectors will need to have a look at my performances." Graeme Swann's analysis of 4-0-17-1 is a marvel. Conventional offspin is supposed to be on the way out; only unorthodox deliveries could prevent a slow bowler being clobbered in Twenty20. Swann's approach to international cricket of 'I'm downright pleased to be here' has filtered through to spectators. He has achieved success while remaining himself.

Kieswetter and Pietersen then dominate. The authority with which Pietersen strikes Mitchell Johnson through the covers is surpassed only by driving a decent, fast ball from Shaun Tait high over long-off for six.

Collingwood, whose move in giving Luke Wright a solitary over in the tournament was rewarded with the wicket of Cameron White, hits the winning runs and the England team run on the field. In the midst of the celebrations one man is not visible – coach Andy Flower. Flower is the Clement Attlee of English cricket. One quote attributed to the former prime minister reads: "Democracy means government by discussion but it is only effective if you can stop people talking." Flower is unafraid to discuss; more importantly, he is unafraid to decide.

The Wisden Cricketer, July 2010

Julian Guyer is a sports correspondent for AFP

1st semi-final May 13, St Lucia †SL 128-6 in 20 ov (AD Mathews 58; SCJ Broad 2-21, GP Swann 1-20); **Eng 132-3** in 16 ov (KP Pietersen 42*, C Kieswetter 39, MJ Lumb 33; NLTC Perera 2-19). **Eng won by 7 wkts.** *MoM: Broad 4-0-21-2.*

2nd semi-final May 14, St Lucia Pak 191-6 in 20 ov (Umar Akmal 56, Kamran Akmal 50); **†Aus 197-7** in 19.5 ov (MEK Hussey 60*, CL White 43; Mohammad Amir 3-35). **Aus won by 3 wkts.** *MoM: MEK Hussey* left 24b, 3x4, 6x6.

Final May 16, Barbados Aus 147-6 in 20 ov (DJ Hussey 59, White 30; RJ Sidebottom 2-26); **†Eng 148-3** in 17 ov (Kieswetter 63, Pietersen 47). **Eng won by 7 wkts.** *MoM: Kieswetter* right 49b, 7x4, 2x6.

ENGLAND v AUSTRALIA five ODIs

Magic masks mistakes

England hid their own flaws and uncovered Australia's – just. By **Richard Hobson**

THE NATIONAL GALLERY has mounted an exhibition of paintings once thought by experts to be the work of great artists only to be exposed as fakes under greater scrutiny. A similar thought emerged, as Australia clawed back respectability in the NatWest Series, that England's one-day team may not be quite the real deal it appeared.

Perhaps that is too harsh a way of interpreting victory over the leading 50-over side in the world, which became guaranteed when they took an unassailable 3-0 lead at Old Trafford. At that point England had a record run of seven successive wins in the format stretching back to South Africa in the winter.

Yet talk of a whitewash proved extremely premature. England did not so much take their feet off any pedals as see a problem come home to roost. The top four had never quite clicked and Eoin Morgan – more Britart in style than Old Master – proved unable to whitewash over the mistakes every time.

Morgan's unbeaten hundred from 85 balls had rescued England from 97 for 4 as they chased a target of 268 at the Rose Bowl and he top-scored again at Cardiff two days later in another four-wicket win. But Australia were only one wicket short in a thriller at Old Trafford, dominated at The Oval, then won easily at Lord's.

A change of strategy to replace the injured spinner Nathan Hauritz with the blinding pace of Shaun Tait proved an inspired decision by the tourists. Tait bowled in short, sharp bursts and recorded 100.1mph in the final game. With Doug Bollinger and Ryan Harris as well, Australia's attack hardly looked depleted, even though it was.

Morgan's invention

There was no doubting the man of the series. Eoin Morgan has gone from strength to strength since the Champions Trophy last September. He is arguably now a better one-day batsman than Kevin Pietersen. KP is without a fifty in the format since his last limited-overs series as captain in India in 2008-09. Over to you, Kevin.

Morgan certainly has more shots. But his real skill is in knowing when to play them. In chess they say the threat is more potent than the deed. So captains have to place fielders for Morgan's reverse hits, leaving space for his orthodox pushes and pulls. It means there will always be a gap somewhere in his range.

When Andrew Strauss described him as "the Michael Bevan-type batsman we have been looking for" he underestimated Morgan. Where Bevan (who played in a better side) placed onus on his lower-order partners to score runs, with his own presence as insurance, Morgan takes personal responsibility for bringing down targets. His partnership with Luke Wright at the Rose Bowl was a case in point. Bevan, of course, can point to the length of his own career. Morgan has just begun.

The real contest

Oh well, they have to be mentioned: the Ashes. Both Strauss and Ricky Ponting played down suggestions that the five matches would have any bearing on the Test series this winter but some of the wickets claimed by England were telling.

England feel they have exploited a chink in Michael Clarke's ability to play the short ball. At Cardiff, after Clarke's nervous pull against a bouncer, Strauss adjusted his field and, even with the mode of attack so glaringly obvious, the Australian could not help gloving one to short leg from Stuart Broad. Broad was a prolific threat and cool in the powerplays.

With his front-foot technique and history of back trouble (which forced him out of the last game) Clarke can expect more of the same this winter. Ponting, too, was twice out pulling. Broad's height is a potent weapon and Australia have yet to meet Steven Finn, who broke off from his strength-and-conditioning programme to bowl in the nets.

Bits and pieces

How do you rate a six to eight of Luke Wright, Tim Bresnan and Mike Yardy? Well, it all depends on the one to five and nine to 11 around them. All three are honest performers with roles to fill: Wright took some key wickets, Bresnan thrashed runs when they were needed and Yardy went for only 4.4 an over across the series.

But England will hit trouble if they need these three for their major contributions, as Ponting pretty much said. Wright is a sixth not a fifth bowler, Yardy a second rather than a frontline spinner. If they go unnoticed, chipping in here and there, the team will be going well. *The Wisden Cricketer, August 2010*

Richard Hobson is deputy cricket correspondent of *The Times*

Scores

1st ODI June 22, Rose Bowl ♀ †**Aus 267-7** in 50 ov (MJ Clarke 87*); **Eng 268-6** in 46 ov (EJG Morgan 103; RJ Harris 3-42). **Eng won by 4 wkts.** MoM: Morgan 85b, 16x4. ODI debut: JR Hazlewood (Aus).

2nd ODI June 24, Cardiff ♀ †**Aus 239-7** in 50 ov (CL White 86*, SR Watson 57, SPD Smith 41; SCJ Broad 4-44); **Eng 243-6** in 45.2 ov (Morgan 52, AJ Strauss 51, PD Collingwood 48; DE Bollinger 3-46). **Eng won by 4 wkts.** MoM: Broad 10-0-44-4.

3rd ODI June 27, Old Trafford **Aus 212** in 46 ov (Watson 61, TD Paine 44; GP Swann 4-37, JM Anderson 3-22); †**Eng 214-9** in 49.1 ov (Strauss 87, Collingwood 40; Bollinger 3-20, SW Tait 3-28). **Eng won by 1 wkt.** MoM: Swann 10-1-37-4.

4th ODI June 30, The Oval ♀ **Aus 290-5** in 50 ov (Clarke 99, RT Ponting 92, Watson 41); †**Eng 212** in 42.4 ov (MH Yardy 57, Morgan 47; Harris 5-32). **Aus won by 78 runs.** MoM: Harris 8.4-1-32-5.

5th ODI July 3, Lord's †**Aus 277-7** in 50 ov (MEK Hussey 79, SE Marsh 59, Paine 54; Broad 4-64, Swann 3-32); **Eng 235** in 46.3 ov (Collingwood 95; Tait 4-48). **Aus won by 42 runs.** MoM: Tait 8.3-0-48-4.

England won the series 3-2 Man of the series: Eoin Morgan

Prepared to strike: Eoin Morgan **left** lines himself up for improvisation during the first ODI at the Rose Bowl

The unorthodox offspinner

Graeme Swann became the No.1 spinner in the world but his bowling is the only conventional thing about him. By **Lawrence Booth**

December 12, 2008, and Graeme Swann is nervous – more nervous than he has ever been on a cricket field. India's reply to England's 316 in the first Test at Chennai is only 13 overs old when captain Kevin Pietersen turns to his debutant offspinner. It is the biggest moment in Swann's career ... but something is wrong. "This ball feels empty," he thinks as he waits for Gautam Gambhir to settle and his nerves to follow suit. "It's like a ping-pong ball!" And thus: a floaty long-hop, cut for four. "It was the best thing that could have happened," he says, more than a year and a half on from the game that launched one of modern Test cricket's most enchanting success stories. "You just think: 'Right, I've got that out of the way.' And then I got two wickets [Gambhir and Rahul Dravid, both lbw] in the same over."

Those six deliveries were gripping drama in their own right but they also served as a microcosm for some of Swann's most seminal moments. Three career-changing episodes stand out. The first came when he toured South Africa in 1999-2000, bowled five overs in a single ODI and did not get another look-in with England until after Duncan Fletcher stepped down as coach in 2007. "I was drunk half the time," says Swann with wry detachment. "I was a 19-year-old with 30 grand in my pocket as a tour fee and I wasn't playing a lot of cricket. I felt like a millionaire. I was staying in five-star hotels and I was more than happy to prop up the bar and talk to anyone who wanted to talk to me."

Swann returned to Northamptonshire under a cloud but there was a silver lining: he had avoided playing Test cricket, which, he fears now, would have exposed him as a "charlatan". And that, as much as missed alarm calls and bar-room japery, could have ruined him.

The arrival of Kepler Wessels at Wantage Road in December 2002 almost did the job instead. Wessels was a disciplinarian from the old school, Swann a free spirit suspicious of authority. The pair clashed and Swann suffered. "I'm sure I was depressed," says Swann. "Turning up to Northampton one day and putting my head on the steering wheel and thinking, 'How am

I going to get out of the car? I can't face walking into the changing room again.' The coach had actually sat people down and said: 'You're not to laugh at any of his jokes, you're not to talk to him.' And being told you're only playing because we've got no one else to play instead ... "

Swann tails off. But not for long: "I don't take well to being bullied and it was a form of bullying. I hated it, my last year. But suddenly going to Notts and discovering how good a county can be – that was an eye-opener. And I went from hating to loving the game overnight."

His eureka moment as an offspinner was yet to come but for now Swann's passion had been reignited. It had all started at the age of seven, when Swann plumped for offspin because it was the only way his small frame could propel the ball far enough to reach his brother at the other end of the back garden. "I can't remember ever deciding to be an offspinner," he says. "I just naturally put a bit of tweak on the ball."

Swann absorbed the lessons of offspin by watching John Wake – now master of cricket at Oundle School – at Northampton Saints. But he never had any specialist coaching, relying instead on that natural tweak and jaunty mindset. Wantage Road's spin-friendly tracks proved both a help and a hindrance. On pitches so helpful that he knew he could get away with landing the ball in the same place over after over Swann's development stalled.

"I remember Darren Lehmann was one of my first ever Championship wickets and I just expected it because I was bowling at Northampton," he says. "But it was Darren Lehmann. If I got him out now I'd be doing cartwheels. When I left Northampton I had to go and learn to bowl properly."

Yet even after moving north to the happier surrounds of Trent Bridge it still took two years to move to the next level. With Nottinghamshire relying on their seam-bowling attack, Swann was limited to 364 Championship overs in 2005 (claiming a modest 30 wickets at 38 apiece), and 401 in 2006 (24 wickets at 46). These were not stats to impress Fletcher. Then he worked out to attack less in the first innings, when conditions were not as helpful, and keep the powder dry for the second. Bowl at the stumps first time, give it more loop thereafter. In 2007 Swann bowled more Championship overs (463) than anyone at the club, taking 43 wickets at 34.

Just as important, Peter Moores had replaced Fletcher. Some eye-catching performances in the NatWest Pro40 in 2007 earned Swann a one-day series in Sri Lanka

66 I was drunk half the time, happy to prop up the bar and talk to anyone 99

that October. This time he was ready: "It just escalated from there."

There is an irrepressible sense of "so what?" John Arlott once said to Mike Brearley: "Mike, you're the only one who understands that it doesn't really matter." Swann may be hewn from something similar. "The main difference as you get older is you get far more pragmatic about things and you realise if you have a shit day, you have a shit day," he says. "You think: 'Sod it. I didn't bowl very well today, I will tomorrow.'" The tomorrows are piling up – and Swann is endearingly happy to go with the flow. ⬛ *The Wisden Cricketer, August 2010*

Lawrence Booth writes on cricket for the *Daily Mail* and is author of the *Top Spin* emailer

Top England spinners and their lbw percentage						
	CAREER	TYPE	TESTS	WKTS	LBWS	LBW %
Derek Underwood	1966-82	SLA	86	297	24	**8.0**
Jim Laker	1948-59	OB	46	193	32	**16.5**
Tony Lock	1952-68	SLA	49	174	21	**12.1**
Fred Titmus	1955-75	OB	53	153	23	**15.0**
John Emburey	1978-95	OB	64	147	16	**10.9**
Hedley Verity	1931-39	SLA	40	144	18	**12.5**
Ashley Giles	1998-2006	SLA	54	143	20	**14.0**
Wilfred Rhodes	1899-1930	SLA	58	127	11	**8.7**
Monty Panesar	2006-09	SLA	39	126	31	**24.6**
(Graeme Swann	2006-10	OB	24	113	38	**33.6)**

Deadly straight: Underwood bowls

Anderson v Mohammads

IT IS NOW five years and 36 matches since Pakistan won two Tests in a row and, if ever there was a game in which they lived up to their label as sport's greatest mavericks, it was this. Barely a week after bowling Australia out for 88 on a gleeful first morning at Headingley Pakistan were themselves steamrollered for 80 on the fourth and final morning at Trent Bridge, as James Anderson capped an outstanding personal performance with his first Test 10-wicket haul.

The result, in terms of runs, was the second-heaviest ever inflicted or received by the competing teams and it caused such great ructions within the Pakistan camp that, within hours of the conclusion, Danish Kaneria had been dropped and the former captain, Mohammad Yousuf, summoned from semi-retirement to bolster the batting.

As ever with Pakistan the headline issues distracted from an entertaining contest that contained some of the most competitive cricket of the summer, in particular as England's top order struggled against superb seam bowling. There were 24 single-figure dismissals – nine of them English – that made the efforts of England's two centuries all the more laudable.

For Ian read Eoin

Eoin Morgan would not have been playing this match had it not been for Ian Bell's foot injury but the seizing of opportunities is international sport in a nutshell and Morgan made his bid for Brisbane with an impressive performance. He needed some luck, most notably on 5 when Kamran Akmal was set too deep to collect a low nick but after an inconclusive debut series against Bangladesh this was the innings that confirmed Andy Flower's suspicions about a player with massive potential.

Morgan's first-class average in 2009 was a measly 24 but, as with Marcus Trescothick and Michael Vaughan 10 years ago, it required the grandest stage properly to whet his competitive juices. Being cast into a dogfight on an overcast first morning, with Mohammads Amir and Asif making the ball talk, was the perfect means to ascertain his character. In fairness Bell in his current mind-set might not have shrunk from the challenge either but it is doubtful whether he would have dictated the game to quite the same effect that Morgan did during his 219-run stand with the admirable Paul Collingwood.

Prior notice

Picking the gaps has never been Matt Prior's forte as a batsman and it has cost him his place in the one-day set-up – at least for now. But in Tests he remains pre-eminent, as his punchy second-innings century amply demonstrated. He came to the crease at 72 for 5, with England threatening to squander their first-innings lead of 172, but responded with a bloody-minded determination that Flower tacitly suggested had stemmed from his ODI omissions.

It was Prior's third Test century but his first since Trinidad in March 2009, which also happened to be the last time that Kevin Pietersen had reached three figures. Prior's barren trot ended with an unlikely ally alongside him, as Steven Finn pressed his lanky frame down the wicket for 50 unbeaten deliveries and helped add 49 runs for the 10th wicket.

No jammy Jimmy

Finn once again impressed in his day job, scooping five wickets in total including three in 19 balls in his opening spell. But in a week in which Pakistan's two Ms, Amir and Asif, had earned comparisons with the two Ws of yesteryear, Wasim and Waqar, Anderson popped up with a performance that might, in a one-off capacity, have trumped the lot.

Bowling with pace, stamina, accuracy and prodigious movement off the seam and through the air in both directions, Anderson celebrated his 28th birthday with his ninth five-wicket haul, then followed up that effort with a shattering second-innings onslaught of 15-8-17-6.

Reviews and reprieves

The Umpire Decision Review System was in use for the first time in a Test in England but, no matter how many replays are used, there is no way of exonerating Kamran Akmal for a desperately poor performance. A five-ball pair was the least of his concerns; Akmal's cymbal gloves gave Collingwood a life in each innings, including a comical drop in front of first slip in the second innings, the delivery after he had held a screamer to dismiss Pietersen.

Most unforgiveable was Akmal's inept management of the UDRS. As wicketkeeper he had a key role to play in determining which appeals were worthy of second opinions but on his watch Pakistan squandered both lifelines in five minutes. England, by contrast, simply played it more cannily – in every respect. *The Wisden Cricketer, September 2010*

Andrew Miller is UK editor of Cricinfo

Perfect: Anderson bowls Imran Farhat

Scores

1st Test July 29 – August 1, Trent Bridge
†**Eng 354** (EJG Morgan 130, PD Collingwood 82; Mohammad Asif 5-77) **and 262-9 dec** (MJ Prior 102*); **Pak 182** (Umar Gul 65*; JM Anderson 5-54) **and 80** (Anderson 6-17). **Eng won by 354 runs.** MoM Anderson 27-15-71-11

Headlines

Day One
The Guardian

Morgan makes careless Pakistan pay

Day Two
The Times

Anderson and Finn force the pace

Day Three
Sunday Telegraph

Prior leaves Pakistan in hopeless position

Day Four
Daily Telegraph

Anderson's art sends Butt back to drawing board

Over the top: Prior on his way to 102*

ENGLAND v PAKISTAN 2nd Test Edgbaston by **Lawrence Booth**

No wizardry, no contest

THE PAKISTANI taxi driver heading for Birmingham's New Street station not long after England wrapped things up in front of a strangely sparse and placid crowd was in little doubt. "The reason no Asians came to watch," he said, "is because they know their team's rubbish." It was tempting to point out his side might have threatened England if they had held even half the 14 chances their captain Salman Butt believed they missed. Yet well though they bowled to induce an England collapse on Saturday afternoon, and spiritedly though they batted on Sunday evening, Pakistan still lost by nine wickets. The taxi driver may just have been on to something.

Wizard of swing
England in effect won the game on the first day, when the Pakistanis departed from a script that usually casts them in the roles of preternatural wizards or enthralling fools. Now, following the traumas of Trent Bridge, they unveiled a new identity and decided to block their way to lunch – so badly that they dined on 37 for 6. Soon after, from 72 all out – a new Pakistani low in England five days after the previous one – it really didn't matter how many wizards they had.

Fight back: Zulqarnain Haider hits out

Their struggles, after bravely batting first under grey skies, were never starker than against Jimmy Anderson, who knows that repeatedly being called the best swing bowler in the world comes with implicit caveats but had nonetheless risen to No.4 in the rankings by the end. His spells with the first new ball in two Tests now added up to an eye-watering 41-22-51-11, with barely a stroke played in anger and the upset at being ignored at the World Twenty20 beginning to fade.

Zero to hero
In the absence of Shoaib Akhtar, Younis Khan and Mohammad Yousuf – who arrived in Birmingham on the eve of the match but was ruled out because the monsoon back home had washed away any chance of practice – the few Pakistan fans who did bother to turn up craved a hero. That it almost turned out to be the bloke who, for a few seconds, seemed to have registered his country's first king pair (and on debut too), seemed chaotically typical. But Zulqarnain Haider has known darker moments than the second-innings lbw decision that momentarily made history.

With his father only just emerging from a hepatitis-induced coma back home, Zulqarnain was grateful that Hawk-Eye had Graeme Swann's leg-before shout just missing leg stump rather than grazing it. Half an inch the other way and he would have been another grim statistic. But his spirited 88, full of cheeky sashays towards the seamers, prompted comparisons with Javed Miandad and helped Pakistan's last four wickets nearly triple their score. Beaten captains can strain credulity in their never-ending search for positives but Zulqarnain felt like the real deal.

Dancing with death
For a while the fate of the Pakistanis seemed involved in a grim *danse macabre* with that of Kevin Pietersen. To

sum up: KP kept nicking it, the Pakistanis kept dropping it – five times in all, the most comical on 36 when Umar Amin, possibly distracted by a misguided lbw appeal, spilled the mother of all sitters in the gully. It somehow felt right that Pietersen again fell short of a hundred.

For Alastair Cook there was no such luck and all he achieved was to leapfrog a couple of names on the list of batsmen who could miss out at Brisbane. His failure to get fully forward to Mohammad Amir on the fourth morning as England set off in pursuit of a tricky 118 told of a batsman in technical turmoil.

Standards!
Stuart Broad's decision to hurl the ball back in the vague direction of Zulqarnain on the third afternoon finally earned him a fine from the match referee and prompted concerns about England under pressure. The same petulance from the bowling unit had been on show at Chittagong, and there were worries now that successive series against Bangladesh (away and home) and now an enfeebled Pakistan were turning victory into an entitlement. When the irrepressible Swann, surpassing himself again on a pitch that lost its nip for the seamers, barked "standards" as Zulqarnain and Saeed Ajmal ran the fielders ragged, he spoke for an era with new expectations.

No illusions
Where did it all leave England? Strauss talked of "room for improvement" and there probably was: the batsmen collapsed for the second Test in succession and the bowlers were half as potent when the sun came out. But the failure of any of Pakistan's top six to reach 30 said as much about the batting as it did the bowling. A Test win is a Test win but far tougher examinations lie ahead.

The Wisden Cricketer, September 2010

Lawrence Booth writes for the *Daily Mail*

Scores

2nd Test Aug 6-9, Edgbaston †Pak 72 (Anderson 4-20, SCJ Broad 4-38) **and 296** (Zulqarnain Haider 88, Saeed Ajmal 50; GP Swann 6-65); **Eng 251** (KP Pietersen 80, IJL Trott 55; Saeed Ajmal 5-82) **and 118-1** (AJ Strauss 53*, Trott 53*). **Eng won by 9 wkts.** MoM Swann 37-20-65-6.

Headlines

Day One
The Times

A tale of wonder boys and the whipping boys

Day Two
Sunday Telegraph

Fumbling Pakistan hand it to England

Day Three
Daily Mail

THE INCREDIBLE ZULQ HOLDS OUT

Day Four
Daily Telegraph

Strauss and Trott seal win for professionalism

Irrepressible: Swann celebrates the wicket of Umar Akmal

ENGLAND v PAKISTAN 3rd Test The Oval by **Nagraj Gollapudi**

Fortunes swing on Oval return

FOUR YEARS on from cricket's first forfeited Test match Pakistan returned to the scene of the crime. Already 2-0 down in the series following huge and demoralising defeats, one could not blame the captain, Salman Butt, if he had other things on his mind, despite the constant questions in press conferences.

"I see no reason why that needs to be discussed. We need to discuss good things," Butt said. And the good things? Traditionally The Oval has been one of the favourite hunting grounds for the tourists. Hence Butt focused on history rather than detritus and it paid off.

Two heavy defeats demanded that Pakistan change things. As well as Butt dropping down to No.3 and Mohammad Yousuf returning the biggest change was handing a Test debut to the left-arm quick Wahab Riaz, who took the injured Umar Gul's place. Riaz, a tall, broad-shouldered 25-year-old, was last seen being taken out of the attack after two beamers in an over against India in an ODI at Karachi in June 2008. He was selected for this tour ahead of Tanvir Ahmed, who had excelled in the domestic Quaid-e-Azam Trophy with 86 wickets. Riaz, who had 14 wickets at 40, had a lot to prove.

The presence of black cloud above London which persisted throughout the four days gave Riaz and the other bowlers a hand. With his slingy action, speed and control, Riaz easily dislodged the England top order. Andrew Strauss, Jonathan Trott and Kevin Pietersen were defeated by movement. After lunch he bowled a jaffa to Eoin Morgan, his best wicket in the match, with a brilliant late outswinger. Soon he would celebrate his five-for.

At 94 for 7 England looked helpless. But Matt Prior, just as he had pulled them back to safety from the precipice of 98 for 6 with his second-innings century in the first Test at Trent Bridge, successfully played the role of firefighter for the hosts with an unbeaten 84. His eighth-wicket stand of 119 with Stuart Broad put England back in the match. But even though Prior had applied a fresh band-aid to stop the bleeding, England could not hide their deficiencies. Those wounds would be re-opened in the second innings by Mohammad Amir.

Before that Pakistan produced their best batting effort of the tour. Suddenly the contest that had been missing all series surfaced. This can be credited to the returning Mohammad Yousuf, playing in his first international match in nearly seven months. He was anything but rusty. He began cautiously, of course, but with every passing minute he regained his old mastery of footwork, hand-eye coordination and the unique sense of when to leave. He showed the youngsters in the dressing room how to play time. He stayed rooted to his crease and played the ball late.

Though Yousuf fell to a simple return catch to Graeme Swann, he had injected belief. Azhar Ali, who made sure Pakistan did not disintegrate after his senior's fall, made a steadfast 92. For the first time in the series Pakistan passed 300.

If Pakistan finally found their mojo, there was one man in the England team who was desperately hunting for some self-belief. In his seven Test innings leading into this match Alastair Cook had compiled a mere 100 runs. Writing in the *Daily Telegraph*, Geoff Boycott said keeping Cook was a "recipe for disaster".

It was obvious that Cook was angry. Determined to prove the detractors wrong, he broke the shackles and played with promise. The weather had improved and he took full advantage – and at a decent strike-rate. It helped to have Jonathan Trott frustrating the Pakistanis with his dour batting at the other end.

Though Cook offered a few chances, he never let doubts defeat him. But for his 110, Pakistan would have won the match on the third day as England lost their last six wickets for 26 runs. The combination of Amir's reverse swing and doosras from Saeed Ajmal was too much.

If 33 runs are needed at lunch with seven wickets in hand, you can bet on any team other than Pakistan to win. And when James Anderson pierced the impenetrable defence of Yousuf with an inswinging yorker – the ball of the series so far – Pakistan shuddered. Pakistan lost three wickets in four overs, bringing Amir to the crease with 16 runs required and four wickets in hand. He and Umar Akmal played out five nerve-racking maidens from Anderson and Swann. Once again Swann was at the Pakistanis, ripping the ball and getting bounce.

He had become the news for various reasons, from drink-driving allegations to receiving an apology from the ICC for initially overlooking him in the nominees for the Cricketer of the Year awards. Swann was far more interested in winning the Test. He was not quite successful. Pakistan's youngest pair – Amir and Umar – were more desperate for headlines. *The Wisden Cricketer, October 2010*

Nagraj Gollapudi writes for Cricinfo

Scores

3rd Test Aug 18-21, The Oval †**Eng 233** (Prior 84*; Wahab Riaz 5-63) **and 222** (AN Cook 110; Mohammad Amir 5-52, Saeed Ajmal 4-71); **Pak 308** (Azhar Ali 92, Mohammad Yousuf 56; Swann 4-68) **and 148-6** (Salman Butt 48). **Pak won by 4 wickets.** *MoM: Mohammad Amir 34-9-101-6*

Headlines

Day One
The Times

Wahab brings fresh spring to step of battered Pakistan

Day Two
Daily Telegraph

Canny Swann keeps England in touch

Day Three
The Guardian

Amir and Ajmal cut through England's flabby middle order

Day Four
Sunday Telegraph

Strauss blames batting as England crash to defeat

New belief: Azhar Ali makes 92*

Wahab grab: Riaz after his 5-for

ENGLAND v PAKISTAN 4th Test at Lord's by **Vic Marks**

Sting in the tail

IN THE Broad family this match will be remembered as the one in which young Stuart came of age as a Test batsman. He hit 169, his maiden first-class century, and with Jonathan Trott shared in the highest partnership for England against Pakistan (332), which ensured a mammoth victory for the home side.

Sadly everyone else will remember this Lord's Test for something else. On a sleepy Sunday morning in St John's Wood, the fourth day of the match, you had to be an early bird to find a copy of the *News of the World* still in the newsagents. Cricket lovers snapped them off the shelves and were subsequently dismayed to the core.

They read of allegations of spot-fixing by some Pakistan players during a Lord's Test that had enthralled spectators. The paper told of a middle-man, Mazhar Majeed, who had won the trust of the players, and an exchange of £150,000, and it implicated the trio of Pakistanis who had been provoking a stream of superlatives throughout their tour.

There was Salman Butt, the soft-spoken emergency captain, who

had stepped into the breach with such composure when Shahid Afridi had resigned so abruptly after the Lord's Test against Australia in July. He was just the man to oversee the reconstruction of Pakistan cricket we all decided while marvelling at the stoic, dignified manner in which he dedicated the Oval victory to the victims of the floods back in Pakistan.

There was Mohammad Asif, the exquisite, old-fashioned swing bowler, who had manipulated the Dukes ball with such finesse throughout the summer. And most tragically of all there was Mohammad Amir, the teenage prodigy. How we had delighted at the carefree expression of his wonderful talent as he swung the ball past Australian and English bats throughout.

It was impossible to take any pleasure from a Test which had begun in such an astonishing manner. Rain ruined the first day when England, put in by Butt, were 39 for 1 at the close. On Friday morning Amir ran riot. He dismissed four English batsmen without any of them being able to score a run. Alastair Cook could not add to his overnight tally; Kevin Pietersen was out for a golden duck; Paul Collingwood and Eoin Morgan both departed to their third deliveries. No-balls or not, here was a spell of brilliant, intuitive swing bowling from the most precocious of teenage cricketers.

At 47 for 5 England were on the ropes; at 102 for 7 the situation remained bleak. The Sunday paper writers – or most of them – were mulling over the crisis within England's middle order, which had now collapsed for a third time in the series. Whither Pietersen and Collingwood and Morgan, we wondered, though not for much longer.

Pakistan would not take another wicket for seven hours. Trott metronomically went about his business, looking assured from the moment he clipped his first ball to the midwicket boundary. He established his right to

start the Ashes series beyond debate.

Broad made a mockery of his No.9 status. He played straight like a proper batsman but, when given width, he crashed the ball through the off-side with a flourish. The records kept falling as this pair batted long into Saturday morning. England's last five wickets had put on 399 runs. It was not surprising that Pakistan were demoralised when they came out to bat even if they had no inkling of the revelations about to hit.

Still, they batted abominably. They were dismissed in 33 overs for 74. The England bowlers merely had to run up and wait for their wickets, though not for very long. As ever Graeme Swann bowled delightfully on a pitch that offered considerable turn, finishing with 4 for 12. Following on, Pakistan could fare no better and were 41 for 4 by the close on Saturday evening. In hindsight it seems as if they must have had an idea that their world was about to fall apart.

So the last day was a surreal affair. There were odd curiosities. Would Pakistan turn up? There was no one practising before play began. What sort of reception would Amir receive? The answer was a solitary boo from the Edrich Stand, a cry of "no-ball" from the Grandstand as he received his first ball and stony silence after he was out.

To the relief of most it was all over before lunch. There were no smiles at the closing ceremony conducted behind closed doors in the Long Room to save the touring team further embarrassment. A look at the scorecard showed England had registered the most astonishing victory but there were no great celebrations. There was barely a smile. There was certainly no smile on the face of the ECB chairman, Giles Clarke, when he handed over the cheque to Pakistan's man of the series, Mohammad Amir.

The Wisden Cricketer, October 2010

Vic Marks writes for *The Observer*

Scores

4th Test Aug 26-29, Lord's **Eng 446** (Trott 184, Broad 169; Mohammad Amir 6-84); Pak 74 (Swann 4-12) and 147 (Umar Akmal 79*; Swann 5-62). **Eng won by inns and 225 runs.** *MoM: Broad 297b, 18x4, 1x6*

Eng won series 3-1

Headlines

Day One
Daily Telegraph

Ponting crows while Strauss toils

Day Two
The Guardian

Broad breathes life into England

Day Three
Sunday Times

Records are shattered and so is Pakistan's spirit

Day Four
The Times

Nothing to celebrate as dark cloud looms large over Lord's

Instant assurance: Jonathan Trott

Allround balance: Broad drives

Pluck of the Irish

Eoin Morgan is in Loughborough contemplating England's Test series against Pakistan. "Is there a chance this Test opportunity has come too early for me? The form I'm in at the moment, absolutely not."

Two days later he made his maiden Test hundred in his third Test innings. There were plenty who doubted his five-day credentials but he was not one of them. He would not have played against Pakistan but for Ian Bell's foot injury. But his innings of 130 was another milestone in the remarkable rise of the man nicknamed 'Superstar' by his Middlesex team-mates. Virtually unknown 18 months ago, he is now the first name on England's limited-overs team-sheet and is making a compelling late case for inclusion in England's Ashes top order.

This time last year Morgan was making seven in the Championship as Middlesex drew at Derby. "I've come a hell of a long way," he says, without a hint of overstatement. Morgan made his first half-century for England in the 6-1 one-day series thrashing by Australia that followed the Ashes last year but has since come to epitomise England's newfound spirit in the shorter form under Andy Flower that culminated with the World Twenty20 win.

"I was over the moon with how the tournament went personally, especially in the earlier parts where my contributions went a lot further. It was great."

But there is no escaping from Morgan's past. His friend and former Middlesex team-mate Ed Joyce once told the journalist David Townsend, "You won't find anyone more Irish than Eoin Morgan." Like Joyce, though, Morgan had no option but to transfer his allegiance to England if he was to play Test cricket.

Morgan says: "It's difficult. Ireland keep producing good cricketers and filtering them into county cricket. Where they fall down is the depth within Irish cricket, the lack of numbers and relative popularity of cricket in Ireland. Irish cricket will progress naturally but it just isn't that popular and it's a shame because there is a lot of talent there."

Playing for England has brought Morgan fame and fortune – in the shape of a £150,000 Indian Premier League contract with Bangalore Royal Challengers. His childhood in Rush in north county Dublin seems a long way away.

Cricket was always the priority for the young Eoin, the third of four brothers and the fourth of six children. "My father was a big fan and a cricket player, as were his father and his father's father." If Jody, a groundsman at Trinity College Dublin, and Olivia Morgan did not quite create an XI, they did their best. Most of their children would play at least age-group level for Ireland, while Eoin's sisters Laura and Gwen have represented their country at senior and under-23 level.

The Morgan success led to comparisons with that other famous Dublin cricketing family, the Joyces. So who would win a family six-a-side? "The Morgans would win, definitely. Through stubbornness."

The young Morgan was sports-mad, playing anything from tennis to golf

66 Irish cricket just isn't that popular and it's a shame 99

to hurling when his brothers were not trying to bounce him out in the back yard. The influence of hurling (a game that encourages flexibility in the wrists) on his game today is, he feels, overplayed. "I was far from a good hurler."

His early cricket had been played at Rush CC. Kevin Jennings, deputy head of the Catholic University School on Dublin's Leeson Street, offered him a scholarship but, concerned that he got some more disciplined cricket, sent him to Dulwich College in London. He was spotted by Middlesex and, by then, Morgan had set his mind on a career in cricket. "I was very driven as a kid and at 14 or 15, coming across, I was a bit nervous but Middlesex made it easy. They put me in accommodation with an old lady in Finchley. I used to come across for four months of the school holidays until I was 18, then moved over full time."

Irish cricket would continue to serve Morgan well until his England selection in 2009. From his Ireland debut as a 16-year-old in 2003 Morgan scored 99 on his one-day international debut against Scotland in 2006 and played 22 more ODIs

including valuable experience in the 2007 World Cup. While he had a miserable tournament personally, he learned. "I did find it a big help. Going through that rough patch makes me realise there's no point in worrying and to play with freedom." So Morgan worked hard in the nets on his array of sweeps. "I started working on them when I first got into the Middlesex T20 team (in 2006) as I couldn't clear the boundaries, so I started sweeping and found it easy. I worked at them and now they just come naturally."

Yet the more successful Morgan became in the game's shorter versions, the more it affected his first-class form. He finished the 2009 Championship season with only 413 runs at 24.29 as Middlesex finished one off the bottom of the second division. Was there a link between his county's struggles and his own form? "There might be. I've certainly looked at it and wondered what happened."

Morgan's moderate first-class record (average 37.73 pre-Trent Bridge) has been no barrier to Test opportunity. The selectors considered his limited-overs success, the composure, big-game temperament and the ability to manoeuvre bowlers and fielders: in 2010 he made match-winning hundreds against Bangladesh and Australia.

So next, the Ashes – the start of a big winter for Morgan, with the World Cup in Asia to follow. He has already beaten Australia in a one-day series and, of course, that World Twenty20 final. So did he take anything away from that? "A gold medal," he says – the verbal equivalent of a reverse-paddle. 🖪 *The Wisden Cricketer, September 2010*

Sam Collins is *TWC*'s website editor

First blood: 110 not out v Bangladesh

THE TWENTY20

PARTY

OVER the past 12 months Twenty20 has moved to a new level: the inaugural Champions League where all the domestic winners from around the world compete in one tournament has given a new context to home competitions while the Indian Premier League continues to enrich some of the biggest hitting players in the world: the face of cricket has never looked so colourful or loud or commercial.

The magazine has tracked the ever-changing moods of Twenty20. At the end of 2008 England played a $20m match against Allen Stanford's XI as part of an arrangement with the ECB. The relationship got embarrassing when Stanford was exposed as a fraud – a year later that glittering ground in Antigua looked somewhat different.

Contrast this with the rise and fall of the IPL's energetic figurehead Lalit Modi. He seemed to be in the process of conquering the world with his hyped brand of Twenty20 but allegations of financial mis-management have halted his progress. That said, an IPL franchise has already got together with a county cricket club – Rajasthan Royals and Hampshire. Is this the shape of things to come: global Twenty20 brands, sharing players, resources and grounds?

England, within this, have worked out Twenty20 cricket and conquered the world in the Caribbean with their intelligent bowling and big-hitting – it seemed the dawn of a new English Twenty20 age. That was until the domestic cup started in its new format of increased fixtures, a fat and swollen event, over twice the size of the original, garnering half the interest.

By the end of the English summer, with the second version of the Champions League taking place in South Africa without any England teams, due to a fixture clash, there was one big question: is this Twenty20 party beginning to drag or has it just started cranking up? ⚡

Edward Craig is deputy editor of *The Wisden Cricketer*

Contents

YOU'VE GOT TWENTY 20 VISION

September, 2010: The new Twenty20 Cup in England drags on and on and on

Big impact: Dwayne Bravo swings and Kumar Sangakkara watches. West Indies v Sri Lanka, Barbados, in this year's World Twenty20

"Only the best,

Edward Craig witnessed the inaugural Champions League in India and saw how Somerset and Sussex matched up to the glamour and noise of the Indian Premier League. It was not even close. He kept a diary

only the champions"

Thursday October 8
In Bangalore it is the opening ceremony followed by the first game and it is a cracker between Cape Cobras and Royal Challengers Bangalore. JP Duminy hits 99 including massive sixes. Lalit Modi, the energy and drive behind all things T20 in India, has got lucky again as his new venture kicks off with the near-perfect spectacle. The only shame for him is that the Indian side lost.

Friday October 9
The pitch at Delhi's Feroz Shah Kotla is dreadful: slow and low, a real concern for the organisers whose fuel is sixes. A slick, well-drilled Australian side in New South Wales dispatch South Africa's Diamond Eagles in the first game but the main course is the home side, Delhi Daredevils, with their imported stars Owais Shah, Glenn McGrath and Tillakaratne Dilshan. The crowd grows and a second slick, well-drilled Australian side (Victoria) complete a comfortable win. Two Indian matches, two Indian defeats.

Sunday October 11
It is a must-win game for the Delhi Daredevils who are up against the one Sri Lankan team, Wayamba. And Delhi turns up to watch. I sit on the edge of the boundary in front of the crowd and now I get it: this is the future. The huge crowd, warmed up and firing thanks to the music, the dancers, the DJ and the fireworks, are expecting Sehwag to deliver. The pitch, still slow and low, does not look right for the Viru brand of batting. He hits his first ball for four back past the bowler and does not

look back: 60 off 40 balls. "Sehwag creates his own conditions," writes an Indian journalist.

Sussex play NSW and have 30-odd spectators – a small south-coast Barmy Army. They have blow-up sharks and flags, all wear Sussex tops and, as they sing 'Sussex by the Sea', they attract an Indian following. So the Sussex band of fans grows from white middle-aged men

66 Sussex followers have come with blow-up sharks 99

singing out of tune to include Indian girls in bright yellow dresses waving Sussex flags and Sikhs playing with the blow-up sharks. But their team cannot live up to the support; NSW are too good. Afterwards a bulging-eyed Ed Joyce looks dazed by the atmosphere and the quality of the opposition. County cricket is beginning to look exposed.

Tuesday October 13
Sussex are confident going into their second game – Luke Wright has landed from the UK, Mike Yardy has regained composure. Chad Keegan has been the talk of the Indian press thanks to his hair cut.
Wright hits his first ball for six and a low-scoring game swings one way then the other, ending in a tie and a 'super over'. Sussex come second, losing both their wickets in succession chasing 8. Yardy looks distraught after the game. He admits they have learned a lot and have a lot to learn.

Thursday October 15
News breaks that Marcus Trescothick has headed home. Somerset make a hash of

communicating the news, being less than straight with journalists, which means the Indian press is less than sympathetic. The IPL chief executive announces Tresco's departure on Twitter a few hours before Somerset deny it.

Friday October 16
Fly to Hyderabad for Somerset's next two matches. Somerset – now without Trescothick – suffer another early batting collapse, lose comfortably to the Eagles and look like a side wanting to go home. As if to ram home the distance between English teams and the others, New South Wales crucify Trinidad and Tobago – until Kieron Pollard comes in, smashes 54 not out from 18 balls and wins the match with nine balls to spare, then celebrates with a primeval roar, before leading a dance around the ground with his team-mates. T&T are winning hearts and minds.

Saturday October 17
It is the remaining IPL sides' last chance to make it through to the latter stages of the tournament. There is a carnival atmosphere around Hyderabad and there is a big trade in fireworks. Suddenly ▷

Reader letter in January 2010:
JOHN STERN (TWC, December) asserts that "our 18-county system was exposed badly in the Champions League Twenty20". This overlooks that Sussex were the only side outside the three Indian teams with supporters at the tournament. The Sussex fans all spent four-figure sums to visit India for the matches, much to the astonishment and admiration of other teams' officials and local spectators. It is support like this that makes county cricket unique and the best domestic set-up in the world.
**Paul Eade
Stockholm, Sweden**

JAMES BOARDMAN

Delhi delight: Sussex fans; left David Warner as NSW win

SACRE BLEU! It seems the appeal of Twenty20 cricket has spread to France where the Champions League was broadcast live on Eurosport. The French have long seen cricket as an English oddity but according to commentator David Crossan, Twenty20 cricket is converting the French. "It's created a real buzz," says Crossan, "and the feedback we're getting – from genuine French people, not expats – is all positive." Cricket commentary during the Champions League was a two-man job, Crossan to provide the technical expertise (in French) and his wingman – always a Frenchman – to give a Gallic slant on the game. "At first the French commentators were sceptical about the idea," says Crossan, "but they've really got into Twenty20. We had one or two teething problems but by the end they were clued up." French viewers liked to see the batting side on top and, if that did not happen, it was up to Crossan to explain why the bowlers were on top. "I don't expect the French to take to Tests," says Crossan, "but the length of a T20 game is just right. The French see parallels between the foot and wrist movement of batsmen and tennis players. There's a shared artistry that appeals." Explaining the lbw law (or jambe devant guichet as Crossan calls it) to his fellow commentators may have earned Crossan nothing more than a Gallic shrug but Eurosport bosses are keen for more.

The Wisden Cricketer, December 2010

Gavin Mortimer

French scoop: Andrew Hodd

the revelry takes a back seat. The first Bangalore game between Cape Cobras and Victoria is delayed because of a bomb scare at the ground. For two hours the tournament looks to be over. Victoria express reservations about travelling to the ground, Herschelle Gibbs stays in the hotel. It is a false alarm. The over-reaction from police and the nervous impulses of the South Africans and Australians illustrate the underlying tensions.

Sunday October 18
Home teams are out but where there are West Indians there is a party. Somerset drag themselves to the Hyderabad stadium for one, last improbable attempt at qualification into the semis. For a team that has

> ### 66 Somerset make a hash of notifying us of Trescothick 99

batted so poorly, been the second-best English team in the tournament and wanted to go home for the last three days, it is remarkable they still have a chance with a convincing win over New South Wales Blues. But the Blues have Brett Lee, Stuart Clark and Nathan Hauritz, Somerset Peter Trego, Charl Willoughby and Omari Banks ... NSW win.

Monday October 19
Head back to Delhi for a final group game, a nearly dead-rubber between Delhi and Cape Cobras. It will decide who plays whom in the semis. Somerset's players are on the flight and do not seem to be hurting. They look shattered at the back end of a county season. "Only the best, only the Champions, only the best," says the tournament's incessant theme tune. In England Somerset are neither.

Thursday October 22
Back to Hyderabad for the last two games. NSW are on the same flight,

looking athletic, lean and meaning business. T&T win their fifth game out of five in exhilarating fashion.

And Lalit Modi is in the building. He walks around the boundary and the stands. The crowd mobs him and chant his name. He waves, flashing a massive watch as his arm reaches up. He signs autographs, has his picture taken with children. Not sure how many autographs Giles Clarke signs.

Friday October 24
The final is spectacular, on and off field. Hyderabad celebrates every wicket taken and every six hit – they do not care who does what. There are double the amount of fireworks and stacks of celebrities (mostly Indian actors). Brett Lee, Herschelle Gibbs and Kieron Pollard are the on-field favourites and all deliver something special – either sixes or wickets or both. NSW win a good game thanks mostly to Lee with the bat. It is an exciting end to a tournament ignored in the UK.

This event has shown that English domestic cricket is behind the times on and off the field, much to the surprise of Sussex and Somerset board members. Word around the county circuit is that it is massive in terms of cricket, exposure, marketing potential and prize funds. English fans may not realise it but the Champions League Twenty20 changes everything. ∎

The Wisden Cricketer, December 2010

Edward Craig is deputy editor of *TWC*

Not so super: Sussex's Dwayne Smith in the super over

EXPERT EYE Andy Nash

India shows counties the way

SIX YEARS since the ECB launched Twenty20 the format is set to smash the game's financial compass and after experiencing the inaugural Champions League in India with Somerset it is time to reflect on where Twenty20 can go from here. We, the county clubs, have an opportunity to strengthen our financial positions and change the nature of our relationship with the ECB for the better.

For a long time the county clubs have received a large proportion of their annual income from the ECB's distribution of funds generated by Team England's media deals and match-day income. Some pejoratively and unfairly call this the 'hand-out' that sustains intrinsically uneconomic counties and preserves an anachronistic structure. A more synergistic relationship is within reach if we develop and implement progressive plans for Twenty20.

In 2009 Somerset's takings on the gate, in the restaurants and bars showed we could make six-figure sums in a few hours as larger crowds came to the county ground for Twenty20; £100,000 is almost a quarter of Somerset's membership income from only a few years ago. These are transformational numbers for a county club and it is enabling us to invest greater sums in cricket, our academy, the recreational game, our ground's facilities and capacity. Moreover, this was achieved with the tournament crammed into a few weeks with three home matches in five days. With improved scheduling, future attendances and income will rise.

Why is Twenty20 so popular? It has a unique combination between the length and nature of the contest. No other mainstream sport can leave fans perched on the edge of their seats for almost three hours. Soccer and rugby can be very exciting but they cannot match Twenty20's 240 occasions every game where something extraordinary

can happen – soccer may have only eight attempts on goal in an average match. As we found against the Deccan Chargers, Twenty20 can take your emotions and thrash them around like a rag doll from the first to the last ball of the game. Every delivery can have a significant impact on the result.

It is this facet – compressed into a consumer-friendly and easily digestible three hours – that underpins the success of Twenty20 and explains its incredible growth around the world. Add to these ingredients the ability for teams to compete across all continents for 12 months of the year and the resulting recipe is a mouth-watering prospect. Then, play some powerful music, sprinkle some celebrity stardust, deploy a large passionate crowd and you have a world-beating recipe and one made

66 Twenty20 can do for cricket what Elvis did for music 99

for TV. Plus, if the grounds are full, then so are the sofas at home and the media commercial deals will surely follow.

I believe the new CLT20 is a big moment. Only 10 nations can play Twenty20 internationals. In club cricket there is a multiple of that number who can play Twenty20 to a very high standard. We are seeing the early stages of some club sides turning themselves into international brands: Trinidad and Tobago did just that. When our deputy high commissioner (a Liverpool FC fan) proudly told me in Bangalore that Liverpool had seven million fans in India, I felt deflated that Somerset have only 6,000 members in England. Another challenge.

So how do the county clubs seize the potential? We must be imaginative and improve our performance in a number of areas. Watching Twenty20 in India, South Africa and Australia, one

is struck by the combination of noise, colour, excitement and movement. Watching Twenty20 in England is not yet the same. Twenty20 can do for cricket what Elvis did for music. We need to give our fans Elvis not Val Doonican in a cardigan, pipe and slippers. We need to set far higher standards of customer service, more reliable match scheduling – 'Friday night is T20 night' – and produce winning teams who play attractive cricket.

It is fashionable in some quarters to believe that the ECB moves at the speed of continental drift. The board executive is comprised of capable people who believe in a successful future for English cricket. They have to play a long game in dealing with the ICC in addressing the domestic international schedule. But the counties should not wait to be led on T20. It is up to us to make it happen.

One idea is to scrap the Twenty20 Finals Day – better to have three days by separating the semi-finals. This guarantees three sell-outs instead of one very long day that has its atmosphere ruined when the losing semi-finalists trudge home early. And will Twenty20 kill Test cricket and the first-class game? No – think of first-class cricket as classical music to Twenty20's rock. Elvis never hurt Beethoven.

The Wisden Cricketer, December 2010

Andy Nash is chairman of Somerset

Reader letter in March 2010:
I HOPE the views of Somerset chairman Andy Nash (TWC, December) do not reflect those of the committee or hierarchy at the club – if they do, then the future of county cricket in Somerset is doomed. Twenty20 is a gladiatorial form of rounders interspersed with hideous music and hysterical commentary that prostitutes the game. I'm not naïve enough to say there is no place for this spectacle – income from the competition does provide great investment opportunities – but Twenty20 will kill Test cricket and the first-class game if it is played to excess because the public will tire of it and attendances will dwindle.
John Prior
Ilchester, Somerset

No sweaters: Fans as Elvis Presley not Val Doonican

Club v country?

No contest

Twenty years on from his first England cap **Mike Atherton** looked over two decades of startling change culminating in the impact of the Indian Premier League

A collection of Alan Gibson's cricket writing for *The Times* has been published under the title *Of Didcot and The Demon* and nothing illustrates better how the times have changed. The majority of his pieces span a decade from the mid-1970s, a period of drunken cricket reporting, missed deadlines, plentiful jokes, generous expenses, rail and newspaper strikes and, for Gibson, an almost exclusive focus on county cricket. Occasionally he was sent to do 'colour' on international matches but he did not much care for it. He would not much like the current state of the game, if his report of a match between Somerset and a World XI at Bristol's Ashton Gate in 1980 was anything to go by: "No doubt floodlit cricket has a future," he wrote, "because this is the age of the sporting stunt. In 10 years' time, mark my words, we will have floodlights at Lord's." Well, he was right, if two decades ahead of time ...

In England the central themes of the 20 years after my Test debut in 1989 have been the dominance, firstly, of the professional game and then of the England team. The ECB was established

in 1997. Nobody benefited more than England players from this transformation of the national governing body into a commercially proactive organisation whose concern, despite protestations to the contrary, has been the first-class game.

If things at a national level have been clear-cut, then domestically the years have been characterised by a complete absence of vision, with one glaring exception: the 'invention' of Twenty20. But the level of tinkering has been staggering: one-day competitions have gone from zonal to regional to knock-out, from 40-over to 50-over and back, with Twenty20 competitions appearing then disappearing with bewildering rapidity. The result is incoherent, a fixture list that few can follow and that neither fulfils England's

66 Clubs can sign whoever they wish, finances and availability allowing 99

needs nor caters for the spectator.

On England's tour of India in April 2006 I did an interview with someone who English cricket followers would have been surprised to learn that I thought was the "most powerful" administrator in world cricket. Lalit Modi was little known in England and held no official position within world cricket. He did control the Indian board's ballooning finances.

It was a prescient piece but for the wrong reasons. Love him or loathe him, Modi became the most powerful man in cricket because of his vision rather than his position. In a game blighted by a lack of visionary leaders Modi's foresight stood out. He saw a football-style environment, where privately financed franchises and domestic clubs with

ambition could compete internationally and, furthermore, compete with players' loyalty to their national boards.

The defining moment of the decade will be April 18, 2008 – the day the Indian Premier League began. This was both a remarkable coup by Modi and an even more remarkable piece of organisational skill, showing administrations hampered by tradition and legislation what could be achieved in such a short time. It was the moment that set cricket on a path where the dominance of the international game will eventually be challenged.

The recent Champions League, which was a natural and inevitable off-shoot of the IPL, might not yet have caught the imagination of English followers but it provided a snapshot of cricket's future. There is one simple reason, I believe, why international cricket will eventually be superseded by club cricket: unless a country (like England) has a liberal immigration policy, then an international team is determined by the talent within its boundaries. That does not leave much scope for high-quality, competitive international cricket. Clubs, on the other hand, can sign whoever they wish, from wherever, finances and availability allowing. Over time competitiveness, which is at the heart of good sport, is much easier to maintain.

Within this, English cricket must work out quickly what it wants to be; to paraphrase the Somerset chairman, Andy Nash, *Under Milk Wood* or Bollywood? The latter requires a radical change to the county game. And that argument is just about the only thing that has not changed in the two decades since I first pulled on an England shirt. 🄰 *The Wisden Cricketer*, January 2010

Mike Atherton writes for *The Times*

Coining it: Modi, KP, Warne at the second IPL; left Mike Atherton calls as Hansie Cronje tosses at Centurion Park in 1995-96

"Twenty20 is just ripe for corruption"

The head of the international players' union **Tim May** talked match-fixing, drugs and Pakistan

Are international players forced to play too much cricket?
With the emergence of the IPL and the Champions League we're seeing the creation of official, or unofficial, windows in the international Future Tours Programme. The international calendar is reduced from 12 months to 10 months. The boards want to maintain revenue. Players can't keep up.

Are you surprised Pakistanis do not play in the IPL?
Nothing surprises me when it comes to the IPL. Other decisions made by the IPL and its franchises, such as the refusal to grant players the ability to review security and the decision of the IPL and its franchises not to recognise or deal

with any players' managers or agents, is self-defeating. Its decision-making is very arrogant. The attitude is that they're the only game in town, they're the biggest game in town and, as long as they pay these huge amounts of money, they can do what they like.

Should cricket sign up to Wada's drugs code?
Sometimes you should dilute your rights for a better good – the last thing we want is drugs in our sport. It's very, very difficult to have an effective drug policy if you don't have the ability to have 'no advanced knowledge testing'. Cricket, historically, is a low-risk sport but you can't be too complacent. You have the emergence of Twenty20 which is a

Pointing the way: chief executive Tim May

power game – we've seen power-skill games such as baseball have problems with doping – so I don't think cricket can put its blinkers on.

Has match-fixing been beaten?
Lord Condon, who headed up the ICC's anti-corruption and security unit, said last year that we can never think we have this cancer beaten. Twenty20 is just ripe for corruption – the shorter the game the more influence each incident can have. It opens up a great deal of opportunities for the bookmakers to try and corrupt players into providing various different outcomes, if not the result itself. Cricket needs to be very, very careful. *The Wisden Cricketer,* March 2010
Richard Edwards

Ranatunga slams T20

A talk at the Oxford Union led to some outspoken criticism of the shortest format

THE FORMER Sri Lankan captain Arjuna Ranatunga has lambasted Twenty20 leagues saying the sums of money involved are a hazard to international cricket. He warned that "a lot of unwanted people have started getting involved. They will come in with Twenty20, they will burn money with Twenty20, then they will vanish".

Speaking at the Oxford Union, he directly accused the Indian Premier League of damaging the integrity of the ICC's international programme. "India lost the Twenty20 World Cup thanks to [IPL commissioner] Lalit Modi. No one else. Lalit Modi and his IPL. When I was playing, there were players who always wanted to achieve something for their

country – we used to play for our clubs for no money. It was an honour to play for our country. Not like nowadays."

He was dismissive of the suggestion that Twenty20 leagues gave opportunities to young players. "Only limited top players benefit and that is just financially. You need a balance between bat and ball for good cricket; Twenty20 will kill that for financial considerations."

Ranatunga, who was sacked as chairman of the Sri Lanka cricket board in December 2009 after a dispute with Lalit Modi, said he became an administrator because of his concern for the purity of the international game. "I love my country and the most disappointing day of my life was when my sports minister

Winning critic: Ranatunga holds the 1996 World Cup as captain

[Gamini Lokuge] gave permission for members of the Sri Lanka team not to play for their country in Test matches in England last year [so they could play in the IPL]. I will fight for my country."

Ranatunga said international cricket should be the priority, adding: "Provided we had proper security, I'd lead a team to Pakistan. Sri Lanka had these problems for 30 years [in the Sri Lankan civil war]. If you're going to stop playing because of terrorism, you're going to end up with a shamed country." He had one final message about why international cricket should matter more than Tweny20 leagues: "You need money to live but you don't live to earn money." *The Wisden Cricketer,* January 2010
Christopher Foxon

OPENERS Winter adventures

When Ravi met Napes ...

Essex team-mates went head-to-head in New Zealand

RAVI Bopara and Graham Napier faced each other in the final of New Zealand's domestic Twenty20 competition in a battle of Essex team-mates. And Napier's Central Districts beat Bopara's Auckland in the HRV Cup final by 78 runs.

Auckland had gone into the final in confident mood, unbeaten by Central Districts in all four meetings this season in all formats, including two wins in the earlier stages of the HRV Cup. But in the most crucial tie Auckland and Bopara lost it. Chasing down an imposing 206 (Bopara had conceded 24 from one over), the game was up for Auckland when Napier clean-bowled his Essex pal for three. It was Napier's second wicket and the scoreboard read 9 for 4. Auckland limped to 128 all out in the 17th over.

Bopara's dismissal meant Napier finished as leading wicket-taker for the competition with 18. It was also sweet revenge for Napier, who was on the receiving end of a Bopara hundred in a 50-over defeat. "I knew better than anyone just how dangerous [Bopara] can be. To bowl him was a key moment in the game. It was a straight ball that nipped back and clipped the top of off-stump, a dream delivery. I didn't get a chance to speak to Ravi [after the game] but hopefully we'll catch up, so I can get his thoughts on the dismissal."

Bopara's average from 10 innings in the competition was only 17.50 – not great preparation for a starting spot with Kings XI Punjab in the IPL. Napier could find himself having to choose from three teams to go to the Champions League later this year, if either Essex or Mumbai Indians make it to the final of their respective Twenty20 competitions. "Essex would be my first choice, Mumbai Indians next, so unfortunately Central Districts would be last call but it's a nice position to be in." *The Wisden Cricketer*, March 2010

David Currie

Local hero: Ravi Bopara bats for the Auckland Aces

Local villain: Bopara falls to Essex team-mate Graham Napier

The T20 draft

JOHN Bracewell **below**, Gloucestershire's director of cricket, says the ECB should introduce a player-recruitment system based on the draft system used in American football to keep the Twenty20 Cup competitive. He says: "We don't have the financial resources to buy in players and simply cannot afford to compete with some other counties."

In American football teams are ranked in inverse order based on the previous season's record: the worst team has first pick from the best college players, the second-worst has second pick and so on. Bracewell says a similar draft system, involving the world's best players, would promote a level playing field and prevent the competition becoming a closed shop with only the wealthy having a realistic chance of winning.

The best overseas players would sign up to an English Twenty20 draft and be paid a flat fee. "The top 40 or 60 players sign up and say 'we want in' and the counties take two or three apiece. If they are all paid the same they are not going to prefer playing for one team over another and money will no longer be a determining factor. It would lead to a more competitive tournament and that will ensure people keep watching. The draft day alone would make the ECB a fortune from television rights and could pay for the competition and the players."

Bracewell says Twenty20 success at present is down to money: "The wealthier counties have a significant advantage. If that continues you risk it becoming like the football Premier League where only a few clubs can win the title and the others make up the numbers." *The Wisden Cricketer*, June 2010

Andy Stockhausen

The rise of the global superclub

Hampshire joined forces with an IPL franchise. **Richard Gillis** found out exactly what was going on

ON A DAMP Monday night in London last summer, Shane Warne led out the Rajasthan Royals of the Indian Premier League in a friendly Twenty20 match at Lord's against hosts Middlesex. The game was a forgettable, one-sided affair but this match may yet be viewed as a watershed for the crowd it drew: 23,000 people, drawn largely from the British Asian community, with many dressed in the distinctive blue-and-orange colours of the Royals, a team created just two years before at the start of the IPL.

"The match was a very profound event for many reasons," says Manoj Badale, chairman of the Royals franchise and a leading figure in the British Asian Trust, a charitable and lobbying group.

"It was put on with three weeks' notice and we filled the place. It was great to look around Lord's and see lots of brown faces and lots of young faces."

Badale quotes figures from an exit poll by his own organisation: "Something like 40% of the people there had never been to a cricket match, around 50% had brought their children to the game and 35% were from a British Asian background but had never been to an English cricket ground."

This Indian diaspora, so the cliché runs, are cricket mad and notoriously hard to reach via traditional marketing. Previously, Indian fans in England have been unable to watch their teams because mainstream television only screens content with mass appeal.

The internet and digital TV have opened up cricket to millions of fans outside the domestic markets. And if you have the right brand (remember the stickiness of the Royals brand is largely untested) money follows.

The broader British Asian community has long been the holy grail of sports administrators desperate to unlock a market representing 3% of the UK

population and up to 6% of GDP. The ECB's last attempt to engage with this audience ended in embarrassing failure. The English T20 Premier League was the board's attempt to build a rival to the IPL. The original plan for the event envisaged each team fielding two Indian players as a means of targeting the audience the Royals are now seeking to reach.

He's back: Rajasthan Royals captain Shane Warne bowls against Middlesex during the Twenty20 at Lord's

Encouraged by the Lord's experiment, Badale is attempting to extend the team's brand from India to four key cricket markets around the world and create the 'world's first global sports franchise'. Hampshire will join the Cape Cobras (South Africa), Trinidad & Tobago (West Indies) and Victoria Bushrangers (Australia) in the new alliance. The deal sees each of the teams re-named as the Royals and wearing the same shirt in Twenty20 matches.

But this is not really about cricket – it's about money. Badale's plan is based on luring bigger companies into the sponsorship market, which beyond the national teams operates largely locally. At the top end of the market, the opposite is true. The global TV coverage of the Premier League means that Liverpool

> **❝ It was great to look around Lord's and see a lot of brown faces ❞**

were recently able to sign a new shirt deal with Standard Chartered Bank, which has no presence on the UK's high street, for £20 million a year.

Nobody is talking those sort of numbers in county cricket. But if Badale's plan works, bigger companies may find the Hampshire Royals shirt more valuable for two reasons: it will be seen by more people and on a more regular basis. Currently, the Royals brand appears only in IPL matches but under the new plan would be 'active' for 83% of the year.

It is very much in the IPL's interests that Badale spread the Royals brand outside India. But will it work? Watching Warne and the (real) Rajasthan Royals at Lord's is one thing. Whether the 'Hampshire Royals' – a marketing conceit – has the same draw is very questionable. What's more, the governing bodies in England and the other Test-playing nations have a vested interest in maintaining the status quo, under which competitions between national teams are the game's cash cow. The rise of clubs threatens cricket's economic structure.

Money from TV and sponsorship flows into the World Cup, World Twenty20 and Test cricket and then makes its way via the boards to the game's grassroots. The IPL is a different model, more akin to Formula 1 and football's Premier League: the money flows in and largely stays with the franchise owners and the players.

India, Pakistan and the small nation states of the Caribbean once used cricket as a symbol of their independence from Britain. The rise of club teams such as the Royals, and of the IPL itself, signals a shift away from all this, toward a new globalised world where money, rather than asserting nationhood, is the aim.

The Wisden Cricketer, April 2010

Richard Gillis is a sports-business writer

EXPERT EYE Keith Bradshaw, MCC

The oncoming train?

The chief executive of MCC was excited but worried by the future

DURING THE past three years the explosion of Twenty20, the increasing influence of money and, generally, challenges to the status quo (from switch hits to floodlit first-class cricket) have made the cricketing world more febrile than ever. I consider myself optimistic but it isn't difficult to look ahead and see the pessimists' apocalyptic version of the future of the game, where Tests are redundant, Twenty20 saturates and players are globe-trotting mercenaries. Maybe we are going through a period of evolution or revolution that other sports have already negotiated (the explosion in English football's finances brought about by the Premier League in 1992; the professionalism of rugby union in 1995) and in the not-too-distant future cricket will settle down into a new order.

Thinking about football is instructive because, increasingly, cricket's power is coming to lie with clubs rather than countries. In football no country has the marketing potential, the revenue generation or the fan-base to match behemoths like Manchester United. In cricket the rise of the IPL, the riches on offer to successful Twenty20 sides and the emergence of multi-national franchises will make clubs rather than countries similarly strong.

I'm not just talking about financial power. We know several players have already forgone playing Tests to prolong more lucrative Twenty20 careers but I believe the more covert long-term problem will be that young players will be schooled purely in the Twenty20 game and be unable to adapt to the demands of cricket played over three, four and five days.

There is no doubt Test cricket still remains the pinnacle of the game in my and many other fans' eyes. Twenty20 and ODI cricket can be scintillating and of the highest quality but, very often,

The future: Afghanistan take on USA in the World Twenty20 qualifiers

DONALD MACLEOD

> **❝ There could be twenty countries capable of playing Twenty20 in five years ❞**

because of the sheer volume, the games begin to merge into one. Twenty20 is fast food – a great hit in small quantities but too much becomes unhealthy and unenjoyable. Achievements over five days hold long-term resonance; players prefer scoring a century in a Test.

So what do I see in my crystal ball for the future of the game? It doesn't have to be the pessimist's outlook. Twenty20 could sound the death knell for Test cricket but it could also prove to be the perfect vehicle for the expansion of the game into other countries. The shorter the game, the greater the leveller and Twenty20 is an excellent pathway into the elite fold – just think of the fairy-tale qualification of Afghanistan for this year's World Twenty20. There could be 20 countries capable of playing competitive Twenty20 cricket within five years – surely something to celebrate.

Is the light at the end of the tunnel a shining hope for a more global game, or simply an oncoming Twenty20 freight train driving the sport to destruction? Unless the administrators manage finances and relationships with cricket's long-term health at the forefront of their minds, there won't be a light.

The Wisden Cricketer, April 2010

Keith Bradshaw is chief executive of MCC

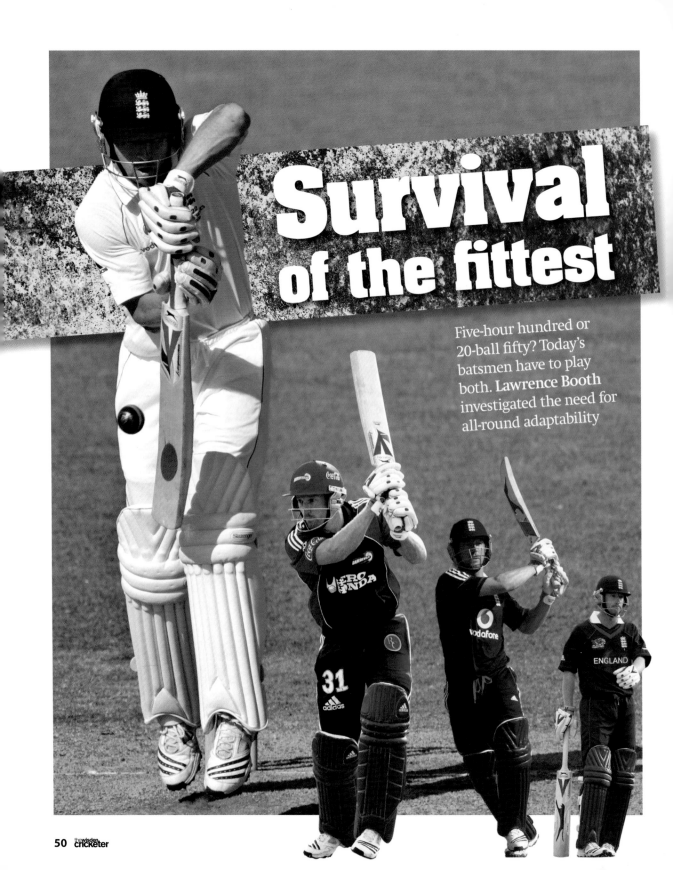

Survival
of the fittest

Five-hour hundred or 20-ball fifty? Today's batsmen have to play both. **Lawrence Booth** investigated the need for all-round adaptability

In a recent newspaper interview Paul Collingwood bit his lip and faced up to the looming prospect of another three months on the road. Since Collingwood was brooding over the thought of more time away from his family, the interviewer presumably decided it was not the time to suggest a different kind of test also lay in wait.

On March 5 Collingwood played in the third of three one-day internationals in Bangladesh. Two days later came a three-day warm-up game in Chittagong, hot on the heels of which was the first of two Tests. And three days after the scheduled finale of the second of them, in Dhaka, he was hoping to be ready for an Indian Premier League Twenty20 match in Bangalore. Three weeks, four tempos: cricketers have never had it so varied.

Cricket's evolution just about squeezes into the Darwinian template. The introduction of a middle stump, the advent of round-arm bowling, WG Grace playing forward and back, the debut of Don Bradman, the arrival of ODIs, coloured clothing, helmets, floodlights and switch-hits – each development has forced players to evolve or perish. But it may well be the 21st century that has taken the doctrine of survival of the fittest to its most logical extreme.

Some players – Ricky Ponting, Andrew Strauss, VVS Laxman – have accepted either their age or their limitations and opted out of the challenge of competing in all formats for their country. Others – Kieron Pollard, David Warner, Eoin Morgan – are polishing reputations without the help of Tests. But for the majority of the world's top players the answer is adaptation. Just ask Collingwood ... plus Brigadier Block and Sergeant Smash, his two alter egos who emerged on last winter's South Africa tour.

This phenomenon of sporting evolution-on-the-make takes place on an almost daily basis in county cricket, where the defined competition blocks have only partially eased a labyrinthine fixture list. Mark Ramprakash, who averages 54 in first-class cricket, 40 in List A one-day games and 31 – with a strike-rate of 127 – in Twenty20 matches may have made light of the potential confusion but he says it isn't the same for everyone. "One day you might have a four-day game at Bristol, where there's a bit of swing and seam around and you're looking to do the basics well, play straight and show the full face of the bat," he says. "The next day it might be a Twenty20 game at Taunton and you have to have the confidence to hit through the line of the ball. Taking the Twenty20 approach into longer forms of the game can liven up the play. But on the negative side I would worry that younger players sometimes get the balance wrong. They say, 'That's just the way I play: I try to be aggressive'. But actually you're not being tough enough on yourself. You need to take responsibility to build an innings."

66 Sehwag just told Collingwood: 'No, no, no. Watch ball, hit ball' 99

If the concern seems apt lower down the food chain, then most international cricketers play down the challenge – not surprising, perhaps, now that Twenty20's money has quelled the uproar over burn-out. Who, since the retirement five years ago of New Zealand opener and perennial self-deprecator Mark Richardson, would cheerfully portray himself as a stick-in-the-mud maker of five-hour hundreds?

Mickey Arthur, who recently stepped down after five years as coach of South Africa, describes the constant realignment of technical and mental skills as "one of my biggest challenges", and cites a difference in Test and one-day batsmen's practice.

"For Tests we'd work on going back and across, covering off stump and playing straight down the wicket," he says. "With the one-day guys we'd look to free them up outside off stump – not covering it, unless the wicket was doing a bit early on. If the wicket was flat, you'd look to stay leg side of the ball. In Test cricket you'd want to stay off side. It's a different guard."

Arthur also talks about the one-day players working on one shot on both sides of the wicket, in addition to a release stroke – the one a batsman can play if he feels bogged down. But he insists "class players will adapt anyway" and claims he never needed more than one session with his batsmen to prepare for a change of format.

Which raises another question posed by the need to adapt: why are England, a middling-to-good Test team, more or less bottom of the heap in Twenty20?

At the 2009 IPL in South Africa the under-employed Collingwood said he tried to pick the brain of Virender Sehwag, a fellow Delhi Daredevil. Collingwood fired a string of technical questions at his team-mate, only for Sehwag to interrupt. "No, no, no. Watch ball, hit ball."

This is more than the advice of a gifted hitter to a self-confessed grafter: it is a clash of cultures, the tendency of over-coached Englishmen to fret over their left elbow than plonk the ball into the stands.

The biggest challenge may be for younger players who come to regard the first-class game as an obstacle to stardom. Could it be that a new generation of players will wrestle less and less with the different problems posed by three formats, staking all on the flick over fine leg or the back-of-the-hand slower ball?

"Unfortunately I see it going that way slightly," says Arthur. "Look at Kieron Pollard. I have a lot of respect for him, but there's no track record there as a player. It's far better to judge a cricketer on a five-hour hundred than a 10-ball 30."

Arthur may soon begin to sound very quaint indeed. 🦅 *The Wisden Cricketer, April 2010*

Lawrence Booth writes for the *Daily Mail*

Collingwood's schedule
How he chopped and changed in 2010

Feb 17-20 T20Is in the United Arab Emirates	2 T20Is
Feb 28 – Mar 24 England in Bangladesh	3 ODIs
	2 Tests
March 29 – April 18 IPL for Delhi Daredevils	8 T20s
May 3-16 World Twenty20 in West Indies	7 T20Is
June 13 – July 20 For Durham	
1 LVCC	2 T20s
June 19 – July 12 Summer ODIs	
	1 ODI v Sco
	5 ODIs v Aus
	3 ODIs v Ban
July 29 – Sept 22 Pakistan in England	
4 Tests	
	2 T20Is
5 ODIs	

Crashing the party

Starting with returning refugees, cricket in war-torn Afghanistan went from zero to the world stage in eight years. **Will Luke** investigated the romance and prospects

Cricket has changed dramatically in the last decade. So fast that it is easy to forget the reason for falling in love with it in the first place. But away from the glitzy facade and big business is a story from one of the world's poorest and most troubled countries. From adversity Afghanistan's cricket team have sprung unlikely success.

The very notion that a war-ravaged country could field a decent side seems ludicrous. Hence everyone's astonishment that such a ramshackle team, built almost solely on hope and dreams, have risen so quickly to a place on the world stage.

Sport has a crucial role to play in the regeneration of the country. A decade ago, under Taliban rule, even the country's most popular sport, buzkashi – a traditional horseback sport where

participants grab goats while at full gallop – was restricted. Women, the perennial victims of Sharia law, were prevented from playing any sport.

It was only in 2002 that cricket began to take a foothold, when refugees returned from Pakistan with their knowledge and new-found love of the game. Their journey began in Division 5 of the World Cricket League, held in Jersey in May 2008, when Taj Malik, the first national coach, boldly proclaimed: "Not only are we going to bring the cup back from Jersey but we are also going to the World Cup." The confidence seemed laughable. But Afghanistan did win in Jersey, before winning Division 4 in Tanzania, Division 3 in Argentina and, in 2009, flicking aside Ireland, Bermuda, Scotland and others but just missing out on making it to the World Cup 2011.

Their greatest achievement to date came in February, winning five out of six matches in the World Twenty20 Qualifiers, a tournament featuring Ireland – the best Associate side by a distance – alongside some less gifted teams, most of whom have been on the scene a lot longer than Afghanistan. They beat Ireland twice – and then came

66 On the streets, everybody knows us and all they talk about is cricket 99

the headline-writers' dream encounter: Afghanistan versus USA or, as *ABC News* put it after the match, "Afghanistan destroys the United States".

Yet these players have come from the humblest, poorest of beginnings. Most have lost a family member or entire

DONALD MACLEOD (3)

Stump splatter: Hamid Hassan v UAE

generations. Most grew up in refugee camps, such as the notorious Kacha Gari in Peshawar in Pakistan's North West Frontier Province, a vast settlement estimated to have homed nearly 50,000 in disgusting conditions enclosed by barbed wire. Playing cricket for their country represents near utopia.

"I am the lucky man," says Raees Ahmadzai, an allrounder apparently in his twenties (his manager says 40 is more likely). "I can do something special for my country. We were not involved in the war. We were not involved in the bad things. I will show my culture to the rest of the world that we are not warrior people."

For a nation accustomed to war and oppression the accomplishments of their cricket team have brought cheer to cities whose walls still echo with gunshots. Hamid Hassan is one of their young, fearless fast bowlers with a future brighter than his parents could ever imagine. Ten years ago, aged 14, he would wag school to play cricket barefooted in the dusty roads of Peshawar; his parents hated the game. In 2009, after Hassan picked up five wickets in South Africa, they sacrificed a goat in celebration, handing it to the poor in his village. Cricket has utterly changed these people's lives.

"People love the game in Afghanistan," Hassan says. "When we go out on the streets, everyone shouts our name, everybody knows us and all they talk about is cricket. Cricket is changing Afghanistan – changing how people view the country. Cricket is everywhere, with children playing on the streets all the time, and it makes for a good future. I'm so proud – yes, of myself. But I'm mainly

proud of my country and so lucky that I get the chance to represent it."

The ICC is no less pleased with Afghanistan's progress, grateful even. "We're ecstatic," says Tim Anderson, ICC's development programmes manager for the region. "We have to be. The story for Afghanistan is great for cricket as a whole, and has put the spotlight on a country most people thought never played cricket.

"So that's a big positive for us. Two years ago they were only just beating teams that were 30th in the world. They're now competing with the likes of Ireland. There has to be something [beneficial] to have changed in their internal structures for that to have happened. Their coach, Kabir Khan, is the one constant who has focused that natural ability."

"I think they have challenges administratively," says Anderson. "I don't say that with any prejudices; when the governance of the country is having difficulties, we can't ask their cricket board to have a fantastic governance. Given that they've got significant interest throughout the country, a lot of people want to get involved and they need to get a local process in place to deal with that interest. And that's difficult. We don't doubt that and we're trying to assist the authorities as much as we can and try to help them out."

Assistance comes in the form of money, up to a considerable £593,400 if the ICC's administrative requirements are correctly carried out. It is not impossible. But it is not terribly likely, either. That said, the team have upset the odds (and a few opponents) with remarkable regularity over the past two years and now have South Africa and India in their sights at the World Twenty20.

Regardless of what happens in the immediate future, the current group of players have done enough to inspire a new generation of Afghans to play the game and disprove the prejudices whose scars they bear. For that alone we should applaud cricket's potential for good in a country tattooed by war. ⟨⟩ *The Wisden Cricketer, May 2010*

Will Luke is a freelance writer and former assistant editor of Cricinfo.com

The Afghan push

The story of Afghanistan's qualification for the 2010 World Twenty20.

SAVE for the occasional gala day, one-day cricket beneath the top 10 is watched by polite little crowds that number in scores or hundreds. How, then, did February's World Twenty20 Qualifier come to feature a pitch invasion by a delirious horde?

Eight teams were summoned to the UAE but only the two finalists would book an onward trip to the West Indies. But this was really the Afghanistan show. By the time of the final, Afghanistan and Ireland already had what they had come for. But the multitudes of Afghan drivers and labourers who live in the UAE did not see it that way and a whisper of interest that had been spreading culminated in a surge.

Afghanistan play cricket for the joy of it. They all bat, they all bowl and they are all exhibitionists. Offspinner Karim Sadiq greets wickets with a forward roll; 18-year-old wicketkeeper Mohammad Shahzad likes to honour a stumping by spinning in a circle with his arms stretched wide. Despite cutting a swathe through the ICC's affiliate ranks and securing ODI status, Afghanistan had never made it onto the world stage proper.

Day one went well, as they benefited from Ireland's rare attack of butterfingers to win by 13 runs. Up the road in Abu Dhabi, Scotland had lost to the USA and the UAE were about to upset Canada. The old guard were wobbling and the Irish were the only team of the three who would regain their footing; the Dutch became the only team to beat Afghanistan. As for those who left early, Canada's efforts were surprisingly bereft. A Scotland side whose Twenty20 limitations are more palpable also lost all three games. Kenya, once the kings of this jungle, have fallen back into the pack.

Defeat in the final book-ended Ireland's efforts and that hurt their pride but their lower order have perfected the format's trademark sweeps and scoops and they keep it simple: get runs on the board and then bowl line and length. How Afghanistan cope with the step-up remains to be seen but nowhere are they not accomplished: Nowroz Mangal has eight or nine bowling options and rotates his openers. They are dashing and daring and they have a canny coach.

Cricket's spirit was alive and well in Dubai and Abu Dhabi. As the remarkable Afghanistan story wound on, even Richard Done, whose job as ICC high-performance manager is to plot a pathway for these countries, confessed with a chuckle: "I don't know where this is going to end."

The Wisden Cricketer, April 2010

Jonathan Coates writes for the *Irish Daily Mail* and *The Scotsman*

Scene of the crime

Before the World Twenty20 the last tournament England played in the Caribbean was the infamous Stanford Super Series. **Nick Hoult** looked back at the whole embarrassing episode

When the World Twenty20 promotional show arrived on the island of Antigua volunteers on the "Bring It" tour bus dished out free T-shirts to locals who by then had probably seen and heard enough about the power of Twenty20.

Just days earlier one of Antigua's former residents, Allen Stanford, celebrated his 60th birthday behind bars in a Texas federal prison. The self-styled "saviour" of West Indies cricket is incarcerated awaiting trial on 21 criminal charges alleging that his banks in Texas and Antigua ran a Ponzi scheme worth billions of dollars ripping off more than a quarter of a million investors.

Meanwhile the SCG (no, not that one) lies underneath a carpet of weeds. The neglect of the Stanford Cricket Ground, adjacent to Antigua's international airport, is perhaps the most fitting

metaphor for a project that crashed when its promoter was accused of a worldwide fraud of "shocking magnitude". That was in February 2009. In January 2011, Stanford is expected to stand trial in Houston, around the same time that Giles Clarke could be campaigning for a third term as chairman of the ECB.

If recent moves to change the ECB's constitution to allow Clarke another year in office without the need for an election are successful, then a potentially awkward clash with Stanford's trial will have been avoided.

That would be great news for Clarke and the board because even now, 14 months since the ECB broke off its relationship with Stanford, those images of Stanford laughing and joking with cricket chiefs on the Lord's turf in front of a helicopter are still shown in the US.

The memory of the only Stanford Super Series week, in late 2008, still lingers because the words "cricket promoter"

follow every mention of Stanford on the US news wires. Stories revolve around the sale of his Panama bank by the US administrators for $14.2m, the stripping of his knighthood by the governor general of Antigua and American Express suing him for an unpaid bill of $115,000.

A detailed investigation by the *Miami Herald* last year alleged that in the weeks leading up to the Super Series, Stanford drove to a mountain top in St Croix, in the Virgin Islands, and burned financial records in a steel drum. The article quoted

> **❝It is alleged he drove to a mountain top in St Croix and burned financial records in a steel drum❞**

Stanford employees detailing his erratic behaviour that included demolishing two mansions he had recently built and replacing them with a one-bedroom apartment. They also told of boozing and temper tantrums as the days ticked

Winning grins: Chris Gayle claims the cheque

Shambolic: Flintoff after Gayle hits a four

by before England's arrival. Stanford was facing an unreal truth. As the stock market crashed – it fell by 18% one week in October 2008 – he faced investors wanting to withdraw money. Money that investigators allege had disappeared.

It was against this backdrop that Stanford proved to be an erratic host during the Super Series, his behaviour lurching from absurd to ignorant. With his bank losing $33.3m per month, dangling a couple of England Wags on his knee was perhaps an understandable escape route. That night on November 1, Antigua's Independence Day, when Stanford's team thrashed England by 10 wickets, cost him a supposed $20m in prize money but his smile was as wide as the Texan plain. It was the last time he would be fêted and celebrated in public. He was lambasted by the British media and the ECB happily leaked, before the week was out, that it was to hold a review into the Stanford deal at the end of the trip.

By the middle of the week Stanford was attempting to repair the damage. "When this was announced in June, I was a hero. Now I'm a skunk in October," he said. But headlines such as 'English cricket is Stanford's Wag' stung both

sides. Stanford was reeling from all the punches as he posed for pictures sporting a moustache that *The Guardian*'s Mike Selvey wrote made him look like a cross between Basil Fawlty and the *Fast Show* character Swiss Tony.

In fact the only Brits happy to be there were the Middlesex team, invited to play Trinidad & Tobago, who had a free end-of-season holiday holed up in an all-inclusive hotel on an Antiguan beach. It was at that hotel in Jolly Beach that Stanford had, six months earlier, lodged three British journalists he had invited to witness his own domestic Stanford tournament. I was one of the reporters sent by my newspaper to cover the final, with Stanford footing the bill. During the weekend we were given an audience with Stanford himself, a rare treat we were told by his staff. The interview was scheduled to last 20 minutes.

It took nearly two hours as Stanford revealed his dream $20m showdown he termed the "OK Corral of cricket". That he was also dismissive of India, who had rebuffed his advances, made him a natural ally for the ECB which at that stage was wary of the IPL's growth.

It is easy to forget now that the deal with the ECB stretched beyond the five Super Series that were originally scheduled. Stanford also had access to naming rights to the proposed English Premier League Twenty20 tournament which would almost certainly have contained a Stanford Superstars side. An annual quadrangular Twenty20 tournament was set to be held at Lord's as another component of the deal.

Stanford was due to be a permanent fixture in English cricket. But his behaviour in Antigua and the inevitable fall that followed led to English cricket dropping its new friend. There was no mention of his name in the ECB's 2009 annual report even though he had actually paid all his dues to the board, worth around $3.5m. Amazingly, the one thing the ECB can claim is that it managed to squeeze money out of Stanford. Investors around the world who have seen life savings disappear, would love to be in that position. ■ *The Wisden Cricketer*, May 2010

Nick Hoult writes for the Daily Telegraph

Publicans and the original IPL

Twenty20 is simply the game returning to its roots

IMAGINE this: two teams, each owned by rich men and made up of highly paid professionals, are about to play a heavily-promoted match in front of a large crowd. There's money on the outcome and a huge amount of side betting going on. The IPL? Allen Stanford? No. This is cricket as played in its birthplace, the Home Counties, in the 18th century. Diehards may complain that Twenty20 is a betrayal of the traditions of the great game. But it is actually cricket reverting to its roots.

As early as July 1697 the *Foreign Post* reported that "The middle of last week a great match at Cricket was played in Sussex; they were eleven of a side, and they played for fifty guineas apiece." By 1700 cricket had become a major spectator attraction.

The promoters were often publicans hoping to attract trade. The purpose of the day was gambling, drink and entertaining sport, in roughly that order. But 'great matches' were organised by landowners: their team against that of a rival. The bulk of their side were professionals – the best village players that they could buy.

The rules were decided between the patrons, as were the number of players per side. Over time this settled at 11 – no one knows why – but there were still plenty of contests which involved far fewer players, anything from one to five. Many of these games were played at Lord's in front of a large crowd.

By the early 19th century cricket had produced real stars and the public loved to see them in what was almost hand-to-hand combat. A few matches were for the 'Championship of England'. There was of course no such championship. It was a marketing ploy. But it packed them in. Just as the IPL does. *The Wisden Cricketer, May 2010*

Julian Norridge is an author

Barmy Army: At Lord's in 1872

The party kings

The World Twenty20 gave the Caribbean the chance to erase the memories of the 2007 World Cup. **Sam Collins** went to Barbados and saw that the West Indies were still dancing

A couple of six-hits from Bridgetown's Kensington Oval stands Herbert House, the home of the Cricket Legends of Barbados. It houses a newly opened museum dedicated to the past of Bajan and West Indies cricket. If you turn too quickly from the portraits of Sobers, Haynes, Greenidge and company that line the walls then you'll get a fright from the freakish life-size cut-outs that immortalise Joel Garner and Wes Hall in their prime. Cuttings detailing two decades of dominance decorate a room at the back. It is a cricketing Pompeii: a preserved reminder of an empire that once ruled the world.

Behind Herbert House is a bar. It looks nothing special, skirting the far-left edge of a converted car park. The rum flows, there is music and dancing in the open air – if it rains a few may lope for the cover of a large hanger but the revelry continues. Beside the dancers, the real Joel Garner towers, smile beaming like a floodlight. In the shade Wes Hall sits chatting. There's also Courtney Browne, Anderson Cummins and Vasbert Drakes moving gently to the beat – no doubt there are more old players. They are all fervently talking cricket.

They are there for a reason – over at The Oval a tournament has been going on and it is an important one. The 2010 World Twenty20 has been the Caribbean's chance to atone for the horror show that was the 2007 World Cup. Back then officious regulations, high ticket prices and over-commercialisation added up to low attendances and lower cheer.

But the organisers learned their lesson. This year, ticket prices are significantly lower – the most expensive seat at the tournament is £26 for the final – and tens of thousands of fans have responded to the invitation to 'Bring It'. The 'Bring It' campaign with theme song of the same name has encouraged spectators to bring their musical instruments, flags, food and personality back to the stands for the authentic Caribbean experience. Attendances have been high, with sell-outs for weekend games and a full-house anticipated for the final.

Gayle Alleyne, a native Barbadian and the event's corporate communications manager, was the media officer in 2007. "A lot of the people who worked on the 2007 tournament wanted to get back involved to show the fans that we could do it the way they expect us to in the Caribbean. We feel the region has embraced this."

One area of contention has been the lack of day-night matches with most games scheduled to start at either 9.30am or 1.30pm local time due to television contracts, which have also prevented games from being shown live on local

> ## The crowds are not as big as they should be. Who's going to get here at 9.30am?

television. Tony Cozier, the voice of West Indies cricket and commentating on the tournament for the BBC, is unimpressed. "The crowds are not as big as they should be. Who is going to get here at 9.30am on a weekday? People should have the opportunity to come down after work and watch under lights in the cool of the evening, the whole atmosphere of limited-overs is ideally suited to day-night cricket. West Indian crowds are again being short-changed but in a different way to the last World Cup. I understand the reasons, we are poor, the money is coming in from TV and we've got to bow and scrape to them."

But even with the Kensington Oval not quite full, the atmosphere is electric. As balls pepper the Greenidge and Haynes stand, flag-bearing supporters from different nations intermingle, causing the scene to change like a traffic light on a wicket or boundary. "It's exactly what we expected," says Josh Dickinson, who has travelled from Western Australia.

The other controversial area has concerned the choice of host islands, specifically Guyana as the third venue alongside Barbados and St Lucia. There was always a chance the choice could backfire given the island's equatorial climate. Yet for Cricinfo's Andrew McGlashan, following England in Guyana, the choice made sense. "Both of the West Indies games there were sold out, the atmosphere was terrific. The Guyanese love their cricket. It was good for the country."

As for the West Indies team itself, they remained a mass of contradictions. Cozier described them "an embarrassment" after defeat to Sri Lanka before a rousing win against India. The travails of the last 15 years have left a scar on the region – the resignation in defeat was as palpable as the joy in victory. Yet while there are few sights like a victorious West Indies crowd, home troubles would not bring down this vibrant tournament. Whatever happens to their team, the West Indies have shown that they still know how to throw a party. ▪

The Wisden Cricketer, June 2010

Sam Collins is *TWC's* **website editor**

The Afghanistan story

MUCH OF the talk in the lead-up to the tournament was of Afghanistan who had beaten Ireland to qualify for the World Twenty20. They could not continue the fairytale in the Caribbean, losing both games comfortably to India by seven wickets and South Africa by 59 runs, where they were 14 for 6 thanks to Dale Steyn and Morne Morkel.

A feature of the Afghan rise has been their unshakeable self-belief, and manager Bashir Khan spoke of the team's disappointment: "The people were happy in Afghanistan and around the world with our performance but the boys were not because they know they could play better cricket. It was very good experience – the players have not faced bowlers of the pace of Steyn and Morkel before."

Yet the Afghans impressed enough for rumours to circulate that new IPL franchise Pune are interested in signing left-arm quick Shapoor Zadran and batsman Noor Ali **left**, who made a fifty against India. Opening bowler Hamid Hassan took 3 for 21 against South Africa to find himself compared to Waqar Younis by Clive Lloyd.

Later in the year Afghanistan played a first-class game against Scotland in Scotland and smashed them by 229 runs.
The Wisden Cricketer, June 2010

The Carnival's collapse

One moment the Indian Premier League seemed too good to be true. The next moment it was. **Dileep Premachandran** found out how it all went wrong

T TOOK a Deep Throat to bring down Richard Nixon's presidency in 1974. All it took to end Lalit Modi's meteoric rise to the apex of cricket administration were a few careless words punched into his BlackBerry, which were then viewed by hundreds of thousands on his Twitter page. By questioning the antecedents of those who had bid for the new IPL franchise in Kochi weeks earlier Modi cast aspersions on Shashi Tharoor, the former UN official who was now India's minister of state for external affairs. The resulting political fallout saw Tharoor resign and the

full weight of the government's investigating agencies bearing down on the IPL.

There were allegations of massive kickbacks from TV companies and in no time income-tax officials and the enforcement directorate started

66 By the end of the tournament Modi's days were numbered 99

probing the finances of each of the eight existing franchises. Stories were leaked to the media on a daily basis of how Modi and his cronies had carved up the juiciest slices of the IPL pie for themselves. By the

time the third edition of the tournament came to an end, with Chennai Super Kings' victory on April 25, Modi's days were numbered. A suspension notice was served to him minutes after the last ball was bowled and the Board of Control for Cricket in India (BCCI) appointed Chirayu Amin, a Vadodara-based businessman, as the IPL's interim chairman even as Modi was given a fortnight to answer the multiple charges levelled against him.

I first came across Modi in the foyer of the Pearl Continental Hotel in Lahore. It was January 2006 and the BCCI had finally been "liberated" from the Jagmohan

WENN (4); PA PHOTOS

168-5 v 146-9
The Final – Chennai beat Mumbai by 22 runs

585
Number of sixes, more than in 2009 (506) but fewer than in 2008 (623)

246-5
Highest total, scored by Chennai v Rajasthan

11.72
Match run-rate from Chennai v Rajasthan, the highest of the tournament

27
Most sixes, hit by Robin Uthappa far left

127
Highest score, by Chennai's Murali Vijay against Rajasthan Royals

618
Most runs, by Sachin Tendulkar

7.66
Best bowling average, by Virender Sehwag

21
Most wickets, by Deccan's Pragyan Ojha right

4.05
Best economy rate, by Virender Sehwag

4-13
Best figures, by Doug Bollinger above left

Dalmiya influence. Modi was seen as one of the right-hand men of Sharad Pawar, the union minister who was now president of the board as well. As one listened to him talk, it was not hard to see why Pawar had chosen him. Most reporters there could still not get their heads round the new TV deal that the board had just signed, worth an astronomical $612m over four years. "You ain't seen nothing yet" was the gist of the Modi message. "Wait till you see what we do with the mobile [telephone] and internet rights," he said smugly.

Pawar may have wanted Dalmiya, the Kolkata construction magnate, out of the way but he had no desire to see the BCCI brand depreciate. After all Dalmiya was the man who had taken both the BCCI and the ICC from penury – the international body had £16,000 in its coffers when he took over – to *nouveau riche* status. In Modi he seemed to have unearthed Dalmiya Mark II, one with an even greater appreciation of how market forces worked in modern-day sport.

Four years on, with Pawar poised to take over the ICC's top job, Modi was a sultan in his own right. The TV rights for the two properties that he lorded it over, the IPL and the

Champions League, were alone worth more than $2.5bn and two new IPL franchises had just been auctioned for a staggering $703m, what Liverpool FC could fetch if sold.

Even those who greatly disliked Modi had labelled him the "most influential and powerful" man in the game. Those within the Indian board who abhorred his 'my-way-or-the-highway' approach kept quiet. He was, after all, their golden goose. The media were just as culpable. TV channels, websites and newspapers gave the IPL and its 'commissioner' saturation coverage.

Mukul Kesavan in the Kolkata-based *Telegraph* put things into perspective after the suspension: "News channels that gloried in partnering IPL franchises, Modi's henchmen at the BCCI, the hitherto house-trained members of the IPL's governing council, have rediscovered reporting, re-grown spines and unearthed scruples; these pigs have wings."

The governing council members have most to answer for. "We should have been aware of what was happening," said Mansur Ali Khan Pataudi, former India captain, in the immediate aftermath of the scandal. "The fact that we didn't question anything is because we

were carried away with how well everything was going … I saw the crowds, the IPL was very popular … the dirt that has been attached to it is sad … but as long as the product was good I was happy."

Ravi Shastri, another member of the council who was also part of the cheerleading commentary team, claimed in an interview that "my job is to ask cricketing questions".

The media were guilty of not digging deeper into the IPL's finances but surely those on the governing council knew that Modi's relatives and friends had a stake in three of the franchises – the Rajasthan Royals, Kings XI Punjab and Kolkata Knight Riders. Are we to understand that no one raised an eyebrow when those three franchises were the cheapest at the auction in 2008? Or was it that, with conflict-of-interest issues plaguing the council as a whole, no one wanted to rock the cash-rich barge?

Having stood back and watched Modi career around like a bowling ball in a roomful of precious Ming vases for five years, reality had bitten the BCCI very late indeed. ◪

The Wisden Cricketer, June 2010

Dileep Premachandran is associate editor of Cricinfo.com

INTERNATIONAL

YEAR

This was the year that Test cricket came back to India. On December 6 an ungainly slog from Sri Lanka's Muttiah Muralitharan flicked the edge of his bat and nestled in MS Dhoni's gloves. India had won by an innings. More significantly the victory pushed them to the top of the Test rankings for the first time. A year on from the Mumbai terror attacks the city was a fitting scene for the coming of age of cricket's greatest nation.

The impact was immediate. Where once India's domestic four-day tournament was watched by fewer people than a 2nd XI match at Derby, now the final brought massive crowds. The Indian board, which had spent the last decade happily feasting on the shorter forms of the game, witnessed the public reaction and realised there was money to be had in Test matches after all.

More Tests were added to a threadbare schedule to ensure India could retain their new-found status. And retain it they did, led by the opening batsman Virender Sehwag. His six centuries in 10 Tests – at a mind-pulverising strike-rate of 97.34 (Mike Atherton finished his career on 37.31) – were symbolic of India's evolution from one-day to Test dominance.

Across the border Pakistan sadly swerved again towards the wayside, where they appear to have an allotted parking space. On top of the ball-biting and spot-fixing allegations were the Test results: L W D L L L L W L L W L. L is for this year's Losers.

Zimbabwe provided the good-news story. As the nation rebuilt in 2009, so did the cricket. A new domestic structure and ODI wins over India, Sri Lanka, West Indies and Bangladesh represented a recovery as gratifying as it was unexpected.

The international game certainly has its problems but a year that saw large crowds turn up for Tests in India, Sachin Tendulkar confirm his genius with the first ODI double-hundred, a Zimbabwean and a Bangladeshi named *TWC*'s players of the month and Sri Lanka play New Zealand in Florida means the decade has started in pretty good shape. 🄻

Daniel Brigham is the assistant editor of *The Wisden Cricketer*

Contents

May 2010: Shoaib Malik admits to marrying an Indian woman over the phone

Leading lights: left MS Dhoni, captain of India the No.1 ranked team, bats at Kolkata against South Africa, the No.2 side; AB de Villiers keeps

The story of the decade

From match-fixing to six-hitting and Mugabe to Bollyline, cricket has rarely changed so dramatically in 10 years. **Lawrence Booth** charted the moments that shaped the Noughties

Say it ain't so, Hansie April **2000**
No one could quite believe it. Hansie Cronje – South Africa's captain, hero and, we thought, moral compass – would never sell his soul, would he? Alas, he would. "Cricket's *annus horribilis*," *Wisden* called 2000, the year that robbed the decade of its innocence almost before it had begun. Whispers about cricket's purity have never gone away.

The Don dies February **2001**
While Bradman was alive, so too, it seemed, were the most vivid memories of 300 in a day at Headingley, Bodyline and the Invincibles, the Hollies googly. His death, at 92, took a disproportionate chunk of an era with him.

India stun Australia March **2001**
Once a century on average, a team – specifically Australia – lose a Test after enforcing the follow-on. The beauty this time lay in the context: Steve Waugh's side had won 16 in a row, including the first Test at Mumbai, and it was looking like 17 when India batted again at Kolkata, 274 adrift. But VVS Laxman (281) and Rahul Dravid (180) put on 376, before Harbhajan Singh – already a first-innings hat-trick hero – took his match haul to 13. Thus was born the Noughties' most gripping rivalry.

The Zimbabwe affair February **2003**
The morality of playing in Robert Mugabe's benighted backyard was troubling enough for Nasser Hussain and his World Cup team-mates. But when a group calling themselves the Sons and Daughters of Zimbabwe threatened the players' families, England forfeited their Harare fixture. Andy Flower and Henry Olonga had already famously worn their black armbands but the rest looked on indifferently.

Counties embrace Twenty20 June **2003**
It started as a marketing ploy to sex up the demographics of the average county audience and finished ... well, it has not finished, not by a long shot. No one – players, fans or hacks – quite knew how seriously to take the tournament but T20 Finals Day became *the* date on the domestic calendar.

Lara goes big. Again April **2004**
Brian Lara rewrote the annals. Almost 10 years to the day since he first claimed the Test batting record with 375 (also against England in Antigua), he hit Test cricket's maiden quadruple-century to usurp Matthew Hayden's 380 against Zimbabwe six months earlier. A monument to individualism but also a paean to a modern great in an age where batsmen went big.

Boxing Day tsunami December **2004**
When a massive underwater earthquake

Leading Test bowlers		
Muttiah Muralitharan 565 wickets @ 20.97		
Makhaya Ntini 380 wickets @ 28.59		
Shane Warne 357 wickets @ 25.17		

Leading ODI bowlers		
Muttiah Muralitharan 335 wickets @ 20.55		
Brett Lee right 324 wickets @ 23.01		
Shaun Pollock 275 wickets @ 24.98		

Leading Test wicketkeepers		
Adam Gilchrist left 397 dismissals (362 ct, 35 st)		
Mark Boucher 383 dismissals (363 ct, 20 st)		
Kamran Akmal 179 dismissals (157 ct, 22 st)		

Leading ODI wicketkeepers		
Adam Gilchrist 362 dismissals (325 ct, 37 st)		
Mark Boucher 353 dismissals (335 ct, 18 st)		
Kumar Sangakkara 313 dismissals (247 ct, 66 st)		

Leading Test batsmen		
Ricky Ponting middle 9458 runs @ 58.38		
Jacques Kallis 8627 runs @ 59.08		
Rahul Dravid 8558 runs @ 54.85		

Leading ODI batsmen		
Ricky Ponting 9103 runs @ 44.18		
Sachin Tendulkar 8823 runs @ 46.68		
Mohammad Yousuf 8494 runs @ 42.25		

The decade that was: left to right flags fly at half mast in Adelaide for the Don; Harbhajan Singh gets the last wicket at Kolkata; Brian Lara reaches 400 in Antigua; Darrell Hair signals a five-run penalty at The Oval; Galle after the tsunami; Yuvraj Singh hits his fourth six, Younis Khan examines Sri Lanka's bus

sent a tidal wave racing to all corners of the Indian Ocean, killing an estimated 230,000 people, cricket was just one of the victims. Sri Lankan players lost relatives and Galle, one of Test cricket's most characteristic venues, was submerged. Not until three years later was the ground ready to stage Test cricket again.

The Ashes, Edgbaston August 2005
The greatest Test in the greatest series? Few were arguing after England came from behind to fill a 16-year urn-shaped vacuum and remind the nation there was more to this sporting life than football. Subsequent results underlined Australia's quality – Adelaide 2006-07 will always haunt the English – but here were the first signs of cracks in the green-and-gold castle.

You think that's big? March 2006
When Australia rattled up a world-record 434 for 4 (Ponting 164 from 105 balls) in the fifth and deciding ODI at Johannesburg, the only question was the size of South Africa's defeat. Not a bit of it – for this was

life in the post-T20 world. Graeme Smith mowed 90 from 55 deliveries, Herschelle Gibbs 175 from 111 and, amid disbelief and delirium, South Africa won with a wicket and a ball to spare.

Ovalgate August 2006
When Darrell Hair, abetted by Billy Doctrove, added five runs to England's total for ball-tampering on the fourth afternoon of the fourth Test against Pakistan, he unleashed cricket's horsemen of the apocalypse. Inzamam-ul-Haq and his men refused to emerge after tea, Pakistan forfeited the game – a first in 129 years of Test cricket. Mud was slung; much stuck.

Yuvraj goes berserk September 2007
Andrew Flintoff may have regretted niggling Yuvraj Singh. When Stuart Broad embarked on the next over, the 19th of India's innings on a steamy night at Durban in the inaugural World Twenty20, Yuvraj became the fourth player to hit six sixes in an over in top-level cricket. India went on to lift the trophy and a nation's

reluctance to embrace Twenty20 gave way to euphoria – and the IPL.

The IPL comes to town April 2008
So much for the quaint revolution of county cricket's Twenty20 Cup. For glitz, glamour and self-importance, the IPL was at least two rungs higher up the evolutionary ladder.

Terrorism November 2008, March 2009
Cricket hotspots, they said, would escape the worst excesses of international terrorism because the terrorists needed whatever public sympathy remained. Then came two bloody episodes. First, with England on tour elsewhere in India, gunmen sailed into Mumbai harbour, went on the rampage and killed 173. Then buses carrying the Sri Lankan team and match officials were attacked on their way to a Test at Lahore. Eight people died. Pakistan has not hosted international cricket since. ◪ *The Wisden Cricketer, February 2010*

Lawrence Booth writes for the *Daily Mail*

AUSTRALIA v WEST INDIES Three-Test series by **Peter English**

Gayle forces a rethink

Home side flattered by 2-0 win as West Indies' captain discovered top form

CHRIS GAYLE arrived in Australia as a symbol of everything bad about West Indies cricket but quickly reminded everyone why they love the Caribbean style. In the beginning he was the man who did not care about Tests and the wrong captain following a divisive player strike. When he left suddenly before the first Test to be with his sick mother in Jamaica there was a feeling that the series was better off without him. Thank goodness he came back.

With his mother's heart condition improving, Gayle landed in Brisbane the day before the first Test and, following the three-day humiliation at the Gabba, inspired his players by following through with talk of redemption at Adelaide a week later. Instead of another forgettable failure, Gayle buried his aggression and displayed rare determination, persistence and courage in carrying his bat for 165 and giving West Indies a chance of winning. Gayle's atypical performance showed he could lead a competitive unit.

The slow and steady demeanour was lost in the final game in Perth. Following Australia's first innings of 520 for 7 declared, Gayle lit up the first 24.1 overs with the fifth-fastest century in Tests in terms of balls faced. For a moment he was on track to beat the 56-ball effort by Viv Richards but he eased back in the middle before speeding to the milestone in 70 deliveries. Gayle could not take the side to victory at the Waca either but, after giving up 208 runs on first innings, his players fought back to dismiss Australia for 150, eventually falling 35 short of a target of 359.

Ranking challenged

The only shame about Gayle's 346 runs at 69.20 was that they were not scored against a great Australian side. Though Ricky Ponting's men succeeded 2-0, they were stretched in the final two games by the world's No.8 side. Australia have won only three of their past six series and are starting to realise that their No.3 ranking is an accurate reflection.

Ben Hilfenhaus won the match award in his only game, repeating the promise he showed in the Ashes. Mitchell Johnson was again inconsistent, despite managing 17 wickets, and Peter Siddle may not be the dominating figure who can bustle through sides. The concentration of the batsmen was also a problem. There were 15 half-centuries but, for the first time since facing New Zealand in 1992-93, no hundreds.

Match fees, please

The "ugly Aussies" made a comeback, with four players reported in the final two Tests. The tag was given to some of Steve Waugh's sides but has not rested on Ponting's team. Doug Bollinger, playing his second Test, delivered an impressive free kick at Adelaide when Brendan Nash was given not out to an lbw appeal and received a reprimand. A week later at Perth Sulieman Benn and Johnson ran into each other sparking a complicated three-way tussle also involving Brad Haddin. And Shane Watson was fined for cheering like an excited gorilla a couple of metres from the dismissed Gayle. "He's that sort of person," Gayle said of Watson. "I didn't expect anything better."

Referrals' first victim

Mark Benson was the first casualty of the new umpire review system, leaving after the opening day at Adelaide when a couple of his tight decisions – an out lbw to Dwayne Bravo and a not-out caught-behind to Shivnarine Chanderpaul – were overturned by the video official Asad Rauf. While the ICC insisted Benson's departure was health-related, colleagues believed he was unhappy with the procedure.

The players were unsure about the system, with Gayle strongly against it and Ponting swaying from believer to cautiously hopeful.

The Wisden Cricketer, February 2010

Peter English is Australasian editor of Cricinfo.com

Capital gain: Skipper Gayle celebrates his century at Adelaide

| Scores |

1st Test Nov 26-28, Brisbane †**Aus 480-8d** (SM Katich 92, MJ North 79, MEK Hussey 66, RT Ponting 55); **WI 228** (TM Dowlin 62, D Ramdin 54) **and 187** (AB Barath 104). **Aus won by inns & 65 runs.** *MoM: BW Hilfenhaus below 23-9-70-5*

2nd Test Dec 4-8, Adelaide †**WI 451** (DJ Bravo 104, BP Nash 92, S Chanderpaul 62) **and 317** (CH Gayle 165; MG Johnson 5-103); **Aus 439** (SR Watson 96, Katich 80, MJ Clarke 71, BJ Haddin 55; SJ Benn 5-155) **and 212-5** (Clarke 61*). **Match drawn.** *MoM: Gayle 285b, 16x4, 1x6*

Over-ruler: Umpire Mark Benson talks to Ricky Ponting

3rd Test Dec 16-20, Perth †**Aus 520-7d** (Katich 99, Watson 89, Haddin 88, Hussey 82) **and 150** (Bravo 4-42); **WI 312** (Gayle 102, Dowlin 55; DE Bollinger 5-70) **and 323** (N Deonarine 82, Nash 65). **Aus won by 35 runs.** *MoM: Gayle 72b, 9x4, 6x6*

Aus won series 2-0

Push comes to shove: Mitchell Johnson and Sulieman Benn

AUSTRALIA v PAKISTAN Three-Test series by **Peter English**

One eye on England

Australia's 3-0 win over Pakistan exposed flaws that needed to be fixed by the Ashes

BEFORE the start of the Australian summer Ricky Ponting said every Test would be a step towards the 2010-11 Ashes and by the end of the 3-0 clean sweep over Pakistan he was optimistic about the long-term prospects of a developing unit. Even when England are not the opponents they remain a focus for Australia, especially in times when they do not hold the urn. But Australia struggled at times to dispose of West Indies and Pakistan, two of Test cricket's lesser lights. Apart from Ponting, the star quality has disappeared and the team's form can swing from great to horrible, a trait which has to be fixed.

Headingley '81 repeat
The season's most memorable moment was Australia's fourth-day miracle at Sydney in the second Test when they started the morning 80 ahead with only two second-innings wickets remaining. Having won the toss, Ponting's side was demolished for 127 to a mixture of seam – on an unusually verdant surface – and poor shot selection. Pakistan's committed reply earned a 206-run advantage and it seemed only the visitors doubted their ability to end the streak of 10 defeats in a row to Australia. Years of scarring could not convince them they were in the better position and, helped by Kamran Akmal's four dropped catches, three from Mike Hussey, they proved themselves right. Hussey scrapped and scrounged an unbeaten 134 and put on 123 with the No.10, Peter Siddle, to set 176.

After a bright start the self-conscious Pakistanis folded as soon as the pressure increased, all out for 139. Nathan Hauritz picked up five of his 18 wickets for the series. "I don't think anyone in the world apart from all the blokes inside our dressing room thought we could win," Ponting said. In days past he might have gloated about the result but in the post-match conference Ponting teasingly asked for a raise of hands from those who did not think a win was possible.

Punter hooked
Life for Ponting was tougher than usual after he was forced to retire hurt from a hit on the elbow by West Indies' Kemar Roach before Christmas. Every bowler above medium pace suddenly sensed a weakness and aimed at Ponting's body, something he encouraged publicly. Hooking and pulling have been a Ponting strength since he surprised Test quicks in the nets as a teenager and he was determined to keep playing the strokes, insisting they were instinctive. Twice he swiped to Pakistan fielders in the deep, including his first-ball exit in Sydney 15 minutes after the toss. Hampered by the elbow problem, he looked older than his 35 years and was confused by his sudden inferiority.

There were calls for him to drop down the order and to shelve the cross-bat shots. Had Mohammad Amir caught Ponting at fine leg before he scored at Hobart, the critics would have roared. Instead Ponting continued to pull and hook compulsively, twice being hit on the helmet. But after stuttering to his half-century the great batsman of the past returned. He recorded 209, his fifth Test double-century. An in-the-mood Ponting can still do anything.

Dropped chances
It is easy to feel sorry for poor, itinerant Pakistan but they contributed to their own demise. Catching was a serious problem, with 16 chances missed in the three Tests, and the batsmen were on the verge of recklessness after spending the last three years in limited-overs mode.

Even when Salman Butt broke through at Hobart with Pakistan's only century it came with the excess baggage of two horrible run-outs. Hope came through Amir, a rapid 17-year-old left-armer, and the supremely confident Umar Akmal. He does not know how to defend but can certainly attack.

The Wisden Cricketer, March 2010

Peter English is Australasian editor of Cricinfo.com

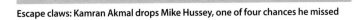
Escape claws: Kamran Akmal drops Mike Hussey, one of four chances he missed

Scores

1st Test Dec 26-30, Melbourne †**Aus 454-5d** (SM Katich 98, SR Watson 93, MEK Hussey 82, NM Hauritz 75, RT Ponting 57) and **225-8d** (Watson 120*; Mohammad Amir 5-79); **Pak 258** (Misbah-ul-Haq 65*, Umar Akmal 51) and **251** (Mohammad Yousuf 61; Hauritz 5-101). **Aus won by 170 runs.** *MoM: Watson below 93r, 191b, 11x4 & 120r, 220b, 10x4, 1x6*

2nd Test Jan 3-6, Sydney †**Aus 127** (Mohammad Asif 6-41) and **381** (Hussey 134*, Watson 97; Danish Kaneria 5-151); **Pak 333** (Salman Butt 71; DE Bollinger 4-72) and **139** (Hauritz 5-53). **Aus won by 36 runs.** *MoM: Hussey 284b, 16x4*

One of six: Mohammad Asif celebrates another wicket

3rd Test Jan 14-18, Hobart †**Aus 519-8d** (Ponting 209, MJ Clarke 166) and **219-5d** (Katich 100, Ponting 89); **Pak 301** (Salman Butt 102, Shoaib Malik 58) and **206** (Khurram Manzoor 77). **Aus won by 231 runs.** *MoM: Ponting below 209r, 354b, 25x4*

Aus won series 3-0

Tamim Iqbal Bangladesh

86, 85, 52 in Tests, 125 in ODIs v England

What was it like playing England?
I thoroughly enjoyed the experience. It was a challenge because they were under the impression that we don't play the short ball well. People were saying all kinds of things without knowing that we have played some of our best cricket in recent times on pitches that had pace and bounce. I worked hard against the short ball and I scored a lot of runs off such deliveries against England. That gave me a great deal of satisfaction.

What are your long-term goals?
To represent Bangladesh as long as possible and to score hundreds against every Test nation in Tests and ODIs.

What sort of cricketer are you?
I think I am a batsman who loves to play his shots and stays aggressive no matter what the situation might be. If the ball is in my zone and is there to be hit then I will go for it 10 times out of 10.

How important is entertaining?
Every player has his own style and my style is an attacking one. I play shots and therefore if I score runs then naturally there will be entertainment.

How has your batting evolved?
I was going along OK in ODIs but at the beginning I struggled to get a balance in Tests. I didn't know whether to start slow or be aggressive. I had no plan. Then I spoke to [coaches] Mohammad Salah Uddin and Jamie Siddons and both told me to trust my natural game. That's what I do now. Some days it might not look pretty but on other days I'll be on top. The biggest change has been in mindset. I pick the right balls to hit.
The Wisden Cricketer, May 2010 **Rabeed Imam**

Virender Sehwag India

131 and 293 in Tests v Sri Lanka

SOME HAVE long stereotyped Virender Sehwag as a cricketing Neanderthal, a creature of instinct and slave to impulse. Those who know him well laugh at this. Sehwag the batsman is as canny as they come, a man capable of thinking on his feet even as his whiplash strokes knock bowlers off their stride. Sri Lanka found that out the hard way.

After two sessions of mayhem at Mumbai had pushed the visitors into a corner Sehwag was on 211 when Rangana Herath speared the ball way down the leg side. Sehwag looked inquiringly at the umpire but there was no response. The next ball was also directed at the rough more than a foot outside leg stump. This time Sehwag jumped towards the on side then carved the ball through extra cover.

If that was extraordinary, what followed was just bizarre. Muttiah Muralitharan pitched one on middle stump and Sehwag quickly switched his hands on the bat handle. But instead of a reverse sweep, he paddled the ball so fine that it went through the space between the keeper and the absent slip.

Seldom can one dropped catch have had such impact. The fourth ball of the Kanpur Test, from Chanaka Welegedara, took Sehwag's outside edge and was heading to Mahela Jayawardene at first slip when Prasanna Jayawardene, the keeper, dived across to obscure his view. Sehwag went on to 131 from 122 balls. That, though, was nothing compared with the beating he gave at Mumbai, where he drove and cut his way to 293 from 254 balls. Both innings won matches. Unthinking slogger? Like calling Lennon just another busker. *The Wisden Cricketer*, January 2010
Dileep Premachandran

Shane Watson Australia
93, 120*, 97 in Tests v Pakistan

How did you feel after getting your first Test hundred, especially when you were dropped on 99?
It's been a long time coming, it's a massive relief. It was nice to see the ball drop out of [Abdur] Rauf's hands, and then I scampered through for the one. I actually didn't get much of a chance to think about it [the drop] because I hit it really well and before I knew it, it was straight at him. Luckily enough he dropped it for me.

Was that your defining moment?
The last six months have been my defining moment. The last six months, being able to string so much cricket together throughout the Ashes, then the one-dayers and going on to the Champions Trophy and then on to India as well. That was a big accomplishment for me.

How did it feel to get out in the 90s against West Indies at Adelaide?
It's the most shattered I've been. To be able to be so close to realising a childhood dream was very shattering. I slept very badly [96 overnight]. I kept thinking about the four runs I needed to get my first hundred. That's what engulfed me when I was out there the next morning.

Mohammad Amir blew you kisses at Melbourne. How do you cope with that sort of attention?
Being an opening batsman, fast bowlers are always going to have a bit of a crack at you. That's the way I love playing – I love getting into a bit of a battle. For me that works perfectly, it gets me really sharp. I know where the point is.

The Wisden Cricketer, February 2010
Peter Stevens

Brendan Taylor Zimbabwe
81, 74, 119* in ODIs v India and Sri Lanka

"IT'S TAKEN me 100 games to find some consistency," says Zimbabwe's opening batsman Brendan Taylor, 24, after being named man of the series in the triangular one-day series involving India and Sri Lanka in Zimbabwe.

Taylor started the series with a match-winning 81 as the hosts chased down India's daunting 285 in the first game at Queen's Sports Club in Bulawayo and followed up with 74 and an unbeaten, career-best 119 as a resurgent Zimbabwe knocked India out before thrashing Sri Lanka in what was a dress-rehearsal for the final.

"Alan Butcher has made a big difference since he took over as coach," says Taylor. "He's very good technically but also in terms of physical and mental preparation. I'm more solid now when it comes to shot selection and thinking about the game."

Taylor first came to prominence as a precocious 18-year-old in the immediate aftermath of Heath Streak's 'rebel' strike in 2003 when 14 white players walked away from the game after a series of disagreements with the administration. Taylor was the only white face in the new-look team.

"That was a long time ago," he says. "I just wanted to play cricket – I didn't really know what the issues were."

His ambitions now are to play a senior and substantial role, to play Test cricket again and to earn an IPL contract. Over-ambitious?

"Maybe, maybe not," he says with a grin. "I believe in myself and, besides, maybe there won't be quite so much money flying around in the IPL for the next couple of years and Zimbabwean players might be bloody good value!"
The Wisden Cricketer, July 2010 **Neil Manthorp**

Come two, gone one

A star-studded, topsy-turvy series full of fast-bowling ins-and-outs

WITH A TAUT and at times thrilling series locked at 1-1, the McLean Park curator at Napier, Phil Stoyanoff, said he had produced a result wicket. This was not because it was unusually hirsute but because both team's top orders were, in his words, "useless". Pakistan's first-innings collapse backed up his words but after that it turned into a typical flat, grinding and, ultimately, boring wicket without a skerrick of life. Still, if rain had not intervened, Stoyanoff's promise might have materialised. New Zealand ended on 90 without loss, chasing 208. It was a sad climax to a great series.

After a two-year absence Shane Bond was back in whites. He was forced out of international cricket through his Indian Cricket League connection. It had been a bleak two years in the longest form of the game without his presence and he hinted at what Daniel Vettori had missed by picking up man-of-the-match honours in the first Test at Dunedin.

There had been some talk that Bond, 34, was down several clicks on the speedometer but he hit the clock at close to 150kph (93mph) at times, exceptional in New Zealand conditions.

Just when the Test was getting away from the hosts, Bond snared the impressive Umar Akmal for 75 and New Zealand were on their way to a thrilling 32-run victory that provided a real fillip in a country that had seemingly fallen out of love with Test cricket.

Less spectacularly, but just as effectively, Mohammad Asif relaunched his Test career. Absent for a variety of reasons since October 2007, he hit an immediate groove and was probably the player of the series. He followed his eight wickets at Dunedin with nine in the second Test at Wellington.

Almost as soon as he was back, Bond was gone again – this time, in Test terms at least, for good. A small tear in a stomach muscle he picked up in the first Test turned out to be a lot larger. As soon

as Bond saw the amount of time he would need to rehabilitate from yet another injury he decided the only sensible course of action was to retire from the form he enjoyed most.

We already knew about Kamran Akmal and his dazzling array of shots. Less familiar was his brother Umar, 19, who displayed an even wider array of breathtaking shots. Umar ended his first Test series with 379 runs next to his name and a Test average of 63.16. The law of averages dictates that this will come down in time but do not expect him to become a one-series wonder. He looks much too good for that.

His double of 129 and 75 should have been enough to see Pakistan through the first Test at Dunedin (not an easy wicket to make one's debut on) but, aside from big brother Kamran, he received little support.

At Wellington his double of 46 and 52 meant he second-top-scored in each innings and in a low-scoring match his contribution was as vital as anybody. After failing in the first innings at Napier, he responded with 77 in the second.

Captain, selector, interim coach, best bowler, best batsman: Vettori did everything bar prepare the sandwiches at tea and all this was while nursing a chronic shoulder injury that will, probably sooner rather than later, require surgical attention. He was not at his sharpest with the ball, taking 10 wickets at a respectable 36.4 runs each. His batting was, once again, staggering in its unorthodoxy and output. He flicked at one too many in the first innings at Dunedin, falling one short of a century, scored 40 in the second innings at Wellington and piled on 134 in Napier. He took some terrific catches and led well. He was the complete player.

The Wisden Cricketer, February 2010

Dylan Cleaver writes for the *NZ Herald*

Victory signs: Danish Kaneria after bowling Grant Elliott

Match winner: Shane Bond during the first – and his last – Test

NEW ZEALAND v AUSTRALIA Two-Test series by **Dylan Cleaver**

All too quick and easy

Australia find New Zealand wanting for speed and strength in depth

THE FEELING in advance was that New Zealand could not be hosting Australia at a better time. The visitors had spluttered in Test series against England, South Africa and India while the hosts were boosted by the return of Shane Bond from an ICL exile.

Instead the series was a sobering experience for those who hoped the gap between minnows and majors was narrowing. Australia won the first Test by 10 wickets and the second by 176 runs; neither result flattered them.

By the time Australia arrived they had rediscovered their mojo against West Indies and Pakistan at home. But Bond's comeback had been spectacular but short-lived. He bowled New Zealand to a dramatic victory against Pakistan, then succumbed, for good as far as the five-day game goes, to a stomach injury. New Zealanders have grown up on a diet of green-tinged pitches, where simply being able to put the ball in the right place can see a player rise through the representative age groups. Little

premium is placed on genuine pace because it has few extra benefits in conditions helpful to steady seam. The problem is that turf culture and pitch technology have reached a point now where, for the most part, New Zealand play on very good, very fair Test wickets.

In those conditions, where for the most part bat is favoured over ball, something a little extra is needed. Australia had three bowlers who made life difficult at the Basin Reserve in the first Test and who got every ounce of life they could muster from a largely unresponsive wicket at Seddon Park. Mitchell Johnson (12 series wickets), Doug Bollinger (12) and Ryan Harris (nine) managed it because they were capable of bowling at 90mph.

While Nathan Hauritz wheeled down some tight, if fairly innocuous, offspin at one end, there was never total respite as one of those three would be charging in at the other. It was a sustained battery from an attack that, though it included only one genuine world-class player in

Johnson, had auxiliaries whose willingness to bend their backs endeared them to Ricky Ponting.

By contrast New Zealand's spearhead, Chris Martin, was seldom hitting 90mph and his seam-bowling colleagues – Tim Southee, Daryl Tuffey and Brent Arnel – were slower. Martin took one wicket in two Tests, Tuffey went wicketless in his only Test, Arnel took five and Southee bounced back from a gruesome first Test at Wellington to take six wickets on his home ground at Hamilton. At times Simon Katich, 291 series runs at 97, and Michael Clarke, 259 at 86.33, made the attack look like net bowlers.

By the end of the series captain Daniel Vettori looked like a man carrying many burdens – and bowling was just one of them. He scored 160 runs at 40 and took seven wickets at 45.57 and showed some captaincy innovations, particularly when his opposite number, Ponting, was batting. Very few of the home players looked as if they know how to play Test cricket whereas the Australians have an innate ability to do the right things at the right times.

New Zealand still have a glass jaw at the top of the order. Tim McIntosh showed some ticker in the second innings at Wellington, scoring 83, but he stacks up far too many failures between the scores. In the end they had to pull the domestically prolific Mathew Sinclair back to fill the troublesome No.3 spot for the second Test, without much success.

It is a real shame because the dynamic Ross Taylor, who scored 206 runs at 51.50 including New Zealand's fastest Test century (82 balls), Brendon McCullum (184 runs at 46), who looks to be coming of age as a Test batsman, Martin Guptill and Vettori deserve better protection. *The Wisden Cricketer, May 2010*

Dylan Cleaver writes for the *NZ Herald*

Blown away: Mathew Sinclair is undone by the speed of Mitchell Johnson

Scores

1st Test March 19-23, Wellington †**Aus 459-5d** (MJ Clarke 168, MJ North 112*) **and 106-0** (PJ Hughes 86*); **NZ 157** (DE Bollinger 5-28) **and 407** (BB McCullum 104, TG McIntosh 83, DL Vettori 77). **Aus won by 10 wickets.** *MoM: Clarke below 253b, 22x4, 2x6*

2nd Test March 27-31, Hamilton †**Aus 231** (SM Katich 88; Vettori 4-36) **and 511-8d** (Katich 106, North 90, MEK Hussey 67, SR Watson 65, Clarke 63); **NZ 264** (LRPL Taylor 138, MG Johnson 4-59) **and 302** (MJ Guptill 58, McCullum 51; Johnson 6-73). **Aus won by 176 runs.** *MoM: Johnson below 36.1-8-132-10*

Aus won series 2-0

When does life mean life?

Osman Samiuddin picked over the disciplinary rulings in Pakistan after the Australia tour

AAMIR SOHAIL might consider adding soothsayer to an extensive CV. The former opener, captain, chief selector and board marketing head warned the board last year not to do it. They ignored him and sacked Shoaib Malik as captain anyway, for being "aloof" and a "loner". Sohail said they would spend the rest of the year changing captains. Given Sohail's own experience in the mid-90s captaincy battles – have Test cap, will captain – they really should have listened.

Over the next year Malik's replacement, Younis Khan, twice stepped down from leadership, Shahid Afridi became the Twenty20 captain, Mohammad Yousuf led the side and even Malik found himself back as captain briefly.

Following the tour to Australia, Pakistan were in the situation only they ever find themselves in: no Test or one-day captain and a Twenty20 leader under probation, appointed for one tournament only. Mostly this is the result of another purge of the team by the board (PCB), almost exactly a year on from Malik's sacking. Seven leading players, including four recent captains, were punished: Mohammad Yousuf and Younis Khan were handed indefinite bans; Malik and Rana Naved-ul-Hasan banned for a year; Afridi and the Akmal brothers heavily fined.

After a fair start Pakistan imploded in Sydney and unravelled horribly from then on. They went winless in nine international matches over three formats in two months. All in all, it was another example of Pakistani slapstick and

What old players said

"Players' power was affecting the team's performance badly. There was no discipline and it had become impossible for the board to tackle the players"
Zaheer Abbas

"Younis and Yousuf should go to court to challenge the decision. The board is not setting a good example"
Inzamam-ul-Haq

"It's a brave step. It's a good decision and will go a long way to arrest the decline"
Abdul Qadir

catastrophe: 1962 to England, 1972-73 to Australia, 1979-80 to India, 1983-84 to Australia, 1994-95 to Zimbabwe, 1999-2000 to Australia, 2002-03 against Australia in Sharjah, 2006 to England. Someone always pays the price. So, with much deliberation the board set up an inquiry committee, interviewed players and officials, collected evidence and finally handed down a judgement.

The precise reasons for the bans – Afridi and the Akmal brothers were fined for specific incidents – were not made clear; nor has the report been made public. This is remarkable, not only because the action was so severe but because the Pakistan board keeps secrets about as well as a gossip columnist.

"It is a confidential report and not one for public consumption," Ijaz

Butt, chairman, said. "We have given everyone a fair hearing. Everything has been done properly and all of it is documented. It was a very thorough and comprehensive process."

Bits have dribbled out which, if pieced together with evidence of the last year, paint a picture of such disharmony and fractiousness that the sweep might just be justified. Through every tour since Malik was dumped talk of players conspiring against whoever was captain has filtered out. And this is not idle chatter. Younis said he had "lost command" of his players when stepping down after a one-day series defeat by New Zealand. Privately he is more scathing.

Yousuf, who subsequently led in Australia, was more forthright, openly calling Malik a malign and scheming influence; Abdul Qadir said much the same when resigning as chief selector last year. At one stage, when the board announced midway through the tour that Yousuf would be replaced after it, he reckoned "six to seven players" began to haggle for leadership.

Names, Malik central among them, recur; Kamran Akmal, Salman Butt and Misbah-ul-Haq are others but it is a nebulous thing. One incident in the report concerns an allegiance up to nine players took on the eve of the Champions Trophy semi-final not to support Younis as captain.

Accusations of players refusing to play and deliberately underperforming to spite captains have also been made. The sanctions

on Younis and Yousuf are likely to be retrospective: the former walked out on the captaincy twice within months, having already done it once in the past and turned it down flat once as well; the latter twice hitched his future to the outlawed Indian Cricket League.

Against this backdrop reaction to the punishments has been mixed, which is revealing in itself: for years now, whatever player indiscretions, the board has always been a clown. Waqar Younis, incoming coach, was, like many, shocked. "It is a big step the board has taken and I hope they have solid evidence for it," he says.

Others hailed the punishments as a crusading blow against unchecked player power. An equal number slammed it, an effort by the PCB to deflect attention away from its considerable ineptitude. This sense is undeniable, enhanced by the PCB's furtiveness. It is, after all, ultimately responsible for running the national team and none of its number got the sack. It has not backed any of its captains over the year and has consistently made questionable managerial appointments. By not making the report public, it has fuelled speculation of the worst kind.

Given that Pakistan have not won a Test series in three years, the loss of key players does not bode well. Younis and Yousuf have scored nearly 30% of Pakistan's Test runs since October 2004.

Yousuf announced an unconvincing retirement after the ban and Younis appears cheerfully unaffected. Yousuf aside, all the punished have written to the board asking for clemency or raising legal points. A formal process of appeal is open to them, a reminder that for every punishment in Pakistan, there awaits an equally thorough redemption round the corner. ◪

The Wisden Cricketer, May 2010

Dumped: Mohammad Yousuf

Osman Samiuddin writes for Cricinfo

The Aussie strut that annoys the Aussies

ON A pleasant and slow train journey from Sydney to Maitland, 120 miles north, I was reading the 150th edition of the Australian magazine *Inside Cricket* wherein is reproduced a 2009 interview with Matthew Hayden. He had just retired from international cricket. Putting on his Aussie face paint, he declared that the best moment of his career was not one of his great hundreds. It was, "singing the team song on top of Table Mountain in Cape Town". Haydos, to give him his changing-room name, said, "to me singing the team song was the ultimate, and that was the ultimate time and place. It was about the mateships". Fortunately I had just put my coffee down.

Hayden was part of the Steve 'Stephen' Waugh era, when sentimentality entered the Australian team to a sometimes excruciating degree. Waugh was asked, facetiously, in another interview in the anthology if he would ever put his "baggy green", a relic as worn as the clichés around it, on eBay. "Never on eBay mate, no. It's something that can't be sold." Also among my reading material on that train journey was an excerpt from Tom Gleisner's latest fictional tour diaries of Warwick Todd, *Up In The Blockhole*, in which our eponymous berk, a some-time dreadful Australian team tourist, reflects on his recall.

"When the selectors called to say, 'Toddy, we need you back,' I remember feeling a range of emotions. Pride, that I once again could be pulling on the precious baggy green. Frustration, that I'd only just sold it on eBay a couple of weeks before. And determination to help Australia regain its rightful place at the top of the international ladder."

I would never accuse Haydos or Tugga of flogging their "baggy greens" but, when reality bumps up against parody, it is disturbing. On the eve of the 2001 Ashes tour I asked Waugh if he had heard of Todd or read any of his fictional diaries. "Yeah, mate, read 'em. Not bad." The message was clear. Ricky Ponting and his team similarly ruthless on the field, have also attracted seeping criticism. An Australian sports columnist wrote in a national newspaper recently that he pretty much could not stand them.

There is an assumption in this team that they have only to "execute their skills", to borrow from the coaching manual of John Buchanan, and they will win. When they lose they hand out barbed compliments about the opposition having played out of their skins. Roger Federer would walk into this team.

Such rare outpourings against them usually follow defeat but this latest insurrection in the sports pages arrived when Australia were inflicting a one-sided beating on Pakistan and would continue to do so right up until the return of West Indies. Maybe Australians are tired of winning. I wonder if they pick up on the national mood, if they ever sense their strutting can annoy even their own supporters. *The Wisden Cricketer, March 2010*

Kevin Mitchell is a sports writer for *The Observer*

Right to win: Mitchell Johnson gets Khalid Latif

The impossible job

Leading men

The four key figures in Pakistan's captaincy tragi-comedy

Abdul Hafeez Kardar

Captain 1952-53 to 1957-58. **W6 L6 D11**

High Led country to victory over all, at the time, Test-playing nations including Pakistan's first Test win against India.

Low The visit to India saw a five-match series drawn 0-0 with both teams petrified of defeat in the wake of political tensions between the two.

Mushtaq Mohammad

1976-77 to 1978-79. **W8 L4 D7**

High An all-round display against West Indies at Port-of-Spain with 177 runs and eight wickets helped to secure victory.

Low Eventual defeat in that series after being bounced out by West Indies.

Javed Miandad

1979-80 to 1992-93. **W14 L6 D14**

High Finest batsman in Pakistan's history led them to series wins against New Zealand, Sri Lanka and Australia.

Low Confrontation with Dennis Lillee at Perth, 1981-82, called by *Wisden* "one of the most undignified incidents in Test history".

Imran Khan

1982 to 1991-92. **W14 L8 D26**

High Led Pakistan to their first Test win v England for 28 years, first-ever series win v England and 1992 World Cup victory.

Low Failure to mention the contributions of the rest of his team during his acceptance of the 1992 World Cup trophy helped to seal his fate.

Test captains since 1990

Imran Khan, Javed Miandad, Wasim Akram, Waqar Younis, Salim Malik, Ramiz Raja, Saeed Anwar, Aamir Sohail, Rashid Latif, Moin Khan, Inzamam-ul-Haq, Mohammad Yousuf, Younis Khan, Shoaib Malik, Shahid Afridi, Salman Butt

Pakistan change their captain as often as most change their underwear. And the majority are doomed to failure. Few succeed. **Osman Samiuddin** examined the reasons why

For every captain in Pakistan there stand 10 scorned and nearly 170 million besides with ready advice and insult. Unreasonable expectations are placed on you and unreasonable requests made of you. Effigies are burnt, stones and abuses hurled the way of you and your house. Within your team there is constant intrigue. Secret oaths are taken by players against you, players write letters to the board and press, threatening they will quit rather than play under you.

The board may support you as staunchly as a toothpick might an elephant. Otherwise it actively undermines your authority, to keep you in your place, a separate tussle of power. Coaches, selectors, managers, all men critical to you and your success, will come and go. Some will interfere, some will require an interpreter, some will hide, some will not think you worthy, some will die on you and leave you defending yourself against the charge of murdering them.

On an almost daily basis some scandal will arise. Reporters will come straight for you, for there is still no media department to handle such things. At best the hacks will be pesky. At worst they will be borderline criminals, kingmakers in this great game, bringing to confluence a circumstance that they, and not you, are content with. Politicians will send feelers about players they want in a squad. They will accuse you of match-fixing and grill you in parliament or the senate in a show of macho public strength.

On special occasions the Prime Minister will call you directly and advise you on team selection before a big game. Immediately after you lose it he will happily call for your head. Big-time bookies and gangsters have you in their radar. Your father can be kidnapped if you lose games and let the wrong people down. You are defender of the nation's honour, though capable of soiling it.

We make much of leadership in Pakistan but mostly to bemoan the lack of it. It is not that we have not tried. Among 21 different prime ministers and 14 presidents, of all shapes, sizes, ethnicities, genders, colours, beard lengths, background and political leanings we have had ample opportunity.

The educated patriarchs

Cricket has not lagged in trying different men either. All told Pakistan has changed captains 61 times and 27 different men have led the Test side. All manner of men have led and, if you put them all in one room, only a few would gravitate to one another. Preventing a scuffle might be the greater concern. From those who have had some success and maintained a degree of control two distinct portraits can be drawn. The first takes in the outline of Abdul Hafeez Kardar and Imran Khan. Both were sketched from a broader,

66 Pakistanis are at their most productive when their behinds are being kicked 99

well-established tradition of Pakistan leadership: eloquent and educated Westernised men, more attractive to the outside world than to their own constituency. Pakistan has had many such men, who hijack the voice of a country rather than speak for a nation.

The entire package was one of unquestioned and mostly unchallenged but charismatic authority and this fits neatly into a compelling theory of how Pakistan works best. It is said often that Pakistanis are at their most productive when their behinds are being kicked.

The fighters

The other type to have had some success in this land of extremes is of more grounded, localised stock. Mushtaq Mohammad and Javed Miandad were polar and geographical opposites of Kardar and Imran. In both was the hardened, sharper ethic of Karachi where respect is, for most, to be earned, not handed out at birth in a family name. Karachi makes you get by, offering you shorter cuts if you are smart, not just rich or landed.

The young experiment

In April 2007 Pakistan chose youth. Having just turned 25, Shoaib Malik was the fourth youngest to lead his country. But the first stints of Miandad and Akram, like that of Malik, were all hamstrung by older, more experienced players, many of whom felt that they should have been captain. Only Bob Woolmer attempted even to broach the subject of age. He started football sessions so that younger players would get used to physical contact with the older, patriarchal Inzamam. This, he reasoned, would lead them to be less deferential. It did not work well.

Left between the old who are disgruntled and the young who are emboldened, the young Pakistan captain is up the creek without a paddle. Never will he succeed. 🅰 *The Wisden Cricketer*, August 2010

Osman Samiuddin is Pakistan editor of Cricinfo

Pedigree: Abdul Kardar at The Oval in 1954

Odd couple: Miandad left and Imran in 1987

A familiar feeling

India and Sri Lanka played two Test series and numerous one-dayers in 2010

Sri Lanka in India: India may be white-ball crazy but they won the No.1 Test spot after a crushing victory over Sri Lanka

LOCAL TV channels had billed it as the 'Battle for the Indian Ocean' but, in the end, it turned out to be as one-sided as each of Sri Lanka's previous visits across the Palk Strait. When India clinched a victory by an innings and 24 runs on the final morning at Mumbai it marked a special moment in the nation's cricket history, the team going to No.1 in the ICC Test rankings. The Indian cricket board and the majority of the fans may worship at the altar of the limited-overs game but for the players who have refused to take their eyes off the red ball in recent seasons it was reward for perseverance.

The 2005 Ashes aside, India were the only team to give Australia a proper game during their years of complete dominance and now find themselves top dogs. Kumar Sangakkara spoke afterwards of how his team had been "outbatted and outbowled", and their failure to win a Test on Indian, Australian or South African soil puts Sri Lanka's own position near the top of the table into perspective. With Sanath Jayasuriya long gone, Muttiah Muralitharan about to follow and few youngsters that raise the collective pulse, there was also the sense that a golden era had passed.

Having amassed the biggest total (760 for 7) ever made in India on an Ahmedabad pitch that was more lifeless than a 3,000-year-old mummy, Sri Lanka had gone to Kanpur full of confidence that a winless record in India, stretching back 27 years and 15 Tests, might come to an end. Virender Sehwag had other ideas and two magnificent exhibitions of his utterly unique Catherine-Wheel strokeplay inspired innings victories at Green Park and then at the Brabourne Stadium. Rahul Dravid, who had saved India with a counter-attacking innings on the first day of the series, chipped in with two hundreds. So did Gautam Gambhir

and Dhoni as India went on a run-spree.

Murali, who needed 17 wickets to get to 800, was savaged, as was Rangana Herath, the left-arm spinner who had starred in series wins against Pakistan and New Zealand. As for Ajantha Mendis, the 26-wicket mystery-bowling star of the previous year's home Tests against India, he played only at Kanpur, where Sehwag slapped him around as though he was a slow-medium trundler. The match was over with well over a day to spare as Sri Lanka's batsmen played two innings where nous, application and grit were conspicuously absent.

At Mumbai, Sri Lanka squandered the advantage that came with winning the toss. In their defence Tillakaratne Dilshan, who made a chancy first-day century, got two shocking decisions in the match, igniting debate about why the richest board in the world had not made an effort to implement the referral system for the series. At one point a total of 393 had looked competitive but Sehwag disabused such foolish notions with another spellbinding innings. He careered along at better than a run a ball, falling just short of what would have been an unprecedented third triple-century. Whether it was driving through the covers, slashing the ball behind point from out of the leg-stump rough or reverse-paddling Murali past the wicketkeeper, Sehwag was in total control. Sri Lanka went down with a whimper. Sehwag took the plaudits but perhaps the real story of the series was the renaissance of Dravid. He struck a glorious 177 to rescue India from the depths of 32 for 4 in Ahmedabad. For those 45 minutes when Chanaka Welegedara was dismantling the top order Sri Lanka dared to dream.

The Wisden Cricketer, January 2010

Form man: Sehwag celebrates at Kanpur before his double-hundred in Mumbai

By **Dileep Premachandran**, Cricinfo

Scores

1st Test Nov 16-20, Ahmedabad †**Ind 426** (R Dravid 177, MS Dhoni 110; C Welegedara 4-87) **and 412** (G Gambhir 114, SR Tendulkar 100*); **SL 760-7d** (M Jayawardene 275, P Jayawardene 154*, TM Dilshan 112). **Match drawn.** *MoM: M Jayawardene 435b, 27x4, 1x6.*

2nd Test Nov 24-27, Kanpur †**Ind 642** (G Gambhir 167, Dravid 144, V Sehwag 131; R Herath 5-121); **SL 229** (S Sreesanth 5-75) **and 269. India won by inns and 144 runs.** *MoM: Sreesanth 33-8-122-6.*

3rd Test Dec 2-6, Mumbai †**SL 393** (Dilshan 109, AD Mathews 99; Harbhajan Singh 4-112) **and 309** (KC Sangakkara 137; Zaheer Khan 5-72); **India 726-9d** (Sehwag 293, Dhoni 100*; M Muralitharan 4-195). **India won by inns and 24 runs.** *MoM: Sehwag 254b, 40x4, 7x6.* **India win series 2-0.**

1st Test June 10-13, Galle †**SL 520-8d** (NT Paravitana 111, KC Sangakkara 103; A Mithun 4-105) **and 96-0; India 276** (V Sehwag 109; M Muralitharan 5-63) **and 338** SL (L Malinga 5-50). **SL won by 10 wickets.** *MoM: Malinga 30-2-105-7.*

2nd Test July 26-30, Colombo †**SL 642-4d** (Sangakkara 219, Paravitana 100, M Jayawardene 174) **and 129-3d; Ind 707** (Tendulkar 203, SK Raina 120, Sehwag 99; BAW Mendis 4-172). **Match drawn.** *MoM: Sangakkara 335b, 29x4.*

3rd Test August 3-7, Colombo †**SL 425** (Samaraweera 137*; PP Ojha 4-115) **and 267; Ind 436** (Sehwag 109, ; S Randiv 4-80) **and 258-5** (Laxman 103*; Randiv 5-82). **India won by 5 wickets.** *MoM: Laxman 149b, 12x4.* **Series drawn 1-1.**

India in Sri Lanka: Murali bowed out with 800 Test wickets then India hit back in a series that laboured before coming to life

BUT FOR this series the Indian players would have been nursing tired bodies, getting ready for a new season that culminates in the World Cup at home. But for this series Sri Lanka would have spent a season without any cricket and with nowhere to go. But for this series Muttiah Muralitharan would have retired in what should – miracles apart – be a one-sided win against West Indies later in the year. As it panned out Indian bodies started giving up one by one, Sri Lankans enjoyed keeping the tired

66 Murali was savaged, Mendis was treated like a trundler 99

visitors in the sun for long durations and Murali left in fairytale fashion. But India found enough fight, enough nerve, to come back in the decider and leave the country with reputations intact.

Sri Lanka hadn't lost a Test at home after winning the toss since March 2001. The first Test at Galle reiterated why. In a ruthless, demoralising manner the batsmen piled up the runs. Galle was all decked up for Murali but for once he was

not alone. Lasith Malinga, playing his first Test in two-and-a-half years, inflicted equal damage – only it was sharper and stingier. Of the seven wickets Malinga took in Galle, five came in the first overs of new spells. Malinga's sudden bursts and Murali's patience, ending in a match-sealing 800th wicket off his final ball he bowled in Tests, worked a treat.

Defensive fields remained a feature of the series. It could perhaps have to do with weak bowling attacks: Zaheer Khan and Sreesanth missed all the Tests, Murali retired after the first, Harbhajan played with flu and a side strain and Malinga, who played two games, could not be made to work like a mule.

After a bore draw, in the decider at the P Sara Oval in Colombo, Sri Lanka from effectively 76 for 7 set India a challenging 257 to win. On the final day the fielding captain seemed short on both bowling stocks and wits. Perhaps it would not be a bad thing if Sri Lanka and India don't play each other for a while – this was the 40th international match between them in two years. But the final day of the series ended beautifully. VVS Laxman created symphonies to make an unbeaten 103 and square the series.

The Wisden Cricketer, September 2010

By **Sidharth Monga**, Cricinfo

Asia Cup 2010

Still in the dark
A raucous final but few clues for the World Cup

DURING the Asia Cup final the jam-packed Dambulla stadium in Sri Lanka and the din created by the many papare bands in the stands gave the impression of a keenly followed tournament. But the preceding 10 days had seen sparse crowds and little more than passing interest from sports fans whose attentions were largely on the football World Cup. Unlike the 2008 final, won by Sri Lanka after awe-inspiring displays from Sanath Jayasuriya and Ajantha Mendis, India emerged victors through a team effort. Six of their batsmen passed 20 to set a decent target before their trio of seamers, led by Ashish Nehra, wrecked the Sri Lankan top order in helpful conditions under the lights.

Throughout the tournament the cricket was mostly riveting except for games involving Bangladesh, walloped in all three of their matches. Pakistan, regrouping after the latest round of disciplinary troubles, were involved in two see-saw matches which showcased the 50-over game at its best: against Sri Lanka Shahid Afridi stroked a majestic century that nearly pulled off a miraculous victory from 32 for 4 chasing 243; against India they went down by three wickets to a Harbhajan Singh six off the penultimate ball.

The captains had spoken of the Asia Cup as a rehearsal for next year's marquee tournament in the subcontinent but they gained precious few insights about their squad make-up. For both India and Sri Lanka the problem area is the lower-middle order but there was no trimming from the list of contenders. In the land of U-turns that is Pakistan cricket, eight months is too far to look ahead. Bangladesh's squad is not going to be too different for the World Cup.

The floodlights were an issue throughout. Lasith Malinga started it off saying that batting second was a disadvantage as it was hard to sight the ball. The only one who did not carp was the man of the series Afridi, who called the lights "perfect". *The Wisden Cricketer, August 2010*

By **Siddarth Ravindran**, Cricinfo.com

Piles and miles: Kumar Sangakkara and Mahela Jayawardene at Colombo

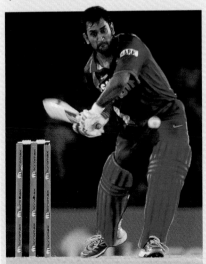

Master blaster: Dhoni hits out against Pakistan

Finished? Really?

India v SA ODI series

1st ODI Feb 21, Jaipur ♀ **Ind 298-9** in 50 ov (SK Raina 58, V Sehwag 46, KD Karthik 44; JH Kallis 3-29) **†SA 297** in 50 ov (Kallis 89, WD Parnell 49, DW Steyn 35). **Ind won by 1 run.** *MoM: Jadeja 22r, 20b, 1x4; 10-2-29-2.*

2nd ODI Feb 24, Gwalior ♀ **†Ind 401-3** in 50 ov (SR Tendulkar 200*, Karthik 79, MS Dhoni 68*); **SA 248** in 42.5 ov (AB de Villiers 114*; S Sreesanth 3-49). **Ind won by 153 runs.** *MoM: Tendulkar 147b, 25x4, 3x6.*

3rd ODI Feb 27, Ahmedabad ♀ **†SA 365-2** in 50 ov (Kallis 104*, de Villiers 102*, HH Amla 87, LL Bosman 68); **Ind 275** in 44.3 ov (V Kohli 57, Raina 49, RG Sharma 48; Steyn 3-37, LL Tsotsobe 3-58). **SA won by 90 runs.** *MoM: de Villiers 59b, 11x4, 3x6.*

Man of the series: Sachin Tendulkar

In 2006 Sachin Tendulkar was fading. Four years later he scored the first 200 in an ODI. By **Dileep Premachandran**

There are times when Sachin Tendulkar reminds you of the intrepid tourist, methodically ticking off places of interest in the tour guide. Even by his standards, though, events at the Captain Roop Singh Stadium in Gwalior were something special, equivalent to turning a corner and coming across the ruins at Machu Picchu.

It had been more than a decade since he finished with 186 not out in a one-day game against New Zealand, eight runs short of the world record set by Saeed Anwar against India in Chennai back in 1997. After ending up with an unbeaten 163 in New Zealand last year he told Virender Sehwag, the man many tipped to breach the 200 barrier: "It will eventually happen if I am destined to do it."

A few months later he was dismissed for 175 as India fell agonisingly short in a mammoth run-chase against Australia. After the peak had been scaled in Gwalior he came back to the dressing room and told Sehwag: "I got what was destined."

Even for someone whose 46 one-day hundreds are scattered across the globe this was an innings to savour. There were a couple of cover-drives in the opening overs that made you gasp, timed and placed to such perfection that the best fielders in the world had no chance. Back-foot punches through point, crisp tucks off the pads and clean swings down the ground frazzled the South Africans but he was just as impressive scampering between the wickets.

He played scarcely a false stroke, and that against an attack that was anything but popgun. Dale Steyn went for 89 in his 10 overs, and looked decidedly bemused as Tendulkar fetched one from outside off stump and whistled it through midwicket. Wayne Parnell's quota cost 95, and there was no joy for Roelof van der Merwe either as he found himself thumped straight down to the sightscreen. By then, Tendulkar was starting to tire and the emphasis shifted to singles with MS Dhoni lashing fours and sixes at the other end.

By the time Tendulkar squeezed one through the hands of the man at point to reach 200 from just 147 balls he had struck 25 fours and three sixes, while running 56 singles and 13 twos. Unlike Anwar, who had a runner for the latter part of his innings, and others like Graeme Smith who have been unable to cope with the demands of batting through, Tendulkar shrugged off cramp, testament to an astonishingly robust physique that has endured two decades of wear, tear and surgery.

With Dinesh Karthik, Yusuf Pathan and Dhoni thriving at the other end, India piled up the sort of total that shut South Africa out of the match and series. Just 40 minutes later, the teams were back out on the field. Instead of an ice bath or the masseur's table, Tendulkar was in the pre-innings huddle with his mates. It said much about a man whose commitment to the game is total.

"It feels good that I lasted for 50 overs, a good test of my fitness." Dhoni, who helped him over the line, said: "It's always good to be on the other side, watching him score 200 runs. When he was tired and couldn't play the big shots, he was very clever to use the pace of the bowler and it's very difficult for the bowlers as they don't know where exactly to bowl."

From all over the world, the tributes poured in. "Nobody else does deserve to get there," said Anwar. "It's only Sachin who deserves to scale that peak." Anil Kumble, another of Indian cricket's quiet achievers, said: "The way he celebrated when he reached his 200 epitomised the man's persona. There was no running laps around the field, no aggressive gestures, nothing over the top."

The World Cup on home soil is now less than a year away and Tendulkar has eyes set on one final expedition: to emulate the 1983 heroes who first fired his imagination. 🄦 *The Wisden Cricketer, April 2010*

Dileep Premachandran is associate editor of Cricinfo.com

Bow down and beaten: Wayne Parnell and Tendulkar

In need of another act

The battle for No.1 was thrilling but all too brief. By **Dileep Premachandran**

IT WAS less than a decade ago that close to 85,000 Kolkatans screamed themselves into needing throat lozenges as Steve Waugh's Australians were defeated in one of the most dramatic Test matches in history. Since then crowds for the five-day game in India have dwindled. When Sachin Tendulkar surpassed Brian Lara to become the highest run-scorer in Tests, there were only a few hundred bussed-in schoolchildren to cheer him at Mohali. And with the Indian board pursuing a rotation policy that grants Test matches to venues where people care little for the longer version, the traditional centres like Eden Gardens in Kolkata and Chepauk in Chennai have been sidelined.

The Valentine's Day Test was thus the perfect occasion for Kolkata's sports-mad populace – 120,000 once turned up to watch Zico's Japan thrash India's footballers – to express its love for a form of the game that was in danger of slipping into irrelevance on the subcontinent in the age of Twenty20 gratification.

India needed vociferous support too. Though the players never used it as an excuse, the abysmal turnout for the opening Test at Nagpur had left them bitterly disappointed. The No.1 ranking was at stake but the new stadium nearly 15 miles from the centre of the city had been devoid of atmosphere as South Africa romped to an innings victory.

Blown away

At times the visitors' jubilant yells drowned out what little crowd noise there was. Any hint of enthusiasm from the stands had long since dissipated by the time India were forced to follow on in a home Test for the first time since 2003 as Dale Steyn blew away the cream of the batting in as lethal a spell of old-ball bowling as you could hope to see. He had already worked his magic with the new ball, having Murali Vijay shoulder arms and after he set up Sachin Tendulkar with a peach of an outswinger the scoreboard read 56 for 3.

The irrepressible Virender Sehwag, sure of eye and deft of hand in any situation, repaired the damage along with the new boy Subramaniam Badrinath but, when he chased an awful wide delivery from Wayne Parnell, the seeds of ruin had been sown. South Africa had the ball changed, Steyn found prodigious reverse swing and 221 for 4 at tea quickly became 233 all out. Tendulkar's 46th three-figure Test knock, cut short by Paul Harris's nagging leg-stump-rough attack, was the only consolation as India failed to make South Africa bat again.

After defeat inside four days on a pitch that was no green-top the smell of recrimination was in the air, especially for the selectors who had picked such an unbalanced squad. With Rahul Dravid nursing a broken cheekbone and VVS Laxman unable to recover from a hand injury India had been dealt a further shock when Rohit Sharma, in line for his debut, sprained an ankle during the morning warm-up. With no other batting reserve in sight Wriddhiman Saha, a wicketkeeper from Bengal who averaged 35 in first-class cricket, gained his spurs.

Scores

1st Test February 6-9, Nagpur †**SA 558-6d** (HM Amla 253*, JH Kallis 173, AB de Villiers 53); **India 233** (V Sehwag 109, S Badrinath 56; DW Steyn 7-51) **and 319** (SR Tendulkar 100). **South Africa won by inns and 6 runs.** *MoM: HM Amla 473b, 22x4.*

2nd Test February 14-18, Kolkata †**SA 296** (Amla 114, AN Petersen 100; Zaheer Khan 4-90) **and 290** (Amla 123*; Harbhajan Singh 5-95); **India 643-6d** (Sehwag 165, VVS Laxman 143*, MS Dhoni 132*, Tendulkar 106). **India won by inns and 57 runs.** *MoM: Amla 237r, 560b, 30x4, 1x6.*

Series drawn 1-1.

66 Steyn blew away the cream of the batting in a lethal spell of old-ball bowling 99

Thirsty work: Kallis and Amla at Nagpur

Big wicket: Parnell gets Sehwag for 109 in the first Test

After offering no stroke to Steyn the first time, India's answer to Darren Pattinson batted bravely in the second innings but South Africa were ruthless in their exploitation of India's chinks.

Faith rewarded

Rather than panic India kept faith as far as possible in those that had not lost a Test since August 2008. In came Laxman and out went Saha but it was again two South Africa batsmen who made all the early headlines. Steyn's bowling had stolen the Nagpur spotlight from Hashim Amla, though there was little doubt that it was his monumental 253 not out, and partnership of 340 with Jacques Kallis after South Africa had slumped to 6 for 2, that set up the charge to victory.

At Eden Gardens Amla carried on where he had left off, with decisive footwork and fluent drives. He added 209 with Alviro Petersen, the Port Elizabeth cabbie's son who made an accomplished century on debut, as South Africa progressed serenely to 218 for 1. Then, on the stroke of tea, Zaheer Khan induced a loose shot from Petersen. After the interval Amla tried to pull a ball he could have left alone and Kallis miscued a slog-sweep off Harbhajan Singh. With Ashwell Prince and JP Duminy struggling for form, India made rapid inroads.

The next morning South Africa were bowled out for 296. By stumps they were already 46 behind, with Sehwag and Tendulkar scoring contrasting hundreds. Reprieved by Duminy at slip on 47 and by AB de Villiers fluffing a stumping – Mark Boucher missed the game with back spasms – when he had 129, Sehwag finished with a buccaneering 165. Tendulkar was chanceless en route to century No.47, and Laxman and MS Dhoni piled on the misery after a cameo from Amit Mishra dented South African morale.

Inclement weather restricted play to 35 overs on the penultimate day but by close of play Mishra had already summoned up Shane Warne-like deliveries to account for Graeme Smith and Kallis and, despite Zaheer missing the final day with a thigh strain, Harbhajan came into his own at a venue he loves as no other. Amla's defiance was magnificent – he batted 1,402 minutes, faced 1,033 balls and scored 494 runs over the two Tests – while both Parnell and Morne Morkel fought with tenacity. But when the end came, with only nine balls to be bowled, the Eden roar could be heard miles away. As with Muhammad Ali and Joe Frazier, this increasingly compelling rivalry will need a third act, this winter in South Africa.

The Wisden Cricketer, April 2010

Dileep Premachandran is associate editor of Cricinfo.com

Leveller: Harbhajan gets the last wicket, Morkel, at Kolkata to tie the series

---

Domestic bliss

The Ranji Trophy, India's four-day domestic tournament, is normally played in front of tiny crowds. All of that changed in this year's final.

OTHERWISE known for its silk and sandalwood, Mysore can be a sleepy town. But for four days in January a little ground called the Gangotri Glades could have been Glastonbury. The Ranji Trophy final, normally a deserted affair, was in town and the inhabitants went to support their state side Karnataka against mighty Mumbai.

The stands heaved with energy and emotion and raucous chants filled the air as the game went to the wire. Over the four days more than 25,000 turned up, many with the Kannadiga yellow-and-red flag. On the fourth day the gates had to be shut with the stands already filled.

Manish Pandey had become the first Indian to hit an IPL century last May and he rounded off a Ranji campaign with a breathtaking century that took Karnataka within a fingertip of glory. But Mumbai are India's canniest side. Ajit Agarkar, who made a Test century at Lord's, took five-wickets and helped end Karnataka's resistance and Mumbai sneaked home by six runs. The capacity crowd were silenced. Mumbai had their 39th Ranji win.

Victory away from home made it sweeter still, especially after the experience of last year when even the presence of Sachin Tendulkar and Zaheer Khan in the ranks wasn't enough to entice the crowds in Hyderabad. That game against Uttar Pradesh convinced the Indian board that the experiment with neutral venues wasn't worth persisting with. Karnataka's games at Bangalore's 40,000-capacity Chinnaswamy Stadium had attracted a mere handful and it was that which forced the local association to opt for Mysore instead. It's been a while since a domestic game received such attention. The season-opening Irani Trophy match between Mumbai and the Rest of India at Chennai in 2003 had seen all the stars turn up and the fans had responded. But with international schedules being what they are the brightest lights in the Indian fraternity have seldom had the time, energy or inclination to turn up for domestic cricket.

Satellite television meant attendances declined especially in cities that host regular international matches. At smaller venues like Mysore, fans starved of big-league cricket are more than prepared to spend a day or two in the sun with next to no facilities to speak of. Wasim Jaffer, who led Mumbai in the final, said shifting the game to Mysore had been an inspired move. "Playing in a small centre, on a good wicket, it was great. The crowd got to see a lot of international players or players who are going to play for India. It was a good advertisement for the game, and especially the Ranji Trophy." *The Wisden Cricketer*, March 2010 **Dileep Premachandran**

Fan base: Karnataka supporters at the final

American nightmare

Sri Lanka and New Zealand became the first Test sides to play in the US. By **Peter Della Penna**

IT WAS just after midday on a bright and sunny Sunday afternoon in south Florida when Sri Lanka's Nuwan Kulasekara was at the top of his mark, getting ready to run in from the Northern End of the Central Broward Regional Park in Lauderhill. A thrilling bit of cricket was moments away from happening as Kulasekara devastated New Zealand's top order to take three wickets in the second over of the second match between two major teams on US soil.

Yet, while USA Cricket Association CEO Don Lockerbie touts 15 million fans living in America, only 700 of them witnessed the magic in person. The rest were stuck in the parking lot, stayed home, or they just don't exist. For an event that was supposed to make history, there was hardly a peep of publicity leading up to it. This is not without precedent from the USACA.

When tickets went on sale May 4 for a three-match T20 series that was supposed to begin just over two weeks later, the only type of marketing in the US since the series was announced on April 23 was free publicity on USACA's own website, news releases on other cricket websites and through fan groups on Facebook. By May 14, only 200 tickets had been

sold for the first match scheduled for the following Thursday, which is when the decision was made to axe it from the event schedule. The three games became two.

Authorities cited inadequate lighting for a night game and the threat of thunderstorms as reasons for calling it off. The match was scheduled for 4pm. Sunset in Lauderhill on May 20 was 8:02 pm. The first match played two days later began at 3:30pm.

Despite all the bumbling by USACA, people in the local community remained optimistic. Right across the street from the stadium lies Bedessee East-West Indian Foods, a well-known shop in the area and one of the biggest sellers of cricket equipment in the US.

"They'll fill up half the place easily," boasted Ravi Bedessee, the owner. "They'll get 10,000 to 12,000 people." Bedessee's shop had several signs telling fans that they could buy tickets. Two days before the first match between, Bedessee was asked how many tickets he had sold in his shop. He replied: "25."

It then didn't help that T20 cricket's biggest selling point for Americans – sixes – were missing thanks to the pitches. Fans just stared at

jugglers, chameleon mimes and a man on stilts sifting their way through the crowd. Was this a circus or a sporting event? These things are geared to distract small children who tend to get bored but if you are like 39-year-old Kishan Patel, you left your kids at home. "I was going to bring my family but because of the high ticket prices and the heat, they decided not to come," says Patel, a native New Zealander living in Jacksonville, Florida.

The second day was even less inspiring. A crowd of 3,483 were in by the time Sri Lanka had scored the winning run via a wide down legside to reach the measly target of 82. Most of them had arrived after all the excitement from Kulasekara had come and gone.

The Sri Lankan team saved the day though when it was announced that they would be sticking around to sign autographs and take pictures. A roar went up and near bedlam broke out when the players walked towards the railings. It was a beautiful scene after the lack of excitement that took place inside the ropes.

The Wisden Cricketer, July 2010

Peter Della Penna is a US freelance writer

BARRY BLAND/PHOTOSPORT

Super bowl: Scott Styris falls to Ajantha Mendis for 10 in the first Twenty20

Moment of mayhem: Sangakkara meets fans

Hard sell: tickets on offer in a local store

Coming up for air

After years fighting bankruptcy and corruption Zimbabwe cricket re-emerged. By **Neil Manthorp**

PROSPER UTSEYA's demeanour reflects the tangle of ironies which Zimbabwe cricket inspires among those who watch and administer. He is quiet and unassuming but not unwise; he would prefer to avoid the spotlight but he is desperate to play at the highest level and, though he will never shout about it, he believes that, as national captain, he has a right and a duty to stake a claim for his country's place at the head table to be restored.

It is hard to imagine the levels of disenchantment and despair that cricketers like Utseya felt two or three years ago when the domestic game had, basically, dissolved, leaving nothing where once there had been hope for a meaningful international career.

In many ways it was the best thing for Zimbabwe Cricket. It needed to reach rock bottom to rebuild. While survivors of the economic crash were still clinging to bits of the old order there was no hope. But at ground zero it was relatively simple to start afresh.

Based on the blueprint of South Africa's successful six-team franchise, ZC's managing director, Ozias Bvute, appointed a committee of largely independent cricket people to build a five-team structure including the previously marginalised areas in the Eastern Highlands, mid-west and far south.

The country's national players were divided among them in a bid to establish equal strength and all five franchises were given a budget of US$750,000 to cover everything from playing fees to mowing the outfield. ZC swore by a policy of ruthless financial management in which there would be no financial handouts to franchises which failed. It is a policy which will rightly raise the eyebrows of Zimbabwe

66 It needed to reach rock bottom to rebuild 99

sceptics, given the allegations of financial irregularity aimed at Bvute and chairman Peter Chingoka during the early and mid-2000s.

"It's time to draw a line in the sand and move forward," says the chief selector, Alistair Campbell. "How long do people want to carry on about what happened in the past? The country has been through a bloody tough time and cricket reached rock bottom. But a lot of people are working their backsides off to rebuild things now and they deserve a chance."

Heath Streak remains the highest profile of those who walked away from the game, having led the so-called 'rebel players' back in 2002. He is now bowling coach with the national team and as fanatical as he ever was. "There were big problems in Zim cricket but most of them have been resolved. It's all very well for people to throw stones at us from 6,000 miles away but they might have something different to say if they came and had a look for themselves."

There is also a deep pride and confidence in the sports minister, Senator David Coltart. After three decades fighting for human rights in the country and suffering personal hardships and imprisonment, Coltart deserves to be listened to: "We have a government of national unity and we are a country in transition. Cricket, in particular, has taken giant strides in the last year." *The Wisden Cricketer*, April 2010

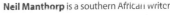

Neil Manthorp is a southern African writer

Leading the way: Prosper Utseya dismisses batsman Mohammad Ashraful in January 2009

Bright days: Heath Streak hits out v Australia

No surprises, no excuses

West Indies once again failed to deliver on their talent. By **Fazeer Mohammed**

WHILE West Indies can rely on Bangladesh blocking the way to the bottom of the Test rankings, many of their players appear to have an unyielding commitment to drag the Caribbean game through the mud of indiscipline and the absence of plain cricketing common sense.

South Africa's 2-0 triumph was hardly unexpected, extending as it did their almost complete Test dominance of the hosts in the six series since readmission. West Indian diehards may seek solace in the dramatic come-from-behind triumph in the historic one-off Test meeting at Kensington Oval in 1992 but the evidence of this latest duel is that those loyalists are also abandoning this team.

Coinciding as it did with the football World Cup, it was inevitable that attendances for the Tests in Port-of-Spain, Basseterre and Bridgetown would suffer. But that just offers a convenient excuse for the apologists desperate to ignore the rising tide of disillusionment.

Both teams performed as expected. Led by Graeme Smith, who once again

tucked heartily into several helpings of West Indian bowling on the way to scoring the most runs in the three Tests (371 at 61.83), South Africa were as South Africa are: disciplined, well-prepared, efficient and determined. AB de Villiers, dismissed only twice in the series, finished with the phenomenal average of 165.00. Jacques Kallis remains massively impressive and Ashwell Prince made two particularly telling contributions in the victories at Queen's Park Oval and Kensington Oval, featuring in century partnerships with de Villiers after five wickets were down for less than 150 runs in the first innings on both occasions.

Yet it was the efforts of fast bowlers Dale Steyn and Morne Morkel that distinguished South Africa's third Test series in the Caribbean. Used in short bursts throughout a series played in energy-sapping heat, they combined for 29 wickets and were thwarted only by the lifeless track at Warner Park.

Offspinner Johan Botha, playing only his third Test four years after making his Test debut, contributed seven wickets to

the series-clinching triumph in Barbados. His inclusion alongside left-arm spinner Paul Harris for that match suggested that the usually conservative South Africans may be more inclined to depart from their metronomic pattern in future.

At least Ottis Gibson, the new head coach, would have had a clearer picture of the magnitude of the challenge ahead of him, the defeats by 163 runs and seven wickets inside four days in the Tests coming hard on a seven-match sweep by the visitors in the shorter contests.

More than anything technical or tactical, though, Gibson's greatest task is coping with a culture of mediocrity and baseless bravado which flourishes in the absence of strong, principled leadership at all levels of West Indies cricket.

It is no coincidence that their only consistent performer with the bat, Shivnarine Chanderpaul (300 runs at 75.00), is the lone survivor of the increasingly distant days when Caribbean cricket was still feared.

There are players of considerable ability still in the West Indies. The problem is too many of them are easily distracted from their primary objective on the field of play while Chris Gayle, the captain, is either disinclined or incapable of doing anything about it other than to complain of a lack of support from persons unknown behind the scenes.

Sulieman Benn's 15 wickets underlined his quality. Yet instead of being a team leader he is invariably the chief rabble-rouser. Apart from the promise of offspinner Shane Shillingford for the home side, nothing new emerged and West Indies will remain grateful that the Bangladeshis are still there to cushion their ignominious fall.

The Wisden Cricketer, August 2010

Fazeer Mohammed is a Trinidad-based writer

Brav-oh: Smith is put down by Dwayne Bravo on the final day of the second Test

Scores

1st Test June 10-13, Trinidad †**SA 352** (MV Boucher 69, AB de Villiers 68, AG Prince 57; SJ Benn 5-120) **and 206-4d** (GC Smith 90; Benn 4-74); **WI 102** (DW Steyn 5-29; M Morkel 4-19) **and 293** (CH Gayle 73). **SA won by 163 runs.** MoM: Steyn 29.3-6-94-8

Big moment: Sulieman Benn gets Smith in the first Test

2nd Test June 18-22, St Kitts †**SA 543-6d** (de Villiers 135*, Smith 132, JH Kallis 110, AN Petersen 52) **and 235-3d** (Kallis 62*); **WI 546** (S Chanderpaul 166, BP Nash 114, N Deonarine 65, DJ Bravo 53, Gayle 50; Morkel 4-116). **Match drawn.** MoM: Chanderpaul below 357b, 10x4, 1x6

3rd Test June 26-29, Barbados †**WI 231** (Bravo 61, J Botha 4-56) **and 161** (Chanderpaul 71*); **SA 346** (Prince 78*, de Villiers 73, Smith 70; Benn 6-81) **and 49-3. SA won by 7 wickets.** MoM: Botha below 39.5-7-102-7

SA won series 2-0

PAKISTAN v AUSTRALIA Two-Test series

Swing and roundabouts

The first neutral Tests in England since 1912 were enthralling. By **Richard Hobson**

THE Pakistan/Australia experience was like the legendary early Sex Pistols concerts: fast, frenetic, newsworthy and seen by relatively small crowds left feeling lucky to have been there. The drawn, sometimes dramatic MCC Spirit of Cricket series was just what the season needed after the one-sided Tests between England and Bangladesh.

Conditions exposed techniques with a wicket falling on average every 42 balls. But the cricket was all the more compelling for bowlers holding sway. Stats charts bore close resemblance to the kind of ledgers familiar in the days of uncovered pitches. Only Simon Katich and Salman Butt averaged more than 35 with the bat.

Australia took a 1 0 lead with a 150-run win at Lord's but that was overshadowed by the resignation as captain of Shahid Afridi minutes after his first Test appearance since 2006. Embarrassed and remorseful at slogging to a fielder for the second time, he admitted to being psychologically ill-suited to the five-day game.

Was the problem, asked John Etheridge of *The Sun*, simply that he could not stop himself from trying to hit sixes? "Yes, that's right," a contrite but candid Afridi replied.

So the teams headed for Headingley, Australia looking to extend their winning run against Pakistan stretching back to 1995 and Pakistan regrouping quickly under the new leadership of a surprised Butt. Surely there was only one winner.

Except that being unpredictable has a positive side. However deep the instability and chaos around Pakistan, they are capable of producing extraordinary cricket. And superlatives were strewn liberally as the two Mohammads, Amir and Asif, and Umar Gul ripped through Australia for 88 in less than three hours on the first day.

Their opponents never recovered, though they tried manfully on the third afternoon and a nail-biting fourth morning when Pakistan lost four wickets before scoring the final 40 runs required. Not for the first time Ricky Ponting could only regret his decision at the toss.

He has refused to insert a side since Edgbaston 2005 but batting first in Leeds was as calamitous as his choice the other way five years earlier. What would Pakistan have liked less – their fragile batting exposed to a swinging, seaming ball or their crafty bowlers unleashed in dream conditions?

Dale Steyn and Morne Morkel are the best new-ball pair in the world but in the right conditions there is no more dangerous trio than Amir, Asif and Gul: left-arm, right-arm, swing and seam with a taller threat in support. The question before the England series concerned their stamina to complete a schedule of six Tests in seven weeks.

The ball by the 18-year-old Amir to dismiss Johnson at Headingley, swinging away and clipping off stump, recalled Wasim Akram at his most devastating. Asif was barely less effective with his deceptively languid approach and ability to hoop the ball both ways. The batting relied on Butt at the top of the order. Imran Farhat played a crucial innings at Headingley after being dropped early and crucially by Shane Watson. Azhar Ali showed promise but Umar Akmal seemed to believe his own publicity and needs to be more discriminating.

More than 40,000 turned up at Lord's but only around 15,000 at Headingley, leaving Yorkshire's departing chief executive, Stewart Regan, bemoaning losses of more than £500,000. The club tried hard and deserved success for gambling on the fixture's viability.

Waqar Younis, the Pakistan coach, attributed the low attendance to supporters being at work but one fan, Dipesh Naik, said that £30 for a ticket was prohibitive. "Especially when you have no idea about the weather," he added.

The Wisden Cricketer, September 2010

Captain's innings: Afridi holes out off North – caught on the boundary for 2

Richard Hobson writes for *The Times*

Scores

1st Test July 13-16, Lord's **Aus 253** (SM Katich 80, MEK Hussey 56; Mohammad Amir 4-72) **and 334** (Katich 83, BW Hilfenhaus 56*; Umar Gul 4-61); **†Pak 148** (Salman Butt 63; SR Watson 5-40) **and 289** (Salman Butt 92; MJ North 6-55). **Aus won by 150 runs.** *MoM: Katich 163r, 312b, 23x4 and Salman Butt 155r, 267b, 27x4*

Substance over style: Simon Katich makes 80

2nd Test July 21-24, Headingley **†Aus 88 and 349** (MJ Clarke 77, SPD Smith 77, RT Ponting 66; Mohammad Amir 4-86); **Pak 258** (Watson 6-33) **and 180-7** (Imran Farhat 67, Azhar Ali 51). **Pakistan won by 3 wickets.** *MoM: Mohammad Amir 38-10-106-7 and Watson below 16-4-51-6*

Series drawn 1-1

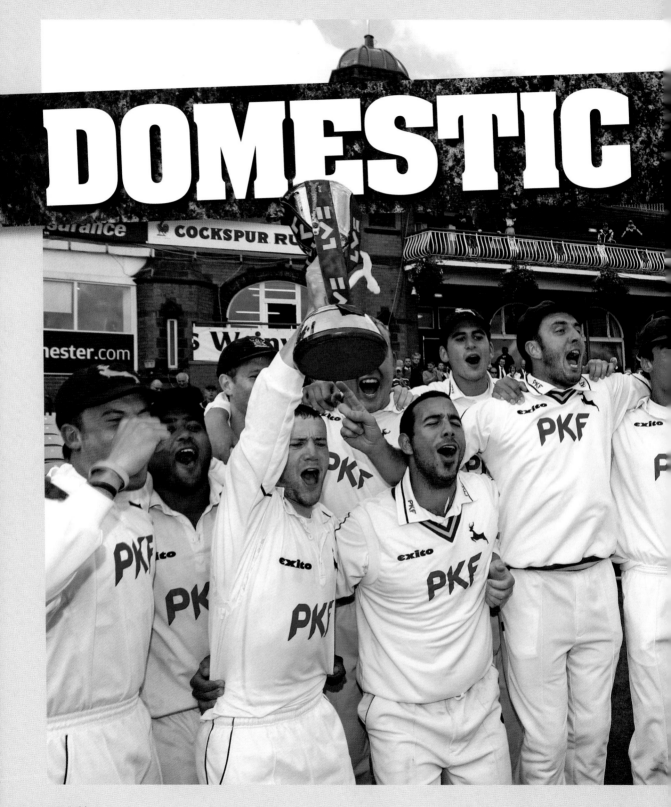

DOMESTIC

BLISS

When Nottinghamshire last won the County Championship, in 2005, it was by two and a half points. That was clearly not hair-raising enough for them. This time they won it by zero points on the final day by virtue of more wins than second-placed Somerset. It was one of the great Championship run-ins.

Two exhilarating domestic finals matched the stirring finale. These bright spots were misleading, though; fresh cherries on stale cakes. It was a season of too much Twenty20 and a 40-over competition that attracted an all too predictably low crowd to its Lord's final.

It was left to the derided Championship to provide consistent summer entertainment and emotions could not have been starker for the winning and losing captains – Chris Read and Marcus Trescothick. Having led Nottinghamshire to second in the table in his two previous seasons, Read topped his county's batting averages for the second successive year to drive them finally to the title. For Trescothick another successful year with the bat could not mask the worst kind of disappointment in his first summer as captain – that of being so close yet so far. Beaten in both the T20 and CB40 finals and missing out on leading Somerset to their first Championship title by the narrowest possible margin seemed horribly unfair.

At least Trescothick's job should be safe. Durham, Middlesex, Northamptonshire, Hampshire, Essex and Derbyshire all finished the season with different Championship captains from those they started with. Even Read stepped aside for the FP t20s as the pressure of so much cricket – and the expectation of immediate success – got too much for many skippers.

But did anyone notice? As the Twenty20 Cup was rebranded into the FP t20, the increase in group games to 144 meant that grounds, which only two years previously were packed, now stood half-empty. It was the perfect illustration of the ECB and counties putting finances before players and fans. As Gloucestershire's Jon Lewis told *TWC*, "The sooner the ECB realises less is more, the better." ⚡

Daniel Brigham is the assistant editor of *The Wisden Cricketer*

Never in doubt: Nottinghamshire left celebrate at Old Trafford after claiming the final bonus point on the final afternoon of the final game to clinch the County Championship ahead of Somerset

Contents

November, 2009: Owais Shah's running is a concern as he gets sent back to the counties

The best county

Robin Martin-Jenkins picks his top Championship side (+ Kolpaks and two overseas)

1 Nick Knight

The glue that stuck the Warwickshire team together and enabled them to win an unlikely Championship in 2004, mainly through sheer weight of runs. Technically very sound, he also had the batting brain to adapt his game to different situations – a vital skill in county cricket when conditions are so changeable. One of four batsmen in the team to average over 50 in the decade, he would also be an intelligent ear for his captain to bend in the slips.

2 Rob Key

In this team for his skill against the new ball. It was a close-run thing between him and Mal Loye but Kent's Key has more experience opening. He is one of the most popular cricketers on the circuit.

3 Mark Ramprakash

The easiest pick of the lot and will happily fill the crucial No.3 position. England's loss has been the County Championship's gain. He was prolific for Middlesex in the first half of his career but a move to Surrey in 2001 turned him into the Bradman of county cricket, scoring 55 first-class centuries for Surrey in nine years. County bowlers who have marvelled at his dancing feet before failing to breach his immaculate defence will forever shake their heads in amazement at why he averaged only 27 in Test cricket.

4 Murray Goodwin

To play either as a second overseas player or a Kolpak (see Stuart Law below), as he has done so successfully for Sussex since 2001. With 1,000 runs seven times in nine years with 37 hundreds (six double and two triple) and twice making the highest score for Sussex, his stats speak for themselves. Just as importantly he has been totally committed to his adopted county both on and, especially, off the pitch.

5 Stuart Law

His qualification as a fair dinkum Brit in the latter part of the decade, having started as an overseas player, caused much mirth. When asked by Chris Adams, sardonically, if he would now be having roast beef and Yorkshire pudding in his lunch break he put on his broadest Queensland accent and replied: "Yeah mate. It's in the veins now, in the veins." But what a player, with match-winning (and saving) innings galore for Lancashire. A sweet timer whose prolificacy was bettered only by Ramps.

XI of the decade

6 Chris Adams (captain)

A team full of interesting characters will need a strong leader. Several batsmen are more qualified to make this team but there has to be a place for the captain of the decade and one of the most successful county captains ever. Bullish and strong, his leadership at Sussex mellowed in later years but an unquenchable will to win burns under his skin. Having seen him on an England tour, Duncan Fletcher once said he was not captaincy material. Adams's glittering trophy cabinet proved him wrong.

7 Nic Pothas (wicketkeeper)

A doughty competitor, hewn from tough Transvaal stock, who is efficient with the gloves rather than stylish but his batting record this decade for Hampshire is second to none among county keepers, averaging 47. Good enough to bat at No.6, he will play as the allrounder and be a fail-safe if the top order misfires, a role he has performed with great determination for Hampshire.

8 Kabir Ali

He may be a surprising choice in some people's eyes but Worcestershire's Kabir has the best strike rate (under 44) of any seamer who has played county cricket during the decade and, if the ball swings, he can be devastating, with enough skidding pace to trouble most county batsmen. He is also a useful, if unfulfilled, lower-order batsman but I am hoping that Adams will be in a position to declare before the tail is needed.

9 Andy Caddick

A good new-ball foil for Kabir, Caddick had, as coaches like to say, 'all the tools': height, a strong action, great wrist and, in the first half of the decade at least, good air speed. He was also one of the grumpiest on-field competitors around with laughably bad batsman-banter, which masqueraded as aggression. A phenomenal county record, built around and after his England career, was all the more remarkable considering he played half of his games on the best batting strip in the country at Taunton.

10 Mushtaq Ahmed

He made Sussex into the team of the decade with his skilful variety of googlies and top-spinners and his insatiable desire to bowl, with a staggering 40 five-wicket and 15 10-wicket hauls in five and a half seasons before his knees gave way. He was the perfect overseas player – available for the full season, a match-winner and a bubbly personality. A typical Mushy day would involve five lots of prayers, five wickets and five vegetarian pizzas.

11 Steve Harmison

Surprisingly he has never taken a 10-wicket haul in county cricket but he is too good for most county batsmen when he is in the mood and he usually is in the mood when playing for his beloved Durham. His very presence in the team was as important in their back-to-back Championship wins in 2008 and 2009 as Mushtaq's wickets were for Sussex in 2006 and 2007. If this team plays in England, he plays. *The Wisden Cricketer, February 2010*

Robin Martin-Jenkins played 16 seasons for Sussex

The county king

Mark Ramprakash has ruled the shires for the last five years but is now reaching the final stages of his playing career. He talked to Sam Pilger about the past, present and future

How have you achieved such longevity?

I suppose I have good genes but above all else it is an overwhelming love for the game. The players who started at the same time as me have retired a long time ago because they don't have that same love. My experience has kept me going as well because eight times out of 10 when I go out to bat I'm not feeling as good as I would like, I am not middling the ball, the feet aren't moving but experience helps you deal with it ... So often when my name and career are spoken about it is in a negative manner. I have to keep reminding myself that I am very proud of what I have achieved in the game.

How has the county game changed?

When I started the bowling was faster. Back then there was an amazing conveyor belt of West Indians, so every team would have a bowler who could bowl at 90mph. Now there are few bowlers who can push you on the back foot. With slow pitches, too, it can be hard work for bowlers.

Does 'Bloodaxe' still lurk in you or is he gone?

Angus Fraser gave me that name because, when I was younger, I was ambitious and, if things weren't going my way, I would get frustrated. But as you get older you learn more about yourself and I have been better behaved in my 30s. I have always walked a fine line between being very competitive and it boiling over.

Who have been the biggest influences on you?

My idol was Viv Richards and I remember him approaching me once in the pavilion when we were playing West Indies. I was upset at how things were going and he told me: "You have got everything as a player but there is clearly something missing." I asked him what and he just said: "Belief." That was so perceptive without even knowing me. To hear him say that was powerful but it didn't sink in for five years. I had a lot of self-confidence until I was 21 but after a tough start in Test cricket, my confidence began to ebb away and then it came back years later.

In your book you write: "An encouraging word [from the England coaches] would have made all the difference."

I don't want to make excuses for not playing well for England. I had lots of opportunities, I tried my best at the time, so I am happy in that knowledge. But, if you look back and analyse it and compare the set-up of the England side in the early 1990s to now, there are big differences in the way new players are welcomed. I was just left on my own but now England are aware of the pressures and they do everything to help new players.

Did you ever think you might be recalled for the fifth Ashes Test at The Oval in 2009?

No, because the selectors did not seem open to the idea of recalling me. And that was disappointing. After being dropped in 2002 I went back to Surrey, continued to work hard, scored runs and developed as a person but the selectors' impression of me is stuck in the past and I have been tagged unfairly. They are out of date in their opinions, they talk about me as if it is 1995 and I have not had success at Test level – but I have. The selectors have said to me the door is always open but it appears to be closed. People say to me all the time, "Ramps, how come you're not being selected, you have scored over 6,000 runs in the last four years and averaging over 90?" It seems unfair.

But you have said you wouldn't swap winning *Strictly Come Dancing* for the chance of playing another Test. Really?

Yes, that's true, I wouldn't swap it because I had such a wonderful time on *Strictly*. I had done cricket for 20 years, so going on the show took me out of my comfort zone. It will stay with me for life.

What changes would you make to counties?

One radical idea, which I don't see happening, is to create nine regional teams and pair counties together, so you could create a London side from Middlesex and Surrey, pair together Essex and Kent, while creating a Manchester side, a Birmingham side and so on. You would produce a strong competition, where you have to perform at your best every game.

How much longer will you go on playing?

Enjoyment is a big thing for me at my age and it hasn't been very enjoyable lately with Surrey bringing up the rear and losing a lot of games. But no longer playing cricket is a scary thought. Being without it and dealing with the transition will be difficult. Going into a career in coaching could help. ◪ *The Wisden Cricketer, November 2009*

Sam Pilger is a freelance writer

Top talent: Ramps bats in 1988

The Kolpak clean-up

Counties could not use Kolpak players so freely in 2010. Was this a good thing? By **Patrick Kidd**

WHEN, in a year or two's time, Channel 4 makes an *I Love the Noughties* show, will the producers find room amid reality shows, Friends Reunited and Gordon Ramsay for an affectionate look back on another curious Noughties' phenomenon that was on the wane: the Kolpak player?

Ah, Kolpakers. Remember them? How they swarmed over, primarily from South Africa, with a bat in one hand, a work permit in the other and that engaging way of saying "jah, boet". When a Slovakian handball player Maros Kolpak got a European court ruling in 2003 that sportsmen from countries with whom the EU had a trading agreement could work unrestricted in Europe, it changed the face of county cricket.

From Claude Henderson, who became the first South African to take advantage of the new freedom when he joined Leicestershire in 2004, to Andre Nel, who retired from internationals to play for Surrey, the Kolpak players have been everywhere. A high (or low) mark was in May 2008 when Northants played Leicestershire with only five players on each side eligible to represent England.

Following a review of work permits and ratification from the UK Border Agency, the ECB rewrote the criteria for professional cricketers, meaning that in addition to the one overseas player allowed per side (two in the Twenty20 Cup) counties could no longer select unproven players on Kolpak visas. If you did not have a European passport, you could earn a 2010 work permit only if you had been with the same county for four years or played recent international cricket (which was carefully defined).

"Work permit criteria have always been there but we've tightened it up," Alan Fordham, the ECB's head of operations, said. "There had been an explosion of Kolpak cricketers, which we wanted to get down to a more sensible

level. We have to make sure that players coming in are the very best possible."

Pedro Collins, the former West Indies fast bowler, signed for Surrey in 2009 on a two-year Kolpak contract but was released because he had not played enough Tests in five years. Dwayne Smith, the allrounder,

Career Kolpak: Kent's Ryan McLaren **below** in the Twenty20 quarter final against Durham in 2009

had to return to the Caribbean for the same reasons despite having a year left on his three-year deal with Sussex.

Kent and Derbyshire released Ryan McLaren and Charl Langeveldt because they did not meet the new criteria but the players immediately won places in South Africa's one-day squad to play England this winter. They may now return but most likely as overseas players.

Paul Millman, Kent's chief executive, was sorry to lose McLaren, who had been with the county for three years and had another year to run on his contract. "We understood the desire by the ECB to

❝It is hard to rip up a contract for someone really loyal❞

reduce Kolpak players but why did the shutters have to come down so soon?" he asked. "I would have preferred the ECB to allow players on existing contracts to see out their time – by which stage Ryan would have been eligible for us under the four-year rule. It is difficult to rip up a contract for someone who has been terrifically loyal."

Stephen Hornsby, a specialist sport lawyer at Davenport Lyons, said these changes suited the PCA as they could mean more money and jobs for its domestic members: "An unrestricted number of Kolpak players kept wages down." The ECB acknowledges that the criteria suggested by the PCA are the ones that have been adopted but denies any pressure was brought to bear.

Another measure to restrict the quantity of overseas players is the introduction of a £1.8m salary cap – welcomed by smaller counties whose income is far less than counties who stage Test matches – and payments from the ECB for producing young, England-qualified players. Those who may lose out, by contrast, are older England-qualified players, whose higher salaries will make them less attractive. Steve Harmison may have signed a new contract worth £125,000 a year but what about the pros who have not played for England?

Vikram Solanki, the chairman of the PCA, expressed his reservations. "If young players are good enough, they will play anyway," he said. "But, if you force them in too early, you may damage their development and cause resentment in the dressing room. Young players can learn by being around experienced players. When I started, I batted between Graeme Hick and Tom Moody but I also learned from David Leatherdale and Stuart Lampitt." *The Wisden Cricketer, December 2009*

Patrick Kidd writes for *The Times*

EXPERT EYE Mark Wallace

Four days, one solution

Should the ECB rejig county cricket? By Glamorgan's **Mark Wallace**

IT'S BEEN A hectic summer already in the shires with the earliest ever start to a county season on April 9 and four County Championship games before May. There has been little time to catch your breath – or wash your thermals.

Much as it pains me to say it, we play too much cricket in this country. I love playing but 11 days' cricket out of 13 (as was scheduled between May 9 and 21) is not improving my game. Two Championship games, three 40-over games and a grand total of zero practice days. Even one of my two days 'off' is spent on a four-hour bus journey to Bournemouth for a 40-over game only to have to hotfoot it back home straight after the game to start a Championship match in Cardiff the next day. Crazy.

This is well-worn ground, of course, and such gripes have been aired in dressing rooms for years now. In fact, when we see the fixture list nowadays it's not resentment you hear but laughter.

But change is in the air and it's no surprise that the competition deemed ripe for slimming down is the much derided and wholly under-appreciated Championship. Sixteen games a year could be a thing of the past. There has already been plenty of dressing-room discussion about the proposed changes.

Firstly, forget the option including three Minor Counties in the competition. Ridiculous. Three divisions initially stands out as a good idea in theory but clubs getting stuck in the third tier could expect to see their best young players cherry-picked and they'd become feeder clubs for the leagues above.

The three conferences idea has been knocking around for a while and gives you 12 games a season but without the competitive element that two divisions has had since its inception. The fear players have is of too many low-intensity, dead games; two divisions eradicated this.

The other two options maintain the two-divisional structure but involve haphazard, unsymmetrical fixturing which has counties playing some sides once and some twice. This is not popular. Imagine playing the worst sides in the division once and the best sides twice. The table would mislead and downgrade the prestige of being county champions.

All five proposals are a compromise. That it's hard to analyse the strengths of each without hitting on a negative proves one thing for me: the current system is very good. Yet surprisingly, sticking with it is not one of the proposals. The competitive nature of

Making his point: Mark Wallace, batting below, is keen to keep the Championship as it is

MATT BRIGHT/PA PHOTOS

66 When we see the fixture list nowadays we just laugh 99

two-divisional cricket has produced a high standard of player for England and brought two home Ashes victories. So is there need for change? There is a strong feeling that by just focusing on cutting the Championship as a means of creating more days for rest, we risk damaging our greatest domestic asset for producing international cricketers. I fear we may be fixing something that ain't broke.

The Wisden Cricketer, June 2010

Mark Wallace keeps wicket for Glamorgan and writes on cricket and rugby for the *Western Mail*

RMJ's view

Spot the difference
Robin Martin-Jenkins, relegated with Sussex last season, makes an early assessment of the gap between the divisions

THE EMBARRASSMENT of relegation from Division One last season was mitigated by the long winter months and, as we gathered for pre-season training, there was only a passing thought or two for what life would be like in the second division.

The trend for modern sports psychologists is to talk about 'staying in the now' and about 'processes not outcome', so we are fairly brainwashed into focusing on the specific tasks that lie moments ahead. It is one of the reasons why a sportsman finds it so hard, when interviewed, not to utter the words "To be honest, mate, I'm just concentrating on the next game".

But, if I defy the trend for a few moments to reflect on the difference between the two divisions, from what I have seen so far with Sussex they are only minor. The relatively healthy crowds seen at Hove in recent years have not diminished. This will please our chief executive, who must be worried about not being able to maintain a profitable 2009.

Is there a difference in the standard of cricket? Perhaps. Our dominance of all our opponents so far, when we struggled last year with a similar team line-up, would suggest so. Our bowlers may have scythed through the opposition batting in a way that would not have happened in Division One but they have performed exceptionally well. We have also played on some sporting wickets, with good coverings of grass that were far from dry on the first day, and therein might be a clue to the major differences between the divisions: teams are much more likely to gamble for a result.

The Wisden Cricketer, June 2010

Five-for ... and, to be honest, none more treasured for RMJ than Mark Ramprakash lbw

From Langer to Banger

Spiky Justin Langer had gone and Somerset felt Marcus Trescothick was robust enough to handle captaincy. **Ivo Tennant** met him

Trescothick's record*					
M	R	HS	AVGE	100s	50s
64	5815	284	**59.94**	19	28

*first-class record since his last Test in 2006

Marcus Trescothick has his back to the revamped county ground at Taunton. He has no need to survey it for, even though he is sitting in the suite named after the legendary Bill Alley, it is hard to imagine any Somerset cricketer could have experienced the same atavistic sense of belonging. He is in reflective mood, for Phil Frost, the head groundsman throughout his career, whose flat pitches have been beloved by all batsmen, has just left the club.

There will still be sunshine and cider at Taunton, for sure, but altogether fewer sixes. Somerset know that, if they are to become county champions for the first time, the lopsided balance between bat and ball must be addressed. To this end the pitches have been top-dressed with local soil from the Mendips. This will result in fewer runs – perhaps fewer even for their star batsman.

Trescothick is unperturbed. He takes over the captaincy this season and is all too aware that Somerset will not win a match in which they score 680 and their opponents respond with 590. "We need more pace and more productive pitches. Sometimes I have found it hard to bat here because these have become slower and I haven't been able to score quickly as captains post sweepers on both sides of the wicket," he says. "Last season I scored more runs away from Taunton."

As with another powerful England opener, Graham Gooch, Trescothick has never required any motivation to play county cricket. He is as fond of Somerset as Gooch was of Essex. Even so, one reason Somerset have asked him to take over the captaincy from Justin Langer – a good friend who understood Trescothick's depressive illness better than any player – is that, at the age of 34, he will have an additional spur now that he will definitely not play Test cricket again. Besides, as Trescothick himself says, "I always wanted to have a go."

Trescothick has yet to read Mike Brearley's acclaimed book *The Art of Captaincy* but did serve as England's vice-captain under Nasser Hussain and talked to Duncan Fletcher when the selectors were deliberating over Michael Vaughan's suitability. "Michael was quite a

relaxed character who let you express yourself and Nasser was a good tactician so it was difficult to separate the two," says Trescothick. "I see myself as a close-contact person. I am concerned whether captaincy will affect my batting. Justin's was affected at times."

Instead of playing international cricket himself, Trescothick will watch his team-mate Craig Kieswetter forge an England career, which will not help him win the Championship. "We are going to lose Craig fairly soon," says Trescothick. "He will play as a specialist batsman at first because Matt Prior has deserved to retain his place as wicketkeeper." Still he anticipates Somerset will field a balanced team when Murali Kartik arrives.

One certainty is that Trescothick will remain in the game when he retires, which will probably not be until he is at

❝ If I had cancer, no one would dream of taking the mick❞

least 40. He discounts umpiring but will take a coaching course next winter. He had an approach from the IPL at the end of last summer but his decision to return early from the Champions Trophy in India in October 2009 quashed that. Since then he has been training and practising in the indoor nets at Taunton. He continues to receive regular letters about his illness. "I am still getting two or three a week. A

doctor recommended my autobiography to a patient and I have done a few interviews to help out Mind [the mental-health charity]. There has been only one negative reaction – when we played Leicestershire, one of the opening bowlers said something, which I shrugged off. I'd have been disappointed if I'd had a great deal more comments. If I had cancer, no one would dream of taking the mick, so why should they over this illness?"

Trescothick's ability to score runs whatever his frame of mind can be misleading. Last September he arrived at the county ground intending to tell his club he was not well enough to go to India for the Champions Trophy. After he scored a century he thought again but mistakenly so.

In all other aspects Trescothick's life is in order: financially, domestically and in the dressing room. His decency as a person and ability and achievements will gain him the respect of the players he will captain. They had a regard for Langer as a player but not all of them liked him. If it were not for his highly publicised illness, Trescothick would be regarded as a typical high-achieving sportsman.

Trescothick signed a three-year contract during the winter, with the option for a fourth year. He has one regret. "I put playing for England ahead of my family for too long. My career is with Somerset now, for as long as they want me. And I want to win trophies." 🏏 *The Wisden Cricketer, April 2010*

Ivo Tennant writes for *The Times*

What England are missing

■ **Trescothick's opening partnership with Andrew Strauss was productive.** They scored 2,670 Test runs together, averaging 52.35 an innings. That tops both Mark Taylor & Michael Slater (51.14) and Matthew Hayden & Justin Langer (51.41) for Australia.

■ **England's starts in ODIs grew sluggish when Trescothick left in 2006.** He and Strauss rattled along at 5.42 an over and the run-rates in his stands with Nick Knight (5.40) and Vikram Solanki (5.30) were almost as brisk. Since then England have used 19 different opening combinations. Only Strauss and Ravi Bopara (5.19) have managed to score at above five an over. (Qualification: five innings together. All stats accurate to March 16, 2010.)

■ **England have struggled to score one-day hundreds without Trescothick.** No England player has come close to Trescothick's 12 one-day centuries. Next best is Graham Gooch, with eight.

Double-ton: Andrew Strauss and Marcus Trescothick both celebrate hundreds against South Africa at Durban in 2004

DERBYSHIRE Mark Eklid					
	LVCC D2	W3	L7	D6	N/R0 9th
	CB40 B	W4	L8	T0	N/R0 4th
	FPt20 N	W6	L8	T0	N/R2 5th
	LEADING CC RUN SCORER				
	Chris Rogers 1285 runs @ 53.54				
	LEADING CC WICKET TAKER				
	Robin Peterson 51 wickets @ 30.70				

Pre-season Skipper Chris Rogers **below** believes being in the frame for Championship promotion all the way to the final game in 2009 will make the crucial difference to Derbyshire this season. "In many respects we should have got promoted last year … I just think we've got a bit of desperation to do well this year. They don't want to be nearly men and I've been really impressed by that."

Mid-season Derbyshire's season-long struggle with their bowlers' fitness took an almost comical turn for the worse when one of their few remaining seamers was put out of contention for six to eight weeks by one of the others. Tom Lungley was left with a broken right forearm when he could not get out of the way of a firm drive from his batting partner Steffan Jones in the closing stages of the Championship match against Surrey at Chesterfield. That put five first-team seamers out of action. ***Bottom line: Disintegrating challenges on all fronts.***

Final verdict Rock bottom of the second division, captain Rogers, who's been a stalwart for a few seasons, disappearing to Middlesex, senior players fleeing: it's all gone a bit wrong this season. The injuries to fast bowlers made things a struggle but a Championship win over Gloucestershire after being dismissed for 44 in the first innings brightened the gloom. Middling limited-overs results didn't help either. ***Bottom line: Only way is up, isn't it?***

DURHAM Andrew Collomosse					
	LVCC D1	W5	L3	D8	N/R0 5th
	CB40 C	W5	L6	T0	N/R1 5th
	FPt20 N	W4	L8	T0	N/R4 8th
	LEADING CC RUN SCORER				
	Michael Di Venuto 1092 runs @ 45.50				
	LEADING CC WICKET TAKER				
	Ian Blackwell 43 @ 28.02				

Pre-season Durham opened the 2010 campaign strongly fancied to become the first team for 42 years to win three successive Championships. For the second year running Durham started the Championship season without an overseas signing, relying on last season's victorious squad augmented by youngsters from their successful academy. "We have a squad of 20 players and it's important those guys feel they are going to be given the opportunity," says coach Geoff Cook. "It's vital to keep the cycle going and, when one or two like Ben Stokes and Scott Borthwick squeeze through, they provide an inspiration for others."

Mid-season Durham's decision to sack their captain, Will Smith **below**, after their first defeat in 23 matches, and four games in, surprised most around the circuit. Durham, it seemed, had chosen to overlook the injuries to five senior seam bowlers that robbed Smith of his most potent weapon. ***Bottom line: Turbulent times at Riverside.***

Final verdict A hat-trick of Championships would have been hard even if the seam attack had not been beset with injury. But Durham never found top gear in the Championship and laboured in both shorter formats. The knee-jerk decision to replace Smith with Phil Mustard after four matches fuelled the perception that all was not well at the Riverside (sorry, Emirates Durham ICG). ***Bottom line: All good things come to an end … for now.***

ESSEX Patrick Kidd					
	LVCC D1	W2	L6	D8	N/R0 9th
	CB40 B	W8	L3	T0	N/R1 SF
	FPt20 S	W11	L7	T0	N/R0 SF
	LEADING CC RUN SCORER				
	James Foster 839 runs @ 32.26				
	LEADING CC WICKET TAKER				
	David Masters 53 wickets @ 23.07				

Pre-season While most Division One counties will be eyeing their matches with Essex as guaranteed wins, two 21-year-old batsmen have other ideas. Tom Westley, who has come through the county academy, and Billy Godleman, signed from Middlesex towards the back end of last season, are likely to find themselves playing a major role this season.

Mid-season Few will not have felt saddened by Mark Pettini's resignation as first XI captain. Pettini is one of the most likeable and hard-working players on the circuit but, having struggled for runs at the start of his third season as captain, he felt the county and his own game would be best served by returning to the ranks. James Foster **below**, the 30-year-old former England wicketkeeper, has succeeded Pettini in all forms of the game. ***Bottom line: Reached T20 Finals Day with a thrilling run-chase against Lancashire and heads are still above water in the Championship.***

Final verdict Two semi-final appearances mask a torrid season: Championship relegation, captain Pettini standing down after a terrible run with the bat, Mervyn Westfield charged with conspiracy to defraud, Ravi Bopara failing to prove he should be back in England's Test team, no signings and, worst of all, the money cynically spent on signing Dwayne Bravo for T20 Finals Day – 5 runs and 1 for 46. ***Bottom line: Yep, Bravo Essex.***

GLAMORGAN Richard Thomas

LVCC D2	W7	L4	D5	N/R0	3rd
CB40 A	W2	L8	T0	N/R2	7th
FPt20 S	W6	L10	T0	N/R0	8th

LEADING CC RUN SCORER
Mark Cosgrove 1187 @ 49.45
LEADING CC WICKET TAKER
James Harris 63 wickets @ 20.52

Pre-season Jamie Dalrymple **below** has revealed that commercial demands are driving the county's priorities this season. Glamorgan's captain says the county chairman, Paul Russell, and the club management have told the squad they want them to concentrate on the one-day arena. That will demand a big improvement on and off the pitch from last season.

Mid-season Having been immersed in a cricket recession for six years, Glamorgan seem to be enjoying considerable growth as they topped Division Two of the Championship at the halfway stage. They had celebrated five victories – as many wins as in 2008 and 2009 put together. "We laid those foundations last year when we became a lot tougher to beat," says Glamorgan's director of cricket, Matthew Maynard. **Bottom line: The team to beat.**

Final verdict Being blanked by a committee-man after failing to gain promotion has left Maynard and Dalrymple vulnerable. And with the club confirming it will have a top-down review of the season before any more recruitment, it'll be an interesting winter. A promotion bid ended in failure on the last day of the season. "I was walking with Jamie and a committee person passed and did not look at us. That suggests they are not happy," says Maynard. At least 2010 was better than the previous year. "We have been happy with the progress. We see development. It is easy to be impatient." **Bottom line: A season to forget.**

GLOUCESTERSHIRE Andy Stockhausen

LVCC D2	W6	L9	D1	N/R0	5th
CB40 B	W9	L3	T0	N/R0	3rd
FPt20 S	W5	L11	T0	N/R0	9th

LEADING CC RUN SCORER
Hamish Marshall 884 runs @ 35.36
LEADING CC WICKET TAKER
Gemaal Hussain 67 wkts @ 22.34

Pre-season If self-belief is to be considered a reliable measure of a team's promotion prospects, then Gloucestershire can be expected to challenge for a top-two finish in the Championship. In the doldrums for so long, Gloucestershire finally rediscovered the art of winning four-day matches in 2009, triumphing on six occasions to finish in the top half.

Mid-season Skipper Alex Gidman **below** claims Gloucestershire must learn to beat their closest rivals if they are to realise their promotion ambitions. Although the county have established themselves as genuine candidates for a top-two finish this summer, the captain says defeats at the hands of fellow contenders Glamorgan, Sussex and Northants suggest further improvement is necessary if promotion is to be achieved. **Bottom line: Batsmen must cope better against spin.**

Final verdict Gidman admits they fell short when it mattered most. The members were entitled to anticipate promotion and a prolonged run in the CB40 and for a while that optimism looked well-founded. But their challenge for honours on two fronts foundered on batting frailties. Gidman concedes: "When we needed to find that little bit extra to get over the finish line, we were not able to. There were games where we were in a position to win and failed to ram home our advantage." **Bottom line: A season that promised much ended in disappointment.**

HAMPSHIRE Pat Symes

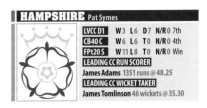

LVCC D1	W3	L6	D7	N/R0	7th
CB40 C	W6	L6	T0	N/R0	4th
FPt20 S	W11	L8	T0	N/R0	Win

LEADING CC RUN SCORER
James Adams 1351 runs @ 48.25
LEADING CC WICKET TAKER
James Tomlinson 46 wickets @ 35.30

Pre-season Hampshire have more links than any other county with the IPL after officially joining with the Rajasthan Royals and losing Dimitri Mascarenhas and Michael Lumb to the competition but coach Giles White dismisses suggestions of a soul being sold. Beginning his second full season in charge, White shares the conviction of his chairman, Rod Bransgrove, that others will forge IPL franchise liaisons.

Mid-season Lumb and Mascarenhas will be looking back on their lucrative involvement in the IPL with mixed emotions. The captain Mascarenhas limped home from the Rajasthan Royals with an ankle injury that later required surgery and has restricted his English season to three overs. He will not play again this summer. Lumb, who also played for Rajasthan, has gone from World Twenty20 winner to not being able to hold his county place. **Bottom line: Thanks to James Vince, Chris Wood and Danny Briggs below.**

Final verdict Hampshire set their hearts on winning the FPt20 on home soil. But White was just as pleased they stayed up. They began the season with six successive defeats in all competitions and, for all the FPt20 euphoria, never quite recovered. White says: "Staying in division one is as satisfying as winning the T20 and maybe it will allow us to challenge for the title next year. To stay up with so many under-21s in the side is as good as winning a trophy." **Bottom line: Cup win made it all worthwhile.**

LVCC D1	W3	L7	D6	N/R 0	8th
CB40 C	W7	L3	T0	N/R 2	2nd
FPt20 S	W7	L9	T0	N/R 0	7th
LEADING CC RUN SCORER					
Martin v Jaars'ld 1082 runs @ 41.61					
LEADING CC WICKET TAKER					
Amjad Khan 38 wickets @ 33.10					

Pre-season Paul Farbrace has been upbeat as new team director considering his first pre-season has proved tough. Record financial losses ruled out an overseas training camp, poor weather led to a three-day pre-season friendly with Nottinghamshire being abandoned and the Australian Stuart Clark withdrew his services as overseas player. Yet Farbrace is buoyant. "It has been a headache but not a distraction and we're in good shape."

Mid-season Competing on three fronts with a small, injury-hit squad and budgetary constraints forced Farbrace to re-evaluate. Patchy top-order batting returns coupled with obdurate injuries for the quicks Robbie Joseph, Dewald Nel and Amjad Khan **below**, have led to a reality check. Inconsistency has left Kent out of T20 contention and fighting to avoid Championship relegation. "It is tough and a bit frustrating right now," says Farbrace.

Final verdict Kent made an immediate return to the Championship's second tier despite a last-gasp win over title-chasing Yorkshire at Headingley. It was a sorry, cash-strapped summer during which the side blew hot and cold in all competitions. Farbrace confirmed Kent will operate on a reduced budget and first-team squad of 16 to 18 players, five of whom will be in full-time education. And they might not be able to afford an overseas player next year. *Bottom line: No money.*

LVCC D1	W5	L3	D8	N/R 0	4th
CB40 A	W6	L6	T0	N/R 0	4th
FPt20 N	W9	L7	T0	N/R 1	QF
LEADING CC RUN SCORER					
Steven Croft 883 runs @ 38.39					
LEADING CC WICKET TAKER					
Glen Chapple 52 wickets @ 19.75					

Pre-season New decade, new Lancashire will be the hope of Red Rose supporters as Peter Moores' side resume their quest for a first major trophy since 1999. The former England coach was obliged to hit the ground running last year with his appointment eight weeks before the start of the campaign. But this time he is hoping the squad's diligent winter preparation and a successful pre-season tour to Barbados will pay off in all formats. "We won a lot of matches last year without going on to win trophies," he says.

Mid-season Luke Sutton **below** was not in Lancashire's T20 squad so hit two hundreds for the 2nd XI before marking his return to Championship action against Durham with a second century of the season. "That was my best knock. Playing against Durham in Durham is the biggest challenge in Division One." *Bottom line: Hanging in there despite lack of runs.*

Final verdict Another muted challenge for that elusive first outright Championship since 1934, another low-key campaign in the one-day league, another quarter-final exit in T20. Lancashire remained difficult to beat and they were still flirting around the fringes of the title race until Glen Chapple's generous declaration in a must-win match at Trent Bridge. Batting was a problem, though Shivnarine Chanderpaul, arriving late, helped with 698 runs at 58.16 in 13 innings. So once again, frustration it is. *Bottom line: Championship title wait goes on.*

LVCC D2	W7	L5	D4	N/R 0	4th
CB40 C	W4	L8	T0	N/R 0	6th
FPt20 N	W6	L9	T0	N/R 1	7th
LEADING CC RUN SCORER					
James Taylor 1027 runs @ 44.65					
LEADING CC WICKET TAKER					
Claude Henderson 56 wickets @ 21.05					

Pre-season Matthew Hoggard's decision to become Leicestershire's new captain suggests that he has no intention of taking life easy in the final years of his career. Hoggard rejected an offer to join Sussex after Yorkshire released him and the captaincy and the chance to help turn around the fortunes of a young, developing side persuaded him to choose Leicestershire. "I might not be very good [at the captaincy] but we will see."

Mid-season There have been challenges for Matthew Hoggard **below** in his first season at the county and as captain, none greater than coping with the shock resignation of the chief executive, David Smith. Smith cited alleged interference in team selection by the chairman, Neil Davidson, for his resignation and urged county supporters to call for a special general meeting. Hoggard successfully distanced the players from the politics. "We are cricket players not office staff or admin staff," Hoggard says.

Final verdict A season of encouraging on-field progress overshadowed by internecine strife. The rise of a young and emerging side from bottom to fourth in the second tier was set against an unstable political situation triggered by the chief executive's resignation. They lost only one of the last eight Championship matches. James Taylor showed maturity by passing 1,000 runs for the second season. *Bottom line: Solid.*

MIDDLESEX Benj Moorehead

LVCC D2	W4	L7	D5	N/R0	8th
CB40 B	W3	L7	T0	N/R2	6th
FPt20 S	W8	L8	T0	N/R0	6th

LEADING CC RUN SCORER
Dawid Malan 1001 runs at 38.50
LEADING CC WICKET TAKER
Tim Murtagh 38 wickets at 36.97

Pre-season "The world's our oyster," reckons Middlesex's new coach, Richard Scott. Fans reeling from the misery of 2009 may scoff at the sentiment but there is an air of renewal about the county: a new management team as well as the plucky New Zealander Iain O'Brien; and, in Twenty20 terms, Middlesex have the best of old and new Australia – Adam Gilchrist **below** and David Warner. But the priority, says Scott, is Championship promotion.

Mid-season Shaun Udal stepped down as captain and Neil Dexter, a batting allrounder who arrived from Kent in 2008, took over after Gilchrist's seven-match T20 run. The task facing Dexter was apparent in his first four games: all were lost. "I'm not going to change anything drastically," says Dexter, who describes himself as "relaxed" and "not the most outspoken person" – a change from Udal. *Bottom line: Staying in Division Two.*

Final verdict Second from bottom in the Championship, little success in any other competition, changes at the top yet a sense of a promising young team. When can supporters expect a challenge? "We made the mistake of prescribing promotion this year, which put us under pressure," says Scott. The damage was done after four straight Championship defeats in April and May. "It was hard clawing it back," admits Scott. *Bottom line: Still promising, still flopping.*

NORTHAMPTONSHIRE Andrew Radd

LVCC D2	W6	L7	D3	N/R0	6th
CB40 B	W4	L8	T0	N/R0	5th
FPt20 N	W7	L6	T3	N/R0	QF

LEADING CC RUN SCORER
Stephen Peters 1296 runs @ 48.00
LEADING CC WICKET TAKER
Jack Brooks 34 wickets @ 36.08

Pre-season The head coach, David Capel, is calling for "soul and spirit" as he embarks on his 31st consecutive season at Wantage Road. And he hopes the return of Mal Loye **below**, his fellow Northamptonian, after seven seasons with Lancashire will help make that happen. "Mal knows this club and knows what I call 'The Northamptonshire Way', which is concerned with quality and standards and the way we do things. It's something from the heart."

Mid-season Rob Newton's Championship debut against Worcestershire at New Road was another plus-point for the Northants Academy. Set up 10 years ago at Wantage Road, it aimed to produce "not just second-team cricketers but players good enough to go straight into the firsts". Newton became the 16th graduate to appear in first-class cricket for the county. *Bottom line: Time to focus on a Championship promotion bid.*

Final verdict Results fell short of expectations in all competitions. A small playing staff and injuries at crucial times gave Capel problems. So 23 cricketers were tried in the Championship – eight of them Northants debutants. Only Stephen Peters passed 1,000 runs in the four-day competition and not one century was scored in one-day cricket. The bowling stats were no more impressive: no one managed 40 Championship wickets. *Bottom line: A seventh successive season in Division Two.*

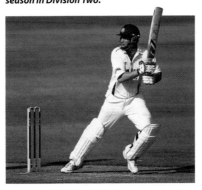

NOTTINGHAMSHIRE Paul Bolton

LVCC D1	W7	L5	D4	N/R0	Champ
CB40 C	W7	L4	T0	N/R1	3rd
FPt20 N	W11	L5	T2	N/R0	SF

LEADING CC RUN SCORER
Chris Read 916 runs at 45.80
LEADING CC WICKET TAKER
Andre Adams 68 wickets @ 22.17

Pre-season Nottinghamshire's director of cricket, Mick Newell, hopes that having a fully fit Darren Pattinson and Charlie Shreck will help deny Durham a third straight County Championship. Nottinghamshire trailed in a distant second to Durham last season when their seam attack, which missed Ryan Sidebottom for all but six Championship matches, lacked a cutting edge because Pattinson and Shreck were rarely at their best.

Mid-season Alex Hales has his sights on filling the place in Nottinghamshire's top order that will be vacated when Mark Wagh **below** retires from first-class cricket midway through next season. It was while Wagh was sitting his exams for the graduate diploma in law that Hales was given his Championship chance this season and he made a maiden century in the competition. "I had a slow start to the season form-wise but I got a score while Mark was away doing his exams and I've managed to keep my slot," he says. *Bottom line: Trophy-hunting.*

Final verdict Notts' nerveless display on the final Championship day lost them the 'chokers' tag. They nearly squandered a 22-point lead when Yorkshire bowled them out for 59 in the penultimate game and rain allowed only 28 overs on the first three days of their last match at Old Trafford. But they held their nerve to collect the six bonus points they needed to pip Somerset. *Bottom line: Definitely not bottlers.*

LVCC D1	W6	L2	D8	N/R0	2nd
CB40 A	W11	L3	T0	N/R0	RU
FPt20 S	W13	L6	T0	N/R0	RU

LEADING CC RUN SCORER
Marcus Trescothick 1397 @ 58.20
LEADING CC WICKET TAKER
Charl Willoughby 58 wickets @ 27.27

Pre-season With Somerset players and members alike coveting a first Championship title, the director of cricket, Brian Rose, says it is dangerous to prioritise and promises an equally robust effort in the one-day competitions. "Our aim is to be really competitive during the first two months of the season in the County Championship and the 40-over … We saw what Mushtaq did for Sussex and we are hoping Murali Kartik **below** can do something similar for us."

Mid-season Rose is talking up Somerset's chances of winning a first Championship after securing the Indian Murali Kartik's services for 2011. A success since joining the county this summer, the left-arm spinner agreed to return. After Kartik claimed match figures of 10 for 107 against Kent at Taunton Rose describes him as "a key weapon in our bid to win the Championship for the first time". *Bottom line: May not quite have what it takes this year.*

Final verdict Somerset were the best county, winning 30 games, yet they contrived to finish runners-up in all three competitions. Sceptics will label them chokers, others will point to a developing side which has still to peak. Captain Marcus Trescothick says: "To come so close and to end up losing three times is devastating for the boys. But we have to learn the lessons from what has happened." *Bottom line: Team of the season without a ruthless streak.*

LVCC D2	W4	L6	D6	N/R0	7th
CB40 A	W6	L4	T1	N/R1	3rd
FPt20 S	W8	L8	T0	N/R0	5th

LEADING CC RUN SCORER
Mark Ramprakash 1595 @ 61.34
LEADING CC WICKET TAKER
Chris Tremlett 48 wickets @ 20.18

Pre-season The developing bond between Rory Hamilton-Brown **below**, the youngest captain in the Championship, and the county's 'senior pro', Mark Ramprakash, is the key to improved performances, according to Surrey's cricket manager, Chris Adams. Hamilton-Brown, 22, impressed during the club's pre-season trip to the UAE. Adams says: "He is showing he is prepared to back his beliefs as a captain."

Mid-season The East Midlands has become something of a happy hunting ground in the county's attempt to avoid lifting this season's Championship wooden spoon. Surrey followed their opening victory of the campaign at Northants in May with a battling display in Chesterfield … a 42-run win secured with 55 balls of the game remaining. Surrey took eight wickets in the final two sessions.

Final verdict When Adams set out on his five-year mission to boldly go where few Surrey coaches have recently been – the club trophy cabinet – he realised that recruiting strong personalities to his ranks would be crucial. That all three of his high-profile signings – Steven Davies, Gareth Batty and Chris Tremlett – settled in so soundly is testament both to the Adams judgement as well as the determination of the players. "We now look a strong seam and pace outfit with Tremlett, Jade Dernbach and Stuart Meaker." *Bottom line: Recruits bedded in. Progress made, albeit slowly.*

LVCC D2	W8	L3	D5	N/R0	Champ
CB40 A	W7	L3	T1	N/R1	2nd
FPt20 S	W9	L7	T0	N/R0	QF

LEADING CC RUN SCORER
Murray Goodwin 1201 runs @ 52.21
LEADING CC WICKET TAKER
Corey Collymore 57 wickets @ 19.87

Pre-season Though Sussex are defending two one-day trophies this season, manager, Mark Robinson, gives short shrift to those who think the county are not prioritising an immediate return to the Championship's top flight. "Relegation hurt us despite the one-day success … There are spots up for grabs so everyone in our squad has a chance of playing."

Mid-season Robin Martin-Jenkins **below** has never been prone to obvious shows of emotion on the field, even though he has had plenty of reason to shed a tear or two given the success he has enjoyed during a career which began when he broke into the Sussex Under-10s. But the allrounder, who is retiring after 15 first-class years, admits he will be a bit dewy-eyed when he walks off a Sussex ground for the last time on July 19. *Bottom line: Championship progress offset by one-day disappointment.*

Final verdict Sussex came up short in the defence of their two one-day titles but the main objective of promotion (as champions) was achieved. But for the second season running only two players passed 1,000 runs and the lower order consistently got them out of trouble – Martin-Jenkins' form before retirement was the most consistent of his career. The enduring consistency of their seam attack was also key to their success and it was good to see Monty Panesar getting his mojo back. *Bottom line: Mission accomplished.*

WARWICKSHIRE Paul Bolton

LVCC D1	W6	L9	D1	N/R0	6th
CB40 C	W11	L3	T0	N/R0	Winners
FPt20 N	W11	L5	T0	N/R1	QF

LEADING CC RUN SCORER
Ian Westwood 726 runs @ 25.92
LEADING CC WICKET TAKER
Imran Tahir 56 wickets @ 24.57

Pre-season Ashley Giles **below right** believes his players need to show less respect for the opposition if they are to become serious challengers for Durham's Championship crown. The director of cricket, Giles, felt that Warwickshire were sometimes in awe of opponents last season. "We almost played the name rather than the team."

Mid-season The honeymoon is over for Giles. A second division trophy in each of his first two seasons in charge at Edgbaston represented a satisfactory start but it has all gone wrong this season. Giles got some of the treatment dealt out to his predecessor Mark Greatbatch when there were calls for him to resign from disgruntled members. ***Bottom line: Struggling.***

Final verdict Warwickshire's season was transformed in five weeks from the despair of a two-day defeat at Trent Bridge to celebrations at Lord's when they won the CB40. When Notts dismissed them twice in a day Warwickshire appeared certain relegation victims but they ended with successive wins over Essex, Kent and Hampshire. They lost nine games – no side had stayed up with as many defeats since two divisions were introduced in 2000. "We slipped under the radar," says Giles. "People thought we were having a nightmare because of the Championship but our one-day form was good. The players showed character in the final weeks." ***Bottom line: It came right in the end.***

WORCESTERSHIRE Paul Bolton

LVCC D2	W7	L4	D5	N/R0	2nd
CB40 A	W4	L8	T0	N/R0	5th
FPt20 N	W5	L10	T0	N/R1	9th

LEADING CC RUN SCORER
Moeen Ali 1260 runs @ 48.46
LEADING CC WICKET TAKER
Alan Richardson 55 wickets @ 24.40

Pre-season Vikram Solanki **below** is backing the exuberance of youth to carry his inexperienced squad through what threatens to be another tough season at New Road. The winter departures of Stephen Moore, Steve Davies, Gareth Batty and Kabir Ali, coupled with the decision to release Simon Jones and Ian Fisher, mean that Solanki, as captain, is leading a team short on experience but full of potential. "There will be tough challenges ahead."

Mid-season The Bangladesh allrounder Shakib-al-Hasan sees himself in a pioneering role as Worcestershire's overseas player. Shakib, who captained his country in the Test series against England this summer, is the first Bangladeshi to play county cricket. He hit 90 on his County Championship debut at Derby and 72 in his first one-day outing against the Unicorns. "I'm enjoying it so far although the results haven't gone our way," Shakib says. "The travelling in county cricket is something that takes some getting used to." ***Bottom line: Poor.***

Final verdict Worcestershire confounded the doom-mongers with an immediate promotion. The inexperienced squad had an outstanding team spirit, Alan Richardson took 55 wickets in his first season and Daryl Mitchell was solid at the top of the order and showed an aptitude for captaincy when he replaced Vikram Solanki five weeks from the season's close.
Bottom line: Job done.

YORKSHIRE Andrew Collomosse

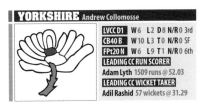

LVCC D1	W6	L2	D8	N/R0	3rd
CB40 B	W10	L3	T0	N/R0	SF
FPt20 N	W6	L9	T1	N/R0	6th

LEADING CC RUN SCORER
Adam Lyth 1509 runs @ 52.03
LEADING CC WICKET TAKER
Adil Rashid 57 wickets @ 31.29

Pre-season Former captain Craig White will be very familiar with his team in his new role as assistant coach. White has played alongside every player in contention for a place in the starting line-up during a 17-year first-team career … "I think Andrew Gale **below** will be in the Graeme Smith mould as a captain and will lead from the front," he says.

Mid-season The success of Gale's young pretenders has revived memories of Yorkshire lifting Championships for fun with a team of homegrown players. Their progress this time has also been built on players born and bred in the county, a policy that the assistant bowling coach, John Blain, believes can bring back good times. Blain says: "I don't see any reason at all why we can't have 10 Yorkshiremen alongside [one overseas]. The talent is there."
Bottom line: Exciting times.

Final verdict Gale's approach fired Yorkshire to early victories and the bandwagon rolled merrily until the wheels came off in the final six days of the season: semi-final defeat by Warwickshire in the CB40 and implosion against Kent with a first Championship since 2001 beckoning. But the standing ovation from the Headingley crowd as Yorkshire's dejected players trudged off provided recognition that the feel-good factor has been restored. "We're reborn as a county," says Gale.
Bottom line: Genuine hope for the future.

Excess
not success

When **Robin Martin-Jenkins** started his career players drank too much. Now booze is not the problem, wrote the Sussex allrounder as he began life after cricket

Robin Martin-Jenkins
Born October 28, 1975, Guildford, Surrey

	M	R	HS	AVGE	100s	50s	W	AVGE	BEST	5w
First-class	184	7448	205*	**31.69**	5	41	384	**31.90**	7-51	8
One-day	229	2014	68*	**15.37**	-	3	234	**30.40**	4-22	-
Twenty20	47	237	56*	**13.16**	-	1	34	**33.91**	4-20	-
Trophies	**County Championship** 2003, 2006, 2007									
	Pro40/National League 2008, 2009									
	C&G Trophy 2006									
	Twenty20 Cup 2009									

ifteen years ago I made my County Championship debut against Yorkshire at Scarborough. The events surrounding the match were more memorable to me than anything that happened on the pitch. Sussex were languishing in the lower half of the table and, with only one more game to go in the season, the mood in the camp was decidedly end-of-termish. From the moment I arrived in my hotel room to hear the senior player, with whom I was sharing, trying to persuade the pretty receptionist to come out that evening I could sense the focus was not on cricket but on Scarborough's nightlife.

Rain limited the match to a single innings and I spent the four days trying to concentrate on cricket – it was my debut after all – and the four evenings following my senior players around from bar to bar, drinking as though we were on a Club 18-30 holiday in Ayia Napa. You could say it was an Ayia-opening experience.

Contrast this with the final away Championship fixture of my career in June this year at Derby. There were similarities. I was sharing a room with a 19-year-old on his first away trip with the senior team. It rained quite a bit, ruining any chance of a result in the match. But there the off-field comparisons end. In Derby players congregated in the evenings to eat in the hotel or nearby restaurants and there was talk of rain in the weather forecasts. But Coke or water was the drink of choice and beds were occupied by 11pm, no receptionists present.

Sussex took 12 players and a manager to Scarborough in 1995. Physiotherapists accompanied the team to away games only occasionally, the opposition's being used if necessary. The players arrived at the hotel on the evening before the game, discussed which restaurants served the best food, went to sleep at a variety of hours, woke up and played. As a young player my first sighting of the captain and coach was next morning at the pre-match nets.

Fast forward to Derby 2010 to see 13 players (two needed for 12th man duties) arrive at the ground on the morning of the day before the match. They are accompanied by two coaches, a physio, a strength-and-conditioning coach and

an analyst. There are nets. Treatment is available for niggles and strains. Fitness programmes are followed through in the gym. The coach will call a meeting in which the analyst delivers a report on the opposition's strengths and weaknesses, including some DVD highlights. The captain will express how he wants us to approach the game. The floor is opened for general comments and then, finally, the players travel to their hotel and collapse in a heap on their beds, exhausted – after a swim and stretch in the pool, that is.

All this might seem far-fetched but it is both exactly as it is and how I remember it. In such ways the county game has changed immeasurably in the past 15 years. It is a change that has mostly been for the better. Some people who have watched cricket for generations bemoan that there are no 'characters' in the game any more. But look at the fitness levels of the modern player; look at the fielding. In

66 Players want to play less to give their bodies more time to rest 99

1993 I watched Martin Speight, the Sussex batsman, sweep Warwickshire's opening bowler Tim Munton for a boundary in a Lord's final and 25,000 people looked on with me in stunned disbelief. These days everybody is sweeping seamers, reverse-sweeping them too and scooping the ball over the keeper's head. This is more fun to watch than David Gower in a Tiger Moth.

Of course, there has been significant structural reform too. The limited-overs league and knockout competitions have had more tinkering than a boy racer's car. Twenty20 has stormed the scene. Whatever people's views on the shortest format, and the vast majority of the players still love it, it has changed the dynamic, created wealth. It is here to stay.

But to the day-in-day-out county stalwart, the kind of player whose ambitions are to play for England but whose talent threshold will forever be just too low – players like me in other words – the most significant change came in the Championship when one division became two. In an instant games such as my debut at Scarborough were banished.

Matches were played with greater intensity throughout the season. It is perhaps the only piece of restructuring that has been an unmitigated success and any future administrations would surely meddle with the two-division structure at their peril.

But none of this restructuring has addressed the hottest issue in the players' minds: the amount of cricket played. At the start of each season the player's collective voice, the PCA, carries out a survey of its members and one of the perennial conclusions is that there are too many matches. Players do not want to play less because they are lazy. On the whole they enjoy playing cricket. It would not be much of a career choice if they did not. They want to play less to give their bodies more time to rest, reduce the frequency of injuries and allow more time for perfecting their craft with controlled practice. They want to avoid inconsistencies in scheduling that sees a week off followed by 12 days of a variety of formats leaving players exhausted and supporters confused.

Over the past 15 years I have come to realise the players are on the bottom rung of what management speak might call the 'stakeholder ladder'. And it appears it was ever thus: consider the following by a 24-year-old county player, writing in 1999 in his local paper: "They just never seem to listen to the players. It makes me wonder whether a bunch of chimpanzees couldn't run English cricket better than the ECB." OK, I was young and naive and, had I thought harder about the implications of criticising my ultimate employers, I might have used subtler language. But 11 years on, retired and so, I trust, immune from being fined again, I hold fast to that view. ∎

The Wisden Cricketer, September 2010

Big hit: RMJ smashes a six during the CB40

Oh captain, bye captain

Seven captains who started 2010 lost their jobs. Bad luck or a culture change? By **Lawrence Booth**

THE GREAT God of football has long rankled with cricket fans fed up with seeing their sport squeezed from the national consciousness. And the resentment may be spreading. The relatively high turnover this season among county captains – a job that, even without rose-tinted spectacles, was once a byword for stability – has provoked comparisons with the treatment long reserved for football managers. Not won for a while? Time for a change.

Shaun Udal could hardly pretend results had been encouraging when he resigned as Middlesex captain in June but – as a 41-year-old who made his first-class debut in 1989 – he is clear about the shift in emphasis. "There was a lot more patience when I first came into the game," he says. "Captains were given a long time in the job but nowadays there does seem to be a massive change. A football-style mentality has crept in. It's true clubs have a right to expect success and captains are paid more than the other players. But county captains have become like managers of football teams. There's a lot less patience than there used to be and a lot more pressure."

Udal's appraisal is eloquent and far from bitter. He even says he has learned to enjoy his cricket once more since returning to the rank and file. But events around the country this summer suggest such equanimity may not always have been in such plentiful supply.

Will Smith stepped down as captain of Durham in May, eight months after captaining his side in an unbeaten, Championship-winning season. Nicky Boje quit soon after at Northants, followed by Udal and Essex's Mark Pettini, whose form with the bat was suffering. Vikram Solanki at Worcestershire went while Chris Rogers at Derbyshire, Chris Read at Notts and Ian Westwood at Warwickshire all relinquished the

captaincy temporarily during the Friends Provident t20 while Hampshire's Nic Pothas – himself a stand-in for the injured Dimitri Mascarenhas – was forced to hand the reins to Dominic Cork.

"County cricket has become like any other professional sport in that regard," says the Durham chief executive, David Harker. "Winning is everything. In the not too distant past it was enough just to play the game: ninth in a division of 18, it wasn't a disaster. If you come ninth in Division One now, it is a disaster. Two divisions have changed the picture. The credibility of the club is at stake."

Harker plays down the football

The cap doesn't fit: Shaun Udal, seen here skippering Middlesex against Surrey at The Oval, resigned in June

analogy, arguing that, while there is greater pressure, it is felt by clubs not individuals. Chris Adams, the former Championship-winning captain of Sussex who is now cricket manager at Surrey, argues for evolution not revolution – especially given his choice of Rory Hamilton-Brown as club captain. "In your early days the job can consume your whole life. How long will we give Rory? As long as it takes," he says.

Surrey's commitment, part of an overall plan to end several years of under-achievement, strikes a rare note. Yet it is partly informed by financial rude

66 I could understand if the odd person turned the job down 99

health. And that may be the problem elsewhere: in an era where Twenty20 promises instant riches and two divisions have created insecurity, less well-off clubs demand success today.

Mick Newell, Nottinghamshire's coach, says: "There's nowhere to hide in two-divisional cricket and now, with two overseas players who need paying, the incentive is to get results more quickly. You want more people through the gate. When Notts are doing well, more people come and watch. So all these things add up to put pressure on a captain."

Udal agrees. "Once there's more money around, as with Twenty20, people get greedier," he says. "Clubs want a piece of it. But you see more and more clubs becoming insolvent and in debt, so they want success straightaway."

Middlesex's managing director of cricket, Angus Fraser, believes the role of Twenty20 is in danger of being overstated but concedes the threat posed by a hire-and-fire attitude. "There is a possibility of things becoming like football but you want to safeguard against that," he says. "If the door becomes a revolving one, then it tends not to be the kind of club that does well."

County cricket seems torn between the world it used to be and the world it fears becoming. Administrators dislike comparisons with football yet demand success as single-mindedly as football chairmen. As a result, while captaincy jobs are not yet regarded as poisoned chalices, a line has been crossed, maybe for good. "If you get approached to be a county captain, it's not something you can turn down," says Udal. "But I could understand it now if people said no because they've seen what's happened and they don't want it to happen to them." *The Wisden Cricketer, September 2010*

Lawrence Booth writes for the *Daily Mail*

LETTERS Having your say

The readers' voice

The letters pages are a forum for celebration, complaint and bemusement in the county game

Thanks Nashy

I'D LIKE to thank Middlesex keeper David Nash. His service and enthusiasm over 12 years has been a pleasure for me and many others. Happy retirement.
John Wischhusen
Enfield, Middlesex
The Wisden Cricketer, November 2009

Sheffield steal

HOW CAN Yorkshire call themselves Yorkshire when they do not play in Sheffield or South Yorkshire? The amount of amateur cricket played in Sheffield has shrunk with the folding of leagues. I believe this is a direct result of no cricket in Sheffield. Does the outdated ECB and county structure not realise there is nobody for South Yorkshire youngsters to look up to? And we all hate Leeds in Sheffield! Where are the new Vaughans, Goughs, Boycotts, Truemans going to come from? Sheffield is one of the 10 largest cities in England – South Yorkshire is the heart of cricket in England. How can it be right there is no first-class cricket here when there is in small towns like Canterbury, Taunton, Worcester and Brighton? Scrap county cricket, rename Yorkshire 'Leeds' and let's have a structure similar to football. Then we may see a decent standard in Sheffield again.
Stuart Burton
Sheffield
The Wisden Cricketer, December 2009

Points for positivity

I WELCOME the ECB's new points system in the four-day game in 2010 as a way of rewarding a more positive approach to matches with the increased points on offer for wins and reductions for draws. But I believe that the bonus points are soft giveaways and too easy to pick up. I'd like to suggest the

following system for the four-day game worldwide: 12 points for a win, three points for a draw. One batting point for a match runs-per-wicket ratio more than 35, one point for a match scoring-rate of more than 3.5 runs an over. One bowling point for taking wickets in the match at a runs-per-wicket ratio under 25, one point for taking match wickets at an average strike-rate of one wicket every eight overs. One bonus point for coming within two wickets or 20 runs of victory in a drawn or lost match. First innings restricted to 120 overs.
Nick Cox
Hinckley, Leicestershire
The Wisden Cricketer, February 2010

Top knock: David Nash during his century for Middlesex against Somerset at Taunton in 2007 **below**

Somerset support

I SHALL soon be 80 and have been on the county ground, Taunton, every year since my grandfather first took me in 1936, including the war years, when I used to play there. I have seen many changes and my father and grandfather would not be able to recognise the ground, which has become a superb modern stadium. A new long room has just been built and I have received an invitation to upgrade my membership. However, I notice that one of the benefits is an "exclusive bar and brassiere". I am just recovering from a heart attack and am wondering if the excitement of my 75th season will be too much.
Jack Endacott
Chippenham, Wiltshire
The Wisden Cricketer, June 2010

Fantastic four days

IN THE LAST two seasons I have seen some of the finest four-day games ever, ranging from battling-against-the-odds draws, successful run chases without resorting to declaration bowling, to last-over victories with nine men

crowded around the bat. Enthralled and substantial crowds invariably watch. These are people who understand and appreciate the finer points of the game. And yet the ECB wishes to tinker with this format by either introducing three regionalised conferences with no promotion or relegation or by reducing the number of counties. Then in the height of summer, when the weather should be at its best and the days are longest, there is seven weeks of Twenty20 played. The PCA views the Championship as the pinnacle of the domestic game. Treat it with the respect it deserves, stop tinkering with the format and return it to the summer.
Stuart Walker
Leigh-on-Sea, Essex
The Wisden Cricketer, June 2010

Fixtures and fitting

I AGREE with Mark Wallace's comments on this season's chaotic fixture lists (Expert Eye, *TWC*, June). This situation has arisen only because six weeks have been set aside to satisfy the ECB's and some county chairmen's obsession with Twenty20. While there is a place in the calendar for that form of the game now that a number of county grounds have floodlights, why cannot these games be played throughout the season instead of crammed into a few weeks? This year the season lasts 161 days and, ignoring matches against the tourists and any knock-out stages of competitions, counties are scheduled to play on 92 of them. This leaves 69 days for rest and practice which, with a properly balanced fixture list, would mean an average of three free days each week and no need to reduce the number of Championship games.
Cliff Simpson
Billericay, Essex
The Wisden Cricketer, July 2010

Saturation point

This year's Twenty20 seemed to be condemned by players and pundits but was it really that bad? **Daniel Brigham** asked those who matter

Meet the experts

Senior player
Jon Lewis
Gloucestershire bowler who has played 48 Twenty20s for his county and played in the inaugural competition

Supporter
Charlotte Evers
Chairman of the Yorkshire Supporters' Association. Has supported the county since 1959

Overseas perspective
James Franklin
Gloucestershire and New Zealand allrounder, playing his fourth season of English Twenty20

Chief executive, non-Test match ground
Richard Gould
Somerset chief executive

Chief executive, Test match ground
Paul Sheldon
Surrey chief executive

Pundit
Nick Knight
Captained Warwickshire to the first Twenty20 Cup final in 2003. Now a seasoned Twenty20 commentator for Sky Sports

This was the summer English cricket was supposed to have India looking over its shoulder. The ECB's Twenty20 masterplan would bring an army of overseas stars, huge crowds and wealth. But as the amount of games increased, crowds dwindled. A flood of critics denounced the format as too long, too tiring and full of dead games. But it cannot all be bad. Crowds were up at some grounds and, relative to the other domestic competitions, healthy. On the field there were a number of batting, bowling and fielding inventions plus plenty of dramatic matches and world-class performances. So what's everybody grumbling about?

Is 144 group games, 16 each, too many?
LEWIS When Twenty20 was introduced, each game was an event, something that people looked forward to. But because it's reached saturation point it no longer has the capacity to enthral.
FRANKLIN Essentially it is a good competition. But there are just too many games in too short a time.
KNIGHT Many times I've been sat at home, turned the TV on and found myself with another game to watch. But the games haven't been the occasions I've seen in the past.
GOULD We're more than happy with 16 games. If you reduced it, it would reduce our earnings significantly. We want it lengthened, so there's more space between home games.

Has the amount of matches and travelling produced poor cricket?
GOULD At the end of July [Somerset captain] Marcus Trescothick said he felt a lot fresher at that stage of the season than he had in previous years because the current format often offers two or three days between games. The players have time to recover, work on their skills and focus on the next game.
KNIGHT Three hours' work on a summer evening in front of a good crowd is not exactly hardship, is it?
LEWIS It is counterproductive. Counties with big squads are able to rotate players but our numbers at Gloucestershire are smaller and the treadmill of games has taken its toll on some of the guys.

If it is taking its toll on players, does that mean standards are slipping?

LEWIS The public are being short-changed when they have to pay to watch fatigued players who are unable to play at their best.

KNIGHT The quality and skill levels are still going up. It is a game for all types now – this year has been an equal balance between bat and ball.

EVERS There's been more innovation this year, especially in the out-fielding. Teams now practise all sorts of ways of fielding and catching on the boundary.

LEWIS Unless changes are made, the standard will continue to suffer.

KNIGHT When we played our first game in 2003 myself and Neil Carter got 10 off the first over and we didn't know whether that was good or bad. So I love seeing all of the innovations and new theories. I never thought you'd see people reverse-sweeping quick bowlers. I love all the scoops and slower-ball bouncers – and there are no camels in the field now. It's all pushing in the right direction.

How has the number of games affected crowds?

SHELDON We've had smaller crowds at The Oval and that's because there are eight games instead of five.

GOULD Although our attendances have been up 15%, there are too many games for the consumers. They can't afford either the leisure time or the finances for every game.

EVERS Attendances have been down at Headingley. We've ended up with three home fixtures in a week, which is wrong. People have said they can't afford to take the family to all of the matches.

FRANKLIN Another issue is that because there are so many games it's difficult for fans – and players – to recall many of them.

EVERS It's also a matter of keeping up with when your team is playing. It's quite easy to miss a game.

LEWIS Quite frankly, the sooner the ECB realises less is more, the better.

Is there a solution to get big crowds?

GOULD Just because you're putting on a Twenty20 doesn't mean you've got a right to attract audiences.

FRANKLIN Fewer games would mean bigger crowds.

SHELDON I think the format of a quick, sharp event attracts the maximum number of people.

EVERS I think they need to look at pricing. If it's going to cost a family £30 or more to go to a game, then we could be talking £120 in a week. Then you add on the costs for food, drink and buying stuff for the kids.

SHELDON A short tournament will offer the opportunity of attracting top overseas players, which is bound to increase interest. But is it really that attractive for the Twenty20 stars of the world to come and play in front of small crowds in a competition that doesn't seem to mean very much?

How important is it that English teams can qualify for the Champions League?

GOULD We went last year and the team learnt a lot from it. It's massive for the players because they get on the market for IPL contracts and international recognition.

EVERS Not many fans would travel to it. They might watch it if it was at Headingley and was included in their membership package!

SHELDON It's terribly important. We need to work closely with overseas boards, to collaborate.

What format would you introduce?

LEWIS Return to three qualifying groups and play on Friday nights and Sunday afternoons.

GOULD Same format, longer period.

SHELDON I'm not keen on extending it at all. We'd like to see games played on Thursday and Friday nights, we don't sell tickets particularly well on weekends. We should seek a window that we use when there isn't international cricket, try and get it agreed with India so we can use Indian players.

GOULD Somerset is one of the best

2010
number crunches

668
Most runs, **Jimmy Adams** (Hampshire)

117
Highest score, **Matt Prior** (for Sussex v Glamorgan)

11 Number of centuries

175.24
Highest strike-rate of those with 300+ runs, **Kieron Pollard** below (Somerset)

29 Most sixes overall, **Kieron Pollard**

9 Most sixes in an innings, **Ross Taylor** (for Durham v Leicestershire)

33 Most wickets, **Alfonso Thomas** (Somerset)

5-13
Best bowling figures, **Andrew McDonald** (for Leics v Notts)

5.93
Best economy rate, 40+ overs, **Robert Croft** (Glamorgan)

Twenty20 sides in the country, as well as one of the best supported, so we don't look at it too kindly when some Test grounds decide that Somerset should not be competing.

SHELDON I imagine that nine teams would mean having a partnership of two clubs and this applies to every county. Surrey joining Kent could be an option. Have three or four Surrey players, three or four Kent players and two overseas.

EVERS Eight matches and have it spread over the season more. I felt they got it about right last year.

SHELDON We should just investigate the possibility of nine or 10 teams. If we don't like it, then we can bin it but don't bin it before we've looked at it. We don't want to overkill Twenty20.

Do counties with internationals and those without want different things?

EVERS Smaller counties see a crowd of 4,000 as a success but that would just look lost at Headingley.

GOULD You walk around international grounds and the only advertising you see is for the next England match. That's an important job to sell their internationals but, if the big grounds want Twenty20 to be a success, they need to focus on them.

SHELDON Internationals and Twenty20 are equally important.

Is T20 still aimed at families?

SHELDON Yes, that's still entirely the point and that's what's still happening. The family audience remains the same but it's been diluted by the extra games.

EVERS This year at Headingley we've made an effort to attract families with a non-alcohol family stand and that's helped. Friday night and Sunday afternoon games are good for children and families.

KNIGHT It should remain the point of Twenty20. That's what it's all about, more so than the money. Somewhere along the line that's been forgotten by too many people. **◼**

The Wisden Cricketer, September 2010

Somerset burned in cool climax

The Bears were bullish on a muted night, condemning their opponents to an unwanted hat-trick

IT WAS appropriate that the season ended with Somerset missing out on another title. Marcus Trescothick, in his first season as captain, had led his side to within one delivery of the Twenty20 Cup and 40 minutes from a first Championship title only for Hampshire and Nottinghamshire to slip past.

After Nottinghamshire's Championship heist two days before the CB40 final Trescothick vowed to come out "swinging from the hip" in a final attempt to secure silverware from a season they had dominated. But they were condemned to a hat-trick of near-misses as the first day-night Lord's final belonged to Warwickshire's stand-in captain, Ian Bell. Chasing a modest 200 under lights, he proved that one-day batting still extends beyond barrel-chested power, calmly steering his side to victory with a masterful 95-ball 107.

Bell enhanced his standing during England's winter tour to South Africa and his stature grew further through his injury-enforced absence from the summer's Test series against Pakistan. His return matched the heightened billing, though, and he appeared to relish the responsibility of leading the side. As the winning target approached, he marked each boundary with an uninhibited fist pump, hammering home, if a touch endearingly, his new-found reputation for toughness when it counts.

Trescothick was as magnanimous as ever in defeat. He said: "You only have to look at the two guys from Warwickshire: Imran Tahir getting five to take the heart out of the game, then Ian Bell. We've got to improve and try to emulate that."

Though Alfonso Thomas, Somerset's opening bowler, was the tournament's highest wicket-taker and the September dew and raucous crowd may have added half a yard of pace to Ben Phillips, on the biggest occasions it is bowlers with

mystery and international quality that prove the difference. The CB40 title crowned a satisfying turnaround in Warwickshire's fortunes. While their limited-overs form was good they had lingered over the Division One trap-door before finding safety with four wins in their last five games.

The tournament, though, encapsulated many of the tensions present in the domestic game. Dwarfed by the glamour and balance sheet of the

IPL, the ECB resolved to overhaul domestic one-day cricket once again, hoping to milk both Twenty20's popularity and the TV revenues from the longer limited-overs game. The result was a scrapping of the 50-over Friends Provident Cup and a reworking of the two-division Pro40 League into a single 40-over tournament to sit alongside a new, inflated Twenty20 Cup. The meddling left supporters bewildered and robbed the tournament of a longer history that should be part of its charm.

The final itself epitomised the spirit behind the tinkering. The floodlights at Lord's made a fine spectacle for fans tucked up at home but the supporters at the ground had to huddle under blankets and jumpers to brave the latter stages. Worse still, with the last train to

Winners and losers: Chris Woakes hits the winning runs as Somerset suffer a third second-place finish

❝ Bell marked each boundary with a fist pump ❞

the West Country departing at 8.30pm, Somerset fans were confronted with a tough journey home. It was no surprise that Lord's was barely half-full.

The intensity of the play nonetheless rose above not only the administrative incompetence but news on the morning of the final that the ICC was investigating Pakistan's ODI victory over England the night before. Thankfully, for this match at least, the ongoing off-field scandals did not overshadow the action. For the likes of Nick Compton, Neil Carter and Arul Suppiah a Lord's final may be the biggest stage they will compete on and the passion they brought was welcome respite from the suspicion that closed the international summer.

The low-scoring encounter was exciting but at odds with the torrent of runs that marked the limited-overs summer. Having been given plenty of practice in Twenty20, batsmen took both the mind-set and technical inventions of the shortest format into the 40-over game and found they could make totals that would have seemed unthinkable a few years ago. While in the 2007 Pro40 summer no team made more than 289, there were 11 scores over 300 this year, with Somerset racking up 368 against Glamorgan, 303 against Surrey and 312 in the semi-final against Essex.

The free scoring was in keeping with the attacking brand of cricket that has underpinned England's recent limited-over transformation. When the CB40 was announced there was plenty of criticism that there would be no 50-over domestic competition to mirror the international one-day game. It would be ironic, then, if England's first World Cup success comes straight afterwards. *The Wisden Cricketer*, November 2010

Sahil Dutta writes for Cricinfo

FP t20 **FINALS DAY** by **Andrew McGlashan** at the Rose Bowl

Uncorking the bubbly

Dominic Cork led a youthful Hampshire to Twenty20 Cup glory

A TOURNAMENT that began way back on June 1 and lasted 151 matches went down to the last possible delivery in mid-August. It was almost as though the competition itself could not quite believe it was over as Dan Christian scrambled a leg bye shortly before 11pm to level the scores and give Hampshire the title by virtue of losing fewer wickets.

Yet even that did not quite do justice to the madness. Somerset could and really should have won. As if the situation was not tense enough, Christian had been forced to call for a runner for the final ball after pulling a hamstring but, when Jimmy Adams sprinted off for the leg bye, so did Christian, only for no one to throw down the stumps even though the umpires waited to see what Somerset would do. "We had the game but just did not think," said Marcus Trescothick.

There was a surreal moment when Hampshire's players, already racing on to the outfield in celebration, paused for an instant as everyone held breath before the umpires removed the stumps to signal the end. "I've never seen a last over like that. It had everything," said Dominic Cork. "Maybe he could have been run out but the umpires declared it match won."

That Christian, already sporting a pair of black eyes after being hit by a bouncer in the Championship game against Somerset two days before, was limping at the conclusion was also apt. Hampshire have been ravaged by injuries this season; Cork, competitive as ever at 39, was leading them only because of Dimitri Mascarenhas's long-term achilles problem and Nic Pothas's absence.

Kabir Ali has also missed most of the season, with his future in doubt, while three days before the final Michael Lumb had his foot broken fielding at silly point. The list of injuries highlights again the condensed domestic schedule. Injuries will always happen in sport but

Unbelievable: Dominic Cork celebrates a spirited FP t20 win with his young charges

> **"We had the game but just did not think"**

Hampshire and Somerset were playing a Championship game two days before this final. Some patched-up players could barely stand – Cork and Sean Ervine also carried niggles. That cannot be the way to prepare for a major event.

But Hampshire could still afford to brush aside Kevin Pietersen and emerge as champions. "Our policy was whoever got us through to the semi-finals plays the final," said Cork. "The club felt it was right that the young guys should do it."

That attitude contrasts sharply with Essex, who flew Dwayne Bravo in for one day as they tried to replace Scott Styris. They did not get value for money; Bravo's bowling cost them as he went for 46 in four overs during Hampshire's chase.

Crowds were down for this year's Cup but the final was a 23,000 sell-out. The Rose Bowl is becoming a fantastic stadium as the chairman Rod Bransgrove's dream comes to fruition. The Somerset-Nottinghamshire semi-final had been lit up by two innings; Trescothick made 60 off 28 balls but the real eye-catcher was 19-year-old Jos Buttler. His 23-ball 55 was breathtaking, especially hitting of Stuart Broad.

The Wisden Cricketer, October 2010

Andrew McGlashan writes for Cricinfo

County Championship

A TIGHT season decided on the final afternoon in the final match with Notts claiming a bowling point that drew them level with Somerset but earned them the title by virtue of number of wins. At one point they enjoyed a 22-point lead but a collapse against Yorkshire had left an opportunity and Somerset nearly took it. Both Essex and Kent went straight back down to Division Two after 2009 promotion, replaced by Sussex and Worcestershire – the two relegated teams from the previous season. Durham's seam-bowling injuries prevented any serious title defence and Yorkshire's home-grown side were in the hunt until a final day collapse against Kent.

Ups and downs: round by round

Scores

CB40 Final Sept 18, Lord's ♀ Somerset 199 in 39 ov (NRD Compton 60; Imran Tahir 5-41 below left); †Warwickshire 200-7 in 39 ov (IR Bell 107; AC Thomas 3-33). Warwickshire won by 3 wkts. MoM: Bell below right 95b 12x4.

FPt20 1st semi-final Aug 14, Rose Bowl Ess 156-7 in 20 ov (ML Pettini 55, AN Cook 38; DR Briggs 3-29); †Ham 157-4 in 19.2 ov (Abdul Razzaq 44, JHK Adams 34). Hampshire won by 6 wkts. MoM: Briggs 4-0-29-3.

FPt20 2nd semi-final Aug 14, Rose Bowl Som 182-5 in 20 ov (ME Trescothick 60, JC Buttler 55*); †Not 117-4 in 13 ov (SR Patel 39). Somerset won by 3 runs (D/L). MoM: Buttler 23b, 6x4, 2x6.

FPt20 final Aug 14, Rose Bowl ♀ †Som 173-6 in 20 ov (C Kieswetter 71, PD Trego 33); Ham 173-5 in 20 ov (NC McKenzie 52, SM Ervine 44*, Adams 34, Abdul Razzaq 33). Ham won by losing fewer wickets. MoM: McKenzie 39b, 3x4, 1x6.

HEROES

& VILLAINS

One might wonder how Oli Broom, a man on an Ashes cycling mission from Lord's to Brisbane, can rub shoulders with Lalit Modi, the Indian businessman who, for good or bad, has done more to change cricket than anyone since Kerry Packer. Yet we instinctively distinguish heroes and villains – no matter how small or big – and the stories of Broom and Modi are unlikely partners in that rich narrative.

Modi's dwindling reputation amid accusations of corruption is a reminder that these distinctions can take on a dark tone. Match-fixing returned in 2010 and it felt like a total eclipse of the summer. Has a cricketer ever gone from hero to villain as quickly as Pakistan's Mohammad Amir?

But note the divided reaction of the public to Amir's case: some painted him a naïve victim, others an example of the abhorrent greed of modern players. And to Muttiah Muralitharan, the smiling assassin who retired as the leading Test wicket-taker. He is, for some, the man who rendered bowling meaningless because of his supposed illegal action. Equally, the response to Mark Nicholas's solution to the escalating disenchantment with the structure of county cricket exposed a sensitive issue that grumbled on all summer: many would throw Nicholas to the lions, others parade him as the messiah. It is our often ambivalent judgement of people and events which expresses the fascinating diversity of our game and its themes.

Then there are those who are simply heroes. Sir Alec Bedser, who died in March, was a champion of English cricket in the 1940s and 50s. But perhaps the quintessential hero was the late David Shepherd, loved as an idiosyncratic umpire and as a flawed big-hitter for Gloucestershire, where he was known as 'Good Old Shep'. "Who cares what his average is?" wrote Alan Gibson, whose own talents were revived in a wonderful book of his work, *Of Didcot and the Demon*. "Doesn't he cheer us up!" ▪

Benj Moorehead is the editorial assistant of *The Wisden Cricketer*

Contents

August, 2010: Nick Newman celebrates Murali's inability to straighten his arm

Murali magic: Muttiah Muralitharan left retired from Test cricket, taking his 800th wicket with his final ball as Sri Lanka beat India at Galle

For the greed not the glory

After the spot-fixing scandal at Lord's **Osman Samiuddin** explained why it happened

THE MODERN Pakistan drama unfolds in several broadly repetitive acts. First there is swift outrage. Someone finds an effigy, another burns it. Then there is some handwringing: why are we like this, what is happening, how will we get out of it? Along the way an inquiry committee is set up. Someone blames India for it. At the end nobody is guilty and nobody is innocent; all concerned are doomed to walk around under their own personalised clouds.

This is applicable to any crisis, from suicide bombs and terror attacks, floods, corruption scams, assassinations. If the spot-fixing crisis goes the same way – a fair few boxes stand checked already – then might it be the biggest tragedy to hit cricket in Pakistan? Probably. Until the next one.

❝Over the last decade the board has, in effect, ceased to exist❞

There is both much complexity and simplicity in the matters of Salman Butt, Mohammad Asif and Mohammad Amir. At the time of writing they stand provisionally suspended from all cricket by the ICC. Soon Pakistan's Test captain and their two best fast bowlers – arguably the best new-ball pair in world cricket – may not play ever again. Not since Hansie Cronje's tears has cricket been so shaken.

First the complex bit. Pakistan's international players are no longer those so romantically and often evoked when such crises are at hand. Majid Khan, Hanif Mohammad, Imran Khan, Fazal Mahmood; ah, who would ever imagine these gentlemen in such scrapes? The game in Pakistan, as it has spread since the late 1970s, has undergone its own

democratisation. Players now come from smaller towns and villages; where once nearly 80% of Test players came from Karachi or Lahore, since 1978-79 not even half come from those cities. They are a different species altogether from the urbane, worldly stars that once made up the national side. To Amir and Asif success, money and fame mean entirely different things from what they did to Imran or Majid or Fazal. They react in different ways. Pakistan itself reacts to success, money and fame in different ways.

Intikhab Alam was too harsh when, as coach on the wholly dysfunctional tour of Australia earlier this year, he called his boys 'retards'. The examples he used – of not being toilet-trained properly or behaving inappropriately in public – were poor ones. But the wider spirit of what he said was not missed. Shoaib Akhtar, no paragon of discipline, once framed it better when touching upon a separate but related point. A happy, outgoing tourist, he wondered in Sydney once why the rest of the team was happy just sitting in their hotel rooms together, eating Pakistani food. "They don't want to go out, to see the country, to meet the people, to make friends, nothing." Essentially these men – boys mostly – are not prepared for the life they must live as sportsmen.

Since the mid-70s these very players have also dealt increasingly with decaying administration. Over the last decade in particular the board has, in effect, ceased to exist. For example, in the four days after the ICC suspended the three players, Ijaz Butt, the PCB chairman, did not issue a single public statement. In the last 30-odd years the players have acquired increasing power. TV has turned them into stars and icons, the only ones this country has apart from some musicians, a handful of actors and

Over-stepping the mark: Mohammad Amir sends down the first of the suspect no-balls at Lord's

philanthropists. Here the decline of other champion-producing sports such as hockey and squash is felt acutely.

So increasingly players are ill-equipped to deal with what they enter into and administrators are ill-equipped to deal with players. In the classic board/player clashes the player has always won, most damagingly in this case in the Qayyum commission, when a host of tainted big names in the first match-fixing scandal was allowed simply to carry on. Shoaib and, until now, Asif are the most current and vivid proofs of this equation. If you know you will not be punished, to what lengths might you go?

But the simplest explanation, of course, is the most overlooked and it took the straightest-talking Pakistani cricketer to point to it. "Greed is endless," Imran Khan said after the scandal broke. "You can't have enough. It is a deficit of the mind." It is easier to be greedy if you are powerful and easier to be greedy if you are unlikely to get caught but it is still greed. And it better explains the one apparent anomaly (in terms of social condition at least) in this group, the alleged ringleader Butt.

Butt is an urban product, comparatively educated, English-speaking and, according to the late Bob Woolmer, "well brought up". He is one of the few of whom it can be said that he is a professional cricketer out of choice. Had he not been, he would likely still have lived comfortably and well, a little like Pakistan's players of the '50s and '60s.

Pakistan's players are very well-paid for the land they come from. They may have missed out on IPL contracts over the last two years – Butt and Asif played and were paid for the first season – but they still make good money from central contracts, endorsements and also their first-class sides, who offer employment and security. Beyond a certain level the individual greed argument is too compelling to ignore.

Ultimately this is a sorry triumph for the paranoid. For 10 years since the first match-fixing storm the ghost of a fix has haunted almost every defeat, every dropped catch, every run-out, every missed run-out, every slog, every failed powerplay, every dodgy selection. It is mostly the public and former players who drive this. Sarfraz Nawaz, who might happily accuse the Don of deliberately falling for a duck in his last innings to avoid the perfect average – Aussies like a punt, don't they? – is the poster-boy for this paranoia.

But after that Australia tour even Intikhab and Aaqib Javed, as coaches, were questioning their players: were they right all along? The *News of the World* sting has changed the game, even if this drama ends unusually with clear, decisive verdicts. The 'glorious uncertainties' of cricket have never meant much in Pakistan. They are now dead. Long live paranoia. *The Wisden Cricketer,* October 2010

Osman Samiuddin is Pakistan editor of Cricinfo.com

No winners: ECB's Giles Clarke and Amir

Just losers: Effigies burn in Pakistan

How football can fix it. By Matthew Engel

INDIA, the second most populous country in the world, lies 138th in Fifa's international football rankings. Bangladesh and Sri Lanka are 152nd and 153rd. Pakistan are 164th, down among the microdots. The 2008 Olympics was considered a triumph for India because they won a gold medal in the 10 metres air rifle, their first ever Olympic individual gold, plus bronzes at boxing and wrestling. The father of the gold medallist, Abhinav Bindra, had installed a shooting gallery in the basement of the family home. Just a typical Indian childhood, then. The three Asian neighbours won nothing, not a brass razoo. Meanwhile the leading subcontinental tennis player is Somdev Devvarman, ranked No.98; and the top golfer is Jeeva Milka Singh, at 136. What has all this to do with the price of no-balls? Quite a lot.

South Asia now has a sporting monoculture in which cricket trumps all other sports put together. It is a cliché to say that Indians and Pakistanis are crazy about cricket. But they have no realistic alternative: no other game offers them any kind of national self-esteem. When the football World Cup is on, people get as involved and obsessed as

66 Match-rigging can be only occasional unless both teams are involved 99

they do elsewhere on the planet. But when the national teams cannot even reliably beat the Maldive Islands, there is not much hope of them being inspirational to the young.

Quite simply, cricket in these countries has got too big for its own good. That is one reason why it is the inevitable focus of illegal betting. This might not matter if players were themselves getting a slice of the riches. Leading Indian players are now so wealthy that it seems unlikely they would jeopardise all that. That is not true of the Pakistanis.

Unable to play at home, currently barred from the IPL, the whole future of their country (never mind the cricket team) now in question, the players are not surprisingly open to temptation. Mohammad Amir might still have had – might still have – a glittering career. That is always a big 'if' for a young player: the end might be one injury away.

Before the fall Amir was reportedly on a basic salary of £15,600 – a fraction of the money available to the leading Indians. As my *Financial Times* colleague Simon Kuper put it: "Athletes who take bribes are underpaid, or think they are ... It's not that they lack a sense of fairness. Rather, they tend to think they aren't being treated fairly." The same motivation sent players into the arms of Kerry Packer.

It seems clear that there is no bookmaker – legal or illegal – taking £150,000 in bets on a no-ball. What was seemingly shown on the *News of the World* video was a demonstration of control: the alleged fixer was showing that he could make things happen if his clients wanted.

Informed sources believe that, to make that level of bribe worthwhile, a whole match would have to be thrown or a substantial feature within it. Match-rigging can be only occasional unless both teams are involved or you have lots of meaningless contests. The 2011 World Cup will last more than a month. The ICC who brought us the 2007 fiasco is about to repeat the trick, even more spectacularly. I cannot imagine who could be interested. Give me a Pakistan v Maldives football match any day. On second thoughts I know just who will be licking his chops. Your friendly neighbourhood match-fixer.

The Wisden Cricketer, October 2010

Matthew Engel is a *Financial Times* columnist and former editor of *Wisden*

Following the story

The *News of the World* put cricket on the front pages again. Here's how other newspapers responded

News of the World
Sunday August 29
CAUGHT!
Match-fixer pockets £150k as he rigs the England Test at Lord's
The *News of the World* has smashed a multi-million pound cricket match-fixing ring which rigged the current Lord's Test between England and Pakistan.

In the most sensational sporting scandal ever, bowlers Mohammad Amir and Mohammad Asif delivered THREE blatant no-balls to order. Their London-based fixer Mazhar Majeed, who let us in on the betting scam for £150,000, crowed "this is no coincidence" before the bent duo made duff deliveries at PRECISELY the moments promised.

And so the story broke and the newspapers tried to make sense of it all.

The Sun
Monday August 30
The Sun says
Cricket's very survival depends on the untarnished integrity of its players. There can be zero tolerance for cheats, even if their dishonesty is genuinely limited to bowling a no-ball to order. If solely the evidence in our sister paper is accepted, immediate life bans must be dished out. Life must mean life.

Daily Mail
Monday August 30
Nasser Hussain
When I heard that Pakistan were involved in a match-fixing scandal I immediately thought two things. The first was: "I'm not massively surprised." The second was: "Please, don't let it be Mohammad Amir."

The Guardian
Monday August 30
Mike Selvey
Pakistan cricket has been given a bad name once more and yet again we wonder whether what we have been seeing is merely the tip of the iceberg of another scandal. Everything – dropped catches, batting collapses, defeats from situations where defeat seemed impossible and now even the most innocuous incidents that are not likely to affect materially the outcome of a match – comes under suspicion. Opposition excellence becomes devalued. And all because two bowlers have quite literally overstepped their mark.

The Times
Monday August 30
Simon Barnes
True, it's not match-fixing. Just three piffling no-balls. But three piffling no-balls, if done on purpose and for cash, destroy your belief in a sincere contest, destroy your belief in sport. Without belief sport is nothing: these allegations make atheists of us all.

Daily Mail
Monday August 30
Martin Samuel
There is no darker force in modern sport than Pakistan cricket. The disciples of the Balco chemical factory, the architects of Bloodgate, cheating footballers, the 'roid-raging big hitters of Major League Baseball all pale beside the institutionalised corruption witnessed year on year when we look at Pakistan cricket ... Pakistan cricket is not maverick or mercurial, it is rotten.

Some writers looked for a solution while asking the simple question: why?

The big splash: above The *News of the World's* cover that started the scandal; below Pakistan captain Salman Butt at Lord's

Financial Times
Monday August 30
Matthew Engel
It would be more useful to reflect on the iniquity that results when governments try to control human behaviour that is inherently uncontrollable, be it drug-taking, prostitution, deviation from sexual norms – or betting. If Asian governments stopped the futile criminalisation of the countless millions of their citizens who choose to gamble, the world would be a better place. And cricket might just become an honest game again.

Daily Telegraph
Monday August 30
Scyld Berry
It is only natural that cricketers – or some of them at least – should reflect the society from which they come. And Pakistan is riddled with corruption ... The military takes most of the country's wealth, leaving far

too little money to fund civilian society: a euphemism for saying the state does not provide its people with schools and hospitals or any real social care. Anyone growing up in such a country therefore sees the state doing nothing for its people, feels no loyalty in return and makes what money he can for himself.

Who is the victim of the scandal? Is it the spectator, the players or the sport itself?

Daily Telegraph
Monday August 30
Derek Pringle
World cricket must not turn its back on Pakistan, who surely deserve one more chance. Many will not want to give them another for they have had plenty in the past, being behind most of the game's leading controversies of the past 30 years. ...

Cricket, especially the Test game, is not in such rude health that it can simply dismiss Pakistan, who have produced some of the most talented cricketers seemingly from nowhere.

The Times
Tuesday August 31
Mike Atherton
Amir is a potent symbol right now, of what was, what is and what might be. He should not be punished as an example to the rest, as everyone seems to suggest; rather he should be made aware of the issues, educated, rehabilitated and held up as an example of what can be achieved. Amir's rehabilitation should be at the heart of the cleansing of Pakistan cricket. He is not the cause of the problem but the most tragic consequence of it.

Pakistan and Indian writers gave an alternative perspective.

The Guardian
Monday August 30
Dileep Premachandran
– Indian journalist
"Two ghosts have haunted Pakistan this decade: Osama bin Laden and

the Fixed Match," wrote Osman Samiuddin in an article on fixing in July. The first remains elusive and the second refuses to go away. We would do well to heed the words of Brian Lara. "I don't think you'd see an indisciplined team if you have a disciplined board."

Daily Telegraph
Monday August 30
Ramiz Raja – Pakistan batsman
Pakistan is only paying the price for its past mistakes. In 1994 I was on a tour to Sri Lanka when there was a lot of match-fixing going on and I did not play a single match. That was because I was not in on the scheme. The manager, Intikhab Alam, told me so afterwards. He sent a report to the PCB but nothing happened. The board was frightened of dealing with the names involved.

What itches most is the hypocrisy in the game: the culture and obsession with money is going to cause problems.

The Times
Thursday September 2
Mike Atherton
An England player uses his profile shamelessly to plug a sponsor's product as he waits in the changing room as next man in; players involve themselves with benefit sponsors no matter how dodgy the reputation; players hold county clubs to ransom; England players sign contracts but expect to be able to play in the IPL; commentators act as players' agents; an England selector is also a county coach. All these things happen ... Conflicts of interest are wide-ranging and numerous. Taken individually, they might not amount to much. Taken as a whole, they paint a picture of a sport in thrall to money. Is it any wonder, in that atmosphere, that players could be led astray? Particularly players from a relatively impoverished country that pays poorly. If everyone is on the gravy train, why should they miss out? *The Wisden Cricketer, October 2010*

At the eye of the storm

Most learned of the spot-fixing allegations at Sunday breakfast. Sam Peters, the News of the World's cricket reporter, found out a bit earlier ...

I HAD just finished eating my lunch at Lord's when my sports editor's name, Paul McCarthy, flashed up on my mobile phone. Working for the *News of the World*, when it's Saturday afternoon and your boss calls, you answer.

"Sam, pack up your gear and get in a taxi to Wapping, now," McCarthy said. "You've got a meeting with the editor in an hour. Don't tell anyone where or what you're doing, just come straight away. And bring Richie." Richie is, of course, Richie Benaud, the *News of the World's* columnist of 50 years. "Richie, we've got to leave," I whispered in the great man's ear. "Why?" was his perfectly reasonable response. "The editor wants to see us immediately. I can't tell you anything else." I made some excuses to my fellow hacks before slipping out down the stairs of the media centre, having told Richie I'd meet him at the North Gate.

I hailed a cab and ushered Richie in. "Richie, I think I know what ... " I started to say. I turned and saw him with one finger pressed to his lips with another pointing in the direction of the cabbie. The great man was more switched on than me. I punched a few words into my phone and showed him the screen so as not to alert the cabbie. "This has to be match-fixing," it read. Richie nodded solemnly.

We were ushered in through the back entrance, where McCarthy met us, and taken directly to the editor Colin Myler's office. After a brief introduction – it was Richie's first visit to the paper he has served for almost 54 years – Myler said. "Tomorrow, gentlemen, the *News of the World* is going to break the biggest story in its history." Myler pointed at a TV in the corner with the cricket on, Pakistan 39 for 3 in their first innings. "It's fixed," Myler said.

We were then handed transcripts and shown the tapes of Mazhar Majeed agreeing to accept £150,000 in £50 notes to influence the outcome of the ongoing Test. He promised Mohammad Amir and Mohammad Asif would deliver 'no-balls' at certain moments of the game. "Do they tally up?" I asked. "Yes," Myler replied, before we were shown the footage of the predetermined 'no-balls'. I sat shaking my head, as did Richie, as we began to take in the magnitude of what we had watched.

"Richie, I want you to write for the front of the book. Sam, you for the back," Myler said. "Just tell me how you feel, write from the heart." I knew how I felt – gutted, angry, depressed. But at the same time I was exhilarated, I was in the middle of something big. "We need 1,000 words," McCarthy said to me. "You've got two and a half hours to write the best piece of your life." I'm not sure I managed that but my phone's not stopped ringing since.

The Wisden Cricketer, October 2010

Well read: Pakistan management at Lord's

The true triumph of
Murali

The man probably least exercised about whether or not Muttiah Muralitharan is the greatest bowler of all time is the bowler himself. When you are that good, modesty is an option geniuses can choose without appearing disingenuous. It is not a quality some of his voluble detractors could boast.

Muralitharan knows how good he is. He has no need to trumpet what is there for all to see, the leading wicket-taker of them all. But critics who qualify their admiration with doubts about the legality of his action diminish their argument by the volume and self-righteousness of their rhetoric.

Even when Muralitharan was cleared of chucking after submitting himself to at least three examinations of his action, even when the Laws were changed to recognise that nearly every bowler, especially finger spinners, threw under the old Laws, the vitriol would not be stemmed. The haters had made their minds up long ago. To admit they were wrong was beyond them.

If Darrell Hair and Ross Emerson thought he was guilty of deliberately breaking the Laws – and who is to say those umpires did not act in good faith? – the small minority of Australian fans who baited him to the point where he hated touring there, and those writers who cast a shadow on his extraordinary deeds, need to ask themselves how fair they have been.

The indignation worked up over his action says everything about people concerned more with legal minutiae than the sheer beauty and potency of a unique bowler. It was left to Shane Warne, his rival and friend, to point out that Murali has been "a real credit to his country and to himself. He was wonderful for the game." It matters not, ultimately, if Murali is better than Warne, or Sydney Barnes or Wilfred Rhodes. They are all great, all different.

There was not much to pick anyway between Murali and Warne. In execution and achievement, too, they were special. To have had one on the scene was a blessing; two was plain greedy. Through invention and technical expertise they raised slow bowling to a level beyond the reach of contemporaries and we will be fortunate to see anything remotely like them again.

As personalities they could hardly have been more different. When The Blond went, it was to considerable fanfare at the MCG in his penultimate Test, on the last Ashes tour. When the master of the doosra

He has never stopped smiling and has never sought to judge others

announced his final Test would be the first Sri Lanka v India Test at Galle, it was through a stiff announcement on his behalf on the Sri Lanka Cricket website. They referred to him as "Mr Muralitharan", as if they were giving him old-fashioned respect, an echo of days gone. Perhaps they were trying to claw back respect for their blighted treasure.

To everyone else he was known as Murali, affectionately of course but also for convenience of spelling and pronunciation. The ICC spelt his surname on the back of a one-day shirt as "Muralidharan". The Telegraph of Calcutta spelt it that way too, perhaps because of some sub-continental anglicising of his name.

And, surprise: Murali did not care. It added to his aura rather than detracted from it. He was, after all, a never-ending mystery, to batsmen and to those priggish purists who hounded him. If being born with a foreshortened and twisted right arm, as well as an unusually supple wrist, loose shoulder and brilliant bowling brain, gave him an advantage, it was one conferred on him from a higher place.

The ever-smiling man from Kandy accepted his minor disability and used it to the full. For his forbearance and his skill he won the hearts of even those among his compatriots who were at war with the minority Tamils. Those possessed of another type of greatness have the ability to rise above rancour and the mundane without appearing to try. Their real soul shines through, whatever the injustices upon them. Mahatma Ghandi had it, as did Nelson Mandela and Muhammad Ali.

While he was not short of passion Murali rarely seemed flustered, either by controversy or by pressure of performance. It is not that he did not put a value on his worth but he played for the joy of it and was uncomfortable talking about himself.

When Ravi Shastri and Michael Slater filmed a revealing experiment that showed Murali bowling in a brace, the bowler remained mute throughout. He has spent his entire career being prodded and questioned. But he has never stopped smiling and has never sought to make a judgement on others. It might be his greatest achievement.

The Wisden Cricketer, August 2010

Kevin Mitchell writes for *The Observer*

Murali in numbers

800 Test wickets (next: Warne 708)

166 Wickets at the SSC in Colombo. Has 117 at Kandy and 111 at Galle. Next highest wickets at one venue: 83 by Heath Streak at Harare.

44039 No. of balls bowled in his 133 Tests

67 Test five-fors

22 Test 10-fors

90 Most Test wickets in a year, 2006 (the most in a year: Warne with 96 in 2005)

Match-winner: Murali bowls John Crawley at The Oval in 1998 on his way to 9 for 65

Home v Away

	O	R	W	5w	AVGE	ER
Home	4176.5	9646	**493**	45	19.76	2.31
Away	3163	8534	**307**	22	27.79	2.70

By opponent

	O	R	W (% of 800)	AVGE
Aus	685.3	2128	**59** (7.38%)	36.07
Bang	452	1190	**89** (11.13%)	13.37
Eng	1102.1	2247	**112** (14.00%)	20.06
Ind	1170	3425	**105** (13.13%)	32.62
NZ	753.2	1766	**82** (10.25%)	21.54
Pak	782.5	2037	**80** (10.00%)	25.46
SA	984.4	2311	**104** (13.00%)	22.22
WI	622.3	1609	**82** (10.25%)	19.62
Zim	786.5	1467	**87** (10.88%)	16.86

How to make 18 go into 12

Mark Nicholas set out his ideas for county reform … and readers responded

THE ONGOING debate about the structure of first-class cricket is undermined by the number of counties that have to be accommodated. If we had a blank sheet, the game would not be run as it is now. To find time for the players to train and practise, to rest and prepare properly for each match, there have to be fewer teams.

It would be no shame for some counties to relinquish their first-class status. The battle to survive is self-serving and damaging to the game's resources. Derbyshire, Northamptonshire, Gloucestershire and Worcestershire – to name four of six or seven – exist for no obviously justifiable reason. County clubs should be centres of excellence but too many are not, employing mediocre cricketers from elsewhere. They stumble along the breadline, sustained by money from Sky. The argument made on their behalf

by the chairman of the ECB, Giles Clarke, is equally self-serving.

An ideal number of county teams would be 12, with a season of 11 four-day Championship matches, a 50-over league/cup competition and a Twenty20 competition with semi-finals and a final. This would provide a fixture list with space to put the three competitions in context, the option of an occasional Test player on view, as well as moments to draw breath.

But 12 counties cannot go it alone as the ECB articles of association call for a three-quarter majority of the full 41-body membership to force change. The trick will be to win a three-quarter majority of the upper house (first-class counties plus MCC) and for those 14 constituents to drive the reform.

At present the nine Test-match grounds are in talks about how best to realise the potential of their

own businesses without culling one another along the way. This terrifies the remaining nine counties. The Test grounds must look outside and structure a way to help support and finance five of the regions, thereby bringing their own number to 14. These organisations could exist with or without private ownership. It is partnerships that are required to blend cricket and commerce in a more elegant and effective 21st-century alliance.

Let us assume that Middlesex go with MCC to play at Lord's and that the remaining eight Test-match grounds, which have the best facilities already in place, are automatically a part of a new Premier League. Geography allows Derbyshire and Worcestershire to merge with Nottinghamshire and Warwickshire respectively, both of whom have the money and facility to sustain progress. Further natural coalitions

Bad Marks
IF THERE is to be a cull of first-class counties, it must not be driven by the assumptions made by Mark Nicholas. Why should the Test-staging counties be guaranteed a place in the new structure? So that it can benefit from the financial and cricketing acumen that has taken Surrey from top to bottom in less than a decade? Or so that we don't miss the one player of true international class that Glamorgan produces every 30 years? How would we manage without Yorkshire's people skills? English cricket would do better with more influence from those counties who have used scarce resources to produce young players of true international potential and less from those whose grandiose dreams have lumbered the game with more international grounds than it needs.
**Peter Hoare
Wellington,
New Zealand**

**Fading grace:
Leicestershire's
home Grace Road
is under threat
from Nicholas'
reform ideas**

come between Northamptonshire and Leicestershire, Gloucestershire and Somerset. If Essex, Sussex and Kent stay as they are, you have 14 teams.

There are other permutations but the balance sheet must determine who lives on. In all honesty, could any of the counties who fail to turn a profit after an annual ECB distribution of £1.5m justify themselves? The trick will be to massage the bruised egos of those who miss out and to manage their future sensitively and productively. Though some heartlands of the game would be among them, their role at every other level can become less distracted by the constant fight for survival, on and off the field, and more relevant and

66 Too many counties stumble along the breadline, sustained by money from Sky99

valuable because of it. But then the first-class game will work as one, with the England team at the top of its pyramid.

England have not been very good for the best part of the last 50 years. Briefly, outstanding captain/player combinations have taken the team near the top – Illingworth with Boycott and Snow; Brearley with Botham; Vaughan with Flintoff – but these exceptional cricketers, and some others born overseas, have papered over the cracks of a system that does not produce the quality it might. English cricket is shored up by outsiders and there is a price to pay. Money is shamefully wasted. The game could and should be better organised, and more organic, than it is.

What if that blank sheet of paper was the first reference? Imagine nine Test-match grounds in eight major cities creating a Premiership of Durham, Leeds, Manchester, Nottingham, Birmingham, London North and South, Southampton, Cardiff. Add three from Bristol, Brighton, Canterbury and Chelmsford and eureka, 12 – job done.

The Wisden Cricketer, July 2010

Mark Nicholas captained Hampshire for 11 years and presents *Cricket on Five*

MARK Nicholas says I follow a county, Northamptonshire, who exist for "no obviously justifiable reason" and so should merge with Leicestershire. Unsurprisingly he sees no need to merge Hampshire with any other county. Where would this combined side play their matches? Has he not been to Wantage Road recently and seen the improvements? Clearly this money can go to waste, whereas Test venues can spend above their means. Maybe he should consider which counties nurtured Broad, Swann and Panesar.
Helen Watts Desborough, Northants

MARK Nicholas is a disgrace. Why should Derbyshire relinquish their first-class status after 140 years? They've spent £700,000 – without borrowing a penny – on redeveloping their ground, have a burgeoning academy, are holding their own in all formats of the game and have shown a profit for the last four years. The only things that exist with no obviously justifiable reason are him and his woeful Cricket on Five.
Robin Hutchison North Finchley, London

MARK Nicholas does not once mention the thousands of members, supporters and spectators who care deeply for county cricket. Calls to amalgamate or destroy counties pay no attention to the very specific nature of supporting English sport, which is always more regional and local than in other countries. Those of us who fork out hundreds of pounds each year do so to watch our counties playing – not to provide time for cricketers to train, practise, rest and prepare. We want to watch county cricket.
Dr Dave Allen Hon Curator, Hampshire Cricket Portsmouth

PRE-ROSE Bowl, Hampshire would have been another of these "unnecessary" clubs and – under his proposals – Nicholas would have been unable to start, let alone pursue, his playing career.
Rowan Cowell Bideford, Devon

As any good gardener will confirm, rose-bushes sometimes need drastic pruning if they are to thrive. Lancashire have won nothing in the last decade and have not won the Championship outright for more than 75 years. Perhaps the pruning should begin in Manchester.
Peter Walker Lichfield, Staffordshire

All letters from TWC

And the banned plays on

Badly behaved club cricketers ...

AN OVERSEAS cricketer banned from the Home Counties League for violence during a match is playing in his native country, highlighting the problems club cricket faces dealing with discipline. Tim Miles, a 19-year-old from Western Australia, was playing for the Oxfordshire club Aston Rowant when he had an on-field fight with Dean Nurse of Basingstoke & North Hants.

"There are some areas where we are too bureaucratic and other areas of the game like this one [discipline] where we haven't got the process in place" was the assessment of the ECB's head of non-first-class development, Paul Bedford.

Miles, banned from the Home Counties League for a year, played grade cricket for Fremantle and took over 20 wickets before Christmas at an average of under 17. A representative of the Western Australia Cricket Association said he was not aware of any incident in the UK.

The situation would be different in rugby or football. If a player receives a ban from a competition, that suspension becomes national and the information is easily available. Bedford says: "[Miles being allowed to play] doesn't help but it's a level of bureaucracy that comes after making sure there are enough opportunities to play the game."

In August Miles and Nurse exchanged words before Nurse, batting, took exception to a yorker-gone-wrong which became a high full-toss. Nurse threw down his bat and charged up the wicket; Miles responded with a rugby tackle and a scrap followed.

Bedford said bans being enforced abroad depends on whether authorities bother to investigate: "There would be ramifications if the home board decide to take it up. I've had a number of instances where a banned player has gone abroad and I've written to the foreign board."

Bedford also thought a banned player in the UK would probably be able to get a game elsewhere in the country and said the ECB was not "a police force". Enforcing bans is down to county boards logging incidents and league registration secretaries checking the records.

Would players banned overseas be prevented from playing in the UK? "No. The level of sophistication in intelligence in cricket is not as high as it should be."

Chris Tucker of the Gloucestershire FA explains how it works in football: "They must request an international transfer from the FA. This procedure prevents suspended players from being active abroad." Likewise in rugby, the RFU would prevent a banned player transferring to a foreign union's competition. Middlesex's Shaun Udal was banned for three years in 2003 after a club-cricket incident. In 2005 an official for the league tried to prevent him touring Pakistan with England for the offence.

The Wisden Cricketer, February 2010 **Alex Winter**

Scrap heap: Miles crouching and batsman Nurse

GEORGE RESZETER

The velvet gloveman

A career that coincided with that of Godfrey Evans meant 'Mac' played only three Tests

A COMRADESHIP of town and country linking three aspiring young men foretold a new beginning for Arthur McIntyre. His friendship with the Bedser twins from Woking stretched back to over 70 years from their first meeting in opposition as Surrey juniors to McIntyre's death in December. The signal to take up wicketkeeping came in a wartime meeting with the twins in Salerno, Italy. He acted upon their advice to submit his credentials to The Oval. The decision would propel a favourite son of Kennington towards a central role in Surrey's great Championship years of the 1950s.

McIntyre passed the crucial test of any wicketkeeper in his ability to stand up to fast-medium bowling, according to Alec Bedser. "Mac was a magnificent keeper who did everything so easily and never made a fuss. He often wore a chest pad but he was rarely hit because his hands were so good and sure." The anticipation and speed of reaction to Bedser's sharply veering legcutters was uncanny.

Yet the distinctions which commended McIntyre as a schoolboy to Surrey were as a legspinner. They gave him a shoal of wickets when he joined the county groundstaff as a 16-year-old in 1934. But as a boy McIntyre harboured the notion of wicketkeeping. He occasionally kept at Kennington Road School and with the London Schools XIs. The transition occurred towards the end of the Second World War. Reports of his keeping with the Central Mediterranean Forces in Italy had not gone unnoticed by the Bedsers. Mac was regarded as a batsman/wicketkeeper when first-class cricket resumed in 1946 and was awarded his 1st XI cap as a batsman. He turned down the tempting offer of Arthur Wellard, the Somerset allrounder, to join him at Taunton. Surrey will be forever grateful.

Variety was the spice of McIntyre's years at The Oval. Encircled by Surrey's brilliant close-fielding cordon, with Stuart Surridge bold and brave at the helm, he revelled in the excitement. "I was fortunate in that I kept to a world-class attack, all Test bowlers. There was always something happening to maintain your interest and keep you on your toes."

Little Mac was fated to linger in the Test shadow of the ebullient Godfrey Evans. He played in only three Tests – twice, against West Indies and South Africa, when Evans was injured, and once solely as a batsman in the storm-affected Test at Brisbane in 1950. Only mildly did he express his disappointment at not being included on other tours after going to Australia in 1950-51. Alec Bedser was less forgiving. He considered it a disgrace that McIntyre was not rewarded for his skills. The workmanlike efficiency contrasted with that of the showman Evans, the big-occasion player whose sustained brilliance made him always first choice.

After retirement he extended his service at The Oval by another 21 seasons as coach.

The Wisden Cricketer, March 2009

Arthur John William McIntyre was born on May 14, 1918 and died on December 26, 2009, aged 91.

Alan Hill is a biographer of England cricketers

Four titles in: McIntyre in April 1956

CAREER RECORD 1938-1963	M	R	HS	AVGE	100s	50s	W	BEST	AVGE	5W	CT/ST
Test	3	19	7	**3.16**	0	0	-	-	-	-	8/0
First-class	390	11145	143*	**22.83**	7	51	4	1-10	**45.00**	0	638/157

Cycling to the Ashes

Oli Broom left Lord's on a bike, destination Brisbane, for the first Ashes Test, all for charity

THE CROWD roared in anticipation as their hero strode from the classroom and approached the crease. His side still needed 68 runs off six overs to retain bragging rights over their arch-rivals. The bowler flung a quick ball that skidded on the concrete towards the batsman. The venue was Jadavpur University in Calcutta. The pitch was Corridor B on the second floor of the Faculty of English Literature. The game was just the latest in a series of cricketing adventures as I make my way by bicycle from Lord's to The Gabba. I have ridden through Europe to Istanbul, through a harsh Middle Eastern winter, into the baking deserts of North Africa as far as Khartoum, across cricket-mad India and Bangladesh to Thailand.

I have sought and found plenty of unsuspecting cricketing accomplices. I played one of the most ethnically diverse matches in Damascus, Syria, alongside two Iraqis, three Syrians, three Palestinian refugees, a Canadian, an American, a Turk, a Brit, two Australians and a few Kurds. In the dusty Sudanese border town of Wadi Halfa I struggled, in the fading light, against the raw bowling ability of a Sudanese man dressed in a traditional floor-length white jalabiya.

And India. I could not fail to be cast under India's spell. From dawn till dusk, as I pedalled through cities, towns, villages and deserted scrub land, faces and shouts appeared: "Cricket Mr! Where you from, good sir? We play here, now, is it not?" I found myself presenting regional knockout trophies in remote villages, performing the toss at a State club game and commentating on a night match between slum children in Sangli. In six weeks I jump on a boat from Jakarta to Darwin and begin the 4,000km outback stretch to Brisbane. Not long to go now.

The Wisden Cricketer, September 2010

Turkish fans

Damascus

Harsh winter

Desert baked

Syrian guards

Indian obsession

OBITUARIES Audrey Collins 1915-2010 by **Sarah Potter**

One-Test women's hero

She played one Test for England but was far more influential in her post-war efforts for the Women's Cricket Association laying foundations for the modern national team

AUDREY COLLINS was unlucky not to play in the first official women's Test in 1934 and the war then ruined her chances of adding to her solitary international appearance, against Australia at The Oval in 1937. Brevity and bad timing, though, did not extend to the rest of her extraordinary cricketing life and it is as an amateur in the finest tradition – even celebrated by an appearance in a Nike advertising campaign when she was a silver-haired and sprightly 80 – that ensures her legendary status.

Born in India in 1915, Collins and her two siblings came to England with their Australian mother in 1920 after their father was killed in the First World War. Chemistry and cricket became her twin passions and she excelled as a leader and organiser after graduating from the University of London and starting as a teacher.

Central to her life was the Women's Cricket Association, which ran the game in England until the merger with the ECB in 1998, and for whom she served stints as secretary, chairman and, between 1983 and 1994, president. Although she was not part of the group who gathered in 1926 in the Herefordshire village of Colwall to set up the WCA, she played her first Cricket Week (the annual festival still enjoyed there today) soon after.

"The founding WCA members all stayed in the Park Hotel," Collins once told me, "but the rest of us were put up in the village. I was in lodgings on the Green and after each day's play I had a tin bath in front of the fire."

Determined to spread cricket's charms, Collins formed the Vagabonds (now Radlett) Women's Club in Hertfordshire when she settled there to teach at St Albans Girls' School. She played until she was 70 and was still eagerly ferrying her beloved club's under-13s to net practice well into her 80s. She had faith in the "presumed order" of things but was not a stickler for the status quo. Collins voted for merger with the ECB and did not object (as some of her peers did) when the playing uniform switched from divided skirts to trousers. She was honoured by MCC in 1999 as one of the first 10 female members.

It is as a seller of chocolate bars that many women's cricket aficionados will remember Collins. In the pre-ECB cash-strapped days the appetite for fundraising was necessarily all consuming. Collins strode purposefully around every boundary she could find, cajoling weary spectators to buy her discounted Nestlé bars.

During the 1980s, when a home tour teetered on the brink of humiliating cancellation, Collins attempted to raise a personal bank loan. Thankfully a sponsor was found and her money was not needed. She did, though, donate her £500 fee for the Nike advert to the East Anglia Under-17 girls team that was so close to her heart.

The campaign, which also featured Joan Whalley, a 74-year-old former footballer, and Barbara Butterick, a 65-year-old ex-boxer, was meant, in Nike's words, "to persuade more women and girls to take up sport". Collins's photograph alone could not possibly achieve that lofty goal but her long and vibrant life most certainly did. *The Wisden Cricketer, June 2010*

Audrey Collins was born on April 14, 1915 and died on February 14, 2010, aged 94.

ALISON McCREEDY

Ninety-one not out: Audrey Collins scoring

Sarah Potter writes for *The Times*

CAREER RECORD 1937	M	R	HS	AVGE	100s	50s	W	BEST	AVGE	5W	CT
Test	1	28	27	**28.00**	0	0	0	-	-	0	0

Tempo, rhythm

and harmony

Philippe Auclair, a football writer from France, could not resist the charms of Abdul Qadir

Cricket," this English friend told me, "is chess on grass." Maybe he'd hoped this cryptic description would discourage me from asking further questions about a game I knew nothing about except that I was quite taken with the idea that you couldn't tell which team a player belonged to by looking at the colour of his shirt. Little did he know that I loved chess and the same would soon be true of cricket.

A copy of the *Dictionary of Cricket* tucked in my music bag, I went to Lord's, where I watched Middlesex and Warwickshire. I sat in the pavilion as a freshly registered overseas member was entitled to, wearing the kind of tie I'd have worn at a Dr Feelgood gig a few years earlier, not ideal but when in Rome ...

I had another book in my bag, a present from the same friend: Mike Brearley's *The Art of Captaincy*, which I read when the game paused for reasons that were still a mystery. I enjoyed those lulls and can think of a few players who managed to make batting itself more boring than the intervals between the deliveries (but this is not a piece about Bill Athey). After all, when playing chess there are times when you let the sand run in the hourglass, calculating the next moves or simply letting your mind drift away. Then the spring is let loose, with devastating and beautiful results. Wayne Daniel I think it was who broke through a batsman's gate to teach me the unique excitement of cricket. The suddenness of the flying stumps was like a sacrificed bishop wrecking a king's castle – a thrilling geometry of violence.

I soon learnt that cricket, unlike any other modern sport, still had room for a type of skill that did not primarily call upon sheer speed and physical prowess to assert itself at the highest level: the art of the spin bowler. It became an obsession. I read about Bosanquet, Tiger O'Reilly and Ian Peebles and that

strange creature, the 'lobster'. The slower the better, it seemed to me. Two spinning fingers up to the established order – I had to love it.

The mid-1980s were not exactly a golden age for spinners. England had Emburey and Edmonds, the arch-pragmatist and the elegant chancer, whose averages seemed distinctly, well, average to a neophyte like me. West Indies had Roger Harper, who bowled flatter than an old pint of English cider. Australia had no one. Spin bowlers were getting older; spin bowling was as good as dead.

It was then, late in the summer of 1987, that I went to The Oval and came upon Abdul Qadir. Emburey and Edmonds had taken zero wickets between them (at a cost of 240) in

66 He fought for a truth that legspin was the supreme form of bowling 99

Pakistan's innings. But Qadir forced England to follow on, with figures of 7 for 96 on a featherbed. I was entranced. I'd read that he was the last of his breed, a mystic engrossed in the intricacies of his craft, a cricketing coelacanth, I suppose, not a harbinger.

This view would soon be proved wrong. Qadir was a bridge thrown between the essentially fallow age of the macho speed merchants and the remarkable blossoming of a new generation of spin bowlers which he made possible. I remember my thrill when Shane Warne went to Lahore to pay homage to Qadir, a gesture that told us much about their love of the game and why we loved them too. Qadir was a keeper of the faith when I, like so many others, the great Warne included, desperately wanted to believe.

Qadir was about tempo, rhythm, harmony. He conducted the game. As he walked and hopped up to the crease in those exaggerated strides he defined a perception of time that was entirely his own: it was the

first trap he could lay for the batsman. His action was close to perfection in that, if it lacked some of the classical fluidity of a Bedi, it allowed him to disguise the variations he had mastered; the only one of his kind who could bowl a wrong'un with as high an arm as when delivering a regulation legbreak. And Qadir had not one but two googlies, one which he would allow batsmen to spot, the other which was virtually indistinguishable from his stock delivery.

But it is also the intensity of Qadir's bowling that captivated me. Every ball brought a hush in the crowd. Which way would it break? Could it really have been a flipper? His appealing, which some judged excessive, seemed a logical extension of his absolute focus on the drama of the delivery.

The Pakistani team of that era was not one easily warmed to; there was a pettiness to their behaviour on the field which tainted admiration. But you did not sense in Qadir the boorishness of a Salim Yousuf: even when his team-mates celebrated one of his wickets, he cut a singular, otherworldly figure. He was fighting for Pakistan, of course, but also for a greater truth: that legspin was the supreme form of bowling. And when he bowled I knew he had to be right. ▣ *The Wisden Cricketer, July 2010*

Philippe Auclair is England correspondent of *France Football* and RMC radio station

To the slaughter: Qadir gets Allan Lamb

The greatest decade

The 2000s produced plenty of great drama and fantastic matches but how does it compare with the last 50 years? *TWC* invited a panel of experts to pick their best post-war decade

The panel **Mickey Arthur** (ex-South Africa coach); **Mike Atherton** (ex-England captain, chief cricket correspondent, *The Times*); **Sambit Bal** (Editor, Cricinfo.com); **Lawrence Booth** (Cricket writer, *Daily Mail*); **Ian Chappell** (ex-Australia captain); **Patrick Eagar** (leading cricket photographer); **David Frith** (former editor, *Wisden Cricket Monthly*); **Gideon Haigh** (cricket writer and historian); **Suresh Menon** (sports writer and editor in India); **Kevin Mitchell** (sports writer, *The Observer*); **Viv Richards** (ex-West Indies captain); **Osman Samiuddin** (Pakistan editor, Cricinfo.com); **Graham Thorpe** (ex-England batsman); **Michael Vaughan** (ex-England captain)

6th 1960s 0 votes

What was so wrong with cricket in the 1960s that meant none of our 14 esteemed judges voted for it? It certainly began well, with Australia and West Indies playing out the first-ever tied Test in 1960-61. Unfortunately it was to be a one-hit wonder, with the pattern of the decade cemented at Old Trafford in 1964: forget the thrill of the Ashes, England and Australia got only two overs into the third innings from five completed days, with Australia's 656 for 8 declared and England's 611 taking over 28 hours. As The Beatles, JFK and miniskirts turned the world upside down, cricket bumbled along at its own pace.

August 19, 1953: Denis Compton at The Oval as England finally win back the Ashes

=4th 1950s 1 vote

James Dean, Grace Kelly and Frank Sinatra infused the 1950s with a post-war glamour and it rubbed off on cricket. Keith Miller and Denis Compton were as prolific and popular in the gossip columns as the sports pages, with the fighter pilot and the Brylcreem Boy encapsulating a decade of entertaining, carefree cricket.

David Frith 66 The 1950s were the best decade: the final years of purity, free of the shameless cash lust that was to warp the game's morality. My temple then was the charming Sydney Cricket Ground, just as Trumper knew it, no logos defacing the sightscreens, picket fence or sacred turf. No helmets obscured batsmen's identities. We had a clean vision of Miller, Harvey, Lindwall, Benaud and O'Neill; Worrell, Weekes, Walcott. It was England's finest period: Hutton, Compton, May, Cowdrey, Graveney, Bedser, Tyson, Statham, Trueman, Laker and Evans 99

=4th 2000s 1 vote

Run-rates that would astonish those present at Old Trafford in 1964, a great Australian side, Twenty20, the 2005 Ashes, eight triple-hundreds, India's remarkable win at Kolkata. That is a decade bursting with quality but still only one vote. Perhaps we are still too close to assess it properly or perhaps bat dominated ball too much.

Mickey Arthur 66 The game has gone to a new level this decade. Test matches have provided many more results than before and are being played at a much faster pace, making for compelling viewing 99

3rd 1980s 2 votes

The decade of the allrounder. The collective talent, ego and flair of Ian Botham, Richard Hadlee, Kapil Dev and Imran Khan was more than enough to make up for the lack of spinning magic. While West Indies did not have an allrounder to match those names, they were happy enough with an infamous pace attack that pummelled the 1980s with more bruises than *Raging Bull*. Their brutal 5-0 assault of England in 1985-86, led by Garner, Holding, Marshall and Patterson, epitomised their intent.

Gideon Haigh 66 Cricket had the balance between Test matches, ODIs and first-class cricket most conducive to the production of broadly skilful players. Tours were undertaken on the basis best for cricket not commerce, competition was also more even: while West Indies were the best team Pakistan challenged regularly and New Zealand beat them 99

Graham Thorpe 66 It was such a great era for rivalries, especially among the allrounders 99

December 8, 1980: Viv Richards at Faisalabad v Pakistan; West Indies won the series 1-0

2nd 1990s 4 votes

The tussle between West Indies and Australia for Test supremacy dominated much of this decade, with tantalising subplots of reverse-swing, legspin, the emergence of Sri Lanka, the re-emergence of South Africa and great World Cups in '92 and '99. It also showcased some of the game's greatest ever batsmen (Lara, Tendulkar) and bowlers (Warne, Akram, Ambrose, Walsh) at their peak. Australia's win in 1994-95 at Kingston, led by Steve Waugh, sealed a momentous series and heralded a new era and a new set of cricketing giants. England did not join in and were mostly rubbish.

Lawrence Booth 66 The renaissance of legspin, more lethal new-ball pairings than at any other time, the passing of the baton from West Indies to Australia, the best World Cup match ever, Lara's 375 and even a half-decent Zimbabwe side. What more could you want? 99

Suresh Menon 66 The 1990s saw the invention of the companion to the googly: the doosra. It might have required a fresh definition of the illegal delivery but in a batsman-dominated game that was a small price to pay 99

Osman Samiuddin 66 The 1990s still had some absolutely outstanding fast bowlers and so cricket had yet to become the bat-dominated and oriented game it is now. The feats of Brian Lara and Sachin Tendulkar meant that much more 99

Michael Vaughan 66 You had Ambrose and Walsh, Waqar and Wasim, Warne and McGrath, Murali and Vaas. Look at all the bowling combinations in the 1990s, plus some truly great batsmen, it puts it above any decade 99

April 23, 1992: Walsh and Ambrose bowl South Africa out for 148 at Bridgetown

November 29, 1975: Greg Chappell hooks Andy Roberts during the first of his two Brisbane 100s

1st 1970s 6 votes

Watergate, three-day weeks and The Osmonds meant the world needed cheering up in the 1970s. And that is what cricket did. It was the most evenly contested decade, with quality English, Indian, Australian and West Indian sides swapping the No.1 position, while New Zealand and Pakistan were both strong and capable of winning abroad. Nearly every year had a gripping series: the 2-2 Ashes in 1972, West Indies winning 3-2 in India in 1974-75, 1-1 between Australia and Pakistan in 1976-77. Great batsmen, great bowlers – both slow and fast – and some of the best keepers the game has produced; international cricket may not see its like again.

Ian Chappell 66 It was a decade where almost 60% of the Tests were decided but no team had greater than a 36% winning record. That's competitive balance. The advent of World Series Cricket produced the toughest cricket I played and changed the game forever 99

Kevin Mitchell 66 We had Bishan Bedi and his Indian spinning mates, the rise of the great West Indies team and the marketing phenomenon that was World Series Cricket 99

Sambit Bal 66 Match-fixing ruined the 1990s, so the 1970s it is. The World Cup arrived but Test cricket ruled; great fast bowlers and great spinners, so runs had to be earned. We didn't watch a lot of it but the radio was enough 99

Viv Richards 66 That period – and you would include WSC in that – couldn't be bettered 99

Patrick Eagar 66 India had four of the finest spinners and the amazing Sunil Gavaskar 99

Mike Atherton 66 No helmets, fast bowlers, pre-professionalism so there were fewer barriers between players and supporters. Players were less plastic, less coached – in cricket and in life. Everything seemed a little more raw 99 *The Wisden Cricketer*, February 2010

No average cricketer

Many will remember David Shepherd the Nelson-hopping Test umpire, who has died aged 68. But Shepherd the batsman thrilled Gloucestershire crowds of the 1960s and 70s and no less so Alan Gibson, former cricket writer for The Times. *In 1975, as 'Shep' was approaching the end of his playing career, Gibson profiled one of his favourite characters*

BROWN, the Gloucestershire captain, is out of the side with a back strain; Procter, the vice-captain, is still some way from fitness, though the reports are encouraging; and therefore Shepherd, the newly chosen senior professional, will lead the county in the match against Glamorgan. Pause here while all Gloucestershire cricketers say "Good Old Shep".

A pity the match is not at Bristol, for there he would have been given a special cheer, but the Cardiff people will do that anyway, for he

is a popular as well as substantial figure in the county cricket scene ("Shep am byth, boyo").

Since the sad retirement of Milburn, David Shepherd has, so far as I can see, no challenger in one respect. Of all current English first-class cricketers he is the bulkiest, plumpest, amplest, tubbiest, best-rounded, most-circumferous – let me cease weighing my words and make, er, no bones of it – he is the fattest.

He is not so fat as he was – he slimmed determinedly the winter before last – but he would still win by several inches any standing race for cricketers when the photo-finish was taken at the start. This is not meant to mock him. He keeps fit, in his own way and shape. He looks fatter than Milburn did, because he carries more weight to the front, but he has often said he would back himself against Milburn over a hundred yards and after watching both field I have no doubt he is right.

66 His sunny nature is often a virtue in time of crisis 99

Shepherd comes from Devon and looks as if he comes from Devon: any film producer making *The Farmer's Wife* or *Lorna Doone* on location would seize upon him as an extra, with double-rate and free cider. His face is pink, tending to purple at strenuous times, like the sun seen from Dartmoor making one of its spectaculars as it goes down across the Tamar. His hair is getting a little grey, like the clouds which hover above the sunset, though he is only 34 and has a sunset or two to see yet.

Devon is a good cricketing county. With a few slightly different twists of luck it might have been a first-class county and would have borne the responsibility quite as well as several which are.

He played cricket for Devon from 1959 to 1964. He scored lots of runs in a boisterous style and was chosen for the Minor Counties

against the 1964 Australians. His first match for Gloucestershire was against Oxford University in 1965. The bowling was perhaps not very good and he scored a hundred, which was not altogether a fortunate thing to happen to him. It took him some time to adjust to the tighter, duller discipline of the three-day game. Indeed he has never quite done that: it is one of the reasons for his popularity and also, I suppose, one of the reasons why, though he has scored 8,000 runs, his first-class average is only 24.

He had to wait until 1969 for his Gloucestershire cap. But he has developed into a good county cricketer. Twice he has scored a thousand runs in a season, not easy nowadays for a middle-order batsman. His sunny nature, hard to ruffle though he is rather a shy man behind that apple face, has often been a virtue in moments of crisis, especially in one-day matches. His fielding, if not speedy, is safe and zealous, and he has a good arm. He has taken two wickets at 34, a figure which occasional captaincy will not tempt him to try to improve.

"Good old Shep," they cry in Gloucestershire when he comes out to bat, one of the West's unmistakable own, usually following a series of much more talented chaps from places like Sialkot and Streatham. "Well done, Shep," they cry, as he chases unflaggingly round the boundary. When those powerful forearms make the ball hum over the bowler's head, how they chortle! When he gets out early through some optimistic bash on a turner, and comes in sorrowfully shaking his head, as if he could not imagine how he of all men could come to do such a thing, there is always a consolatory murmur. "Never mind! 'ard luck. Good old Shep." Who cares what his average is? Doesn't he cheer us up! *The Times*, 1975.

From *Of Didcot and the Demon*, a collection Alan Gibson's work.

The Wisden Cricketer, January 2010

Good old Shep: David Shepherd, batting in 1973, was a popular figure in Gloucestershire

CAREER RECORD 1965-1979	M	R	HS	AVGE	100s	50s	W	BEST	AVGE	5W	CT
First-class	282	10672	153	**24.47**	12	55	2	1-1	**53.00**	0	95
One-day	183	3330	100	**21.34**	1	13	0	-	-	0	34

UMPIRING RECORD 1981-2005
Tests 92* **ODIs** 172 **First-class** 412 **One-day** 505 **Twenty20** 1

*only Steve Bucknor and Rudi Koertzen have umpired in more Tests

TRIBUTES Alec Bedser 1918-2010 by **John Woodcock**

An implacable champion

John Woodcock, cricket correspondent of The Times *from 1954 to 1988, remembers a huge cricketing figure and friend, who died in April*

WITH the death of Alec Bedser, at the grand old age of 91, the game of cricket has lost one of its staunchest and most implacable champions. As a bowler he was true British oak. After his playing days were over he thought few changes were for the better. To him Twenty20 cricket was "tin-pot", a good Bedserian word.

Our own friendship dated from the day I beat him at deck quoits ("slithers" as it was more commonly called) on the ship sailing to Australia on the MCC tour of 1950-51. He had been lying game (the scoring was as in bowls) when, with my last quoit and no doubt flukily, I turned defeat into victory. All he said was "You and your Oxford bloody University", a reaction so genially chippy and hilariously irrelevant

that I laughed and laughed. He laughed, too, when he thought about it and we became and remained the firmest of friends. I tell this story only for what it may say about Alec.

It was on that tour, during the second Test match at Melbourne, that those Australians present who had played against SF Barnes compared Bedser to Barnes, then generally considered the greatest bowler there had ever been. Of the present England attack, Tim Bresnan probably comes closest in pace, though such was Bedser's accuracy that he

❝ To him a ball left alone was not a ball at all❞

always liked to have his wicketkeepers standing up. To him a ball which the batsman allowed to pass was not a ball at all. While watching the modern game, nothing riled him more than to

see the slips clapping, hands above their heads, a succession of balls which the batsman had left alone: if there was no third man, that made it even worse, Alec rarely bowled without one.

Moan as he might, Alec revelled in hard work, however tough the going. He was fortunate, no doubt, to bowl in the days of uncovered pitches, and before short boundaries or nuclear bats. Nor did he have to contend with the exotic batting genius of Sri Lankans, who had still not flown the nest when he played. Being built as he was, it was also merciful that he was spared the need to dive for the ball on the boundary like some bird of prey.

I must have seen him bowl thousands of overs and have no recollection of a loose one. His 69 wickets at something under 17 runs apiece in successive series against Australia, when England were largely dependent upon him – in Australia in 1950-51 and at home in 1953 – brought him his well deserved legendary status. That, and his nature – an amalgam of chauvinism, Puritanism, warmth and wry humour. Off the field he was never "one of the boys", partly because of the constant company of his twin, Eric, whose habit it was to complete a sentence that Alec had started, often with a qualification of his own. When, once, I heard Alec asked whether he considered himself to have been "a strike bowler", his reply was characteristic. "Well, I can't have been, can I," he said, "I didn't run halfway to the pavilion and pitch the thing halfway down the bloody wicket." "Like they all do now," added Eric.

From Alec's first Test match against India in 1946 until the last of his 24 years as an England manager and selector stretched half a century of dedicated service, equalled by few. He never quite forgot the acute disappointment of losing his place in the England side after the first Test in Australia in 1954-55, a matter that Len Hutton, the captain, handled without the compassion due. Much as that hurt him, it was no more than a blip on a monumental career. Sir Alec Bedser was not only a magnificent bowler, he was one of the most revered and distinctive figures in the history of the game and, as such, an irreplaceable part of its tapestry.

The Wisden Cricketer, May 2010

Job done: Bedser leaves the field after taking 7 for 55 in the opening Test of the 1953 Ashes

CAREER RECORD 1939-1960	M	R	HS	AVGE	100s	50s	W	BEST	AVGE	5W	CT
Tests	51	714	79	**12.75**	0	1	236	7-44	**24.89**	5	15
First-class	485	5735	126	**14.51**	1	13	1924	8-18	**20.41**	16	96

Rebels

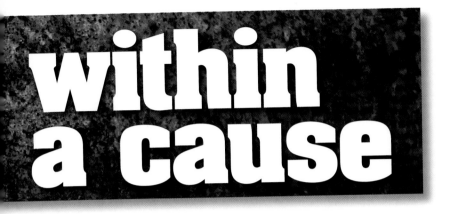

within a cause

It is 20 years since Mike Gatting led a squad of mercenaries to Apartheid South Africa, a desperate and final under-cover tour. **Telford Vice**, then a young journalist, recalls the ill-starred affair

Kimberley brands itself on to the faces of those who live there. Hard eyes gleam with a sliver of the searing sun they have endured for decades. Mouths clench into defiant slashes by the demands of keeping out the town's invasive grit. Staring into faces like those is a challenge. Add a dash of emotion and the average Kimberley visage looms like something out of Faust.

Many such faces confronted Mike Gatting and his English rebels on January 26, 1990. If they thought the Combined Bowl XI they played in the first match of their tour that day would not provide much opposition, they were right (Gatting's team won by 254 runs). But they could not have imagined that their real opponents would be beyond the boundary in the shape of protestors against the tour. They wore their Kimberley faces angrily and they made their presence felt far more effectively than the willing but wanting team of second-division players the tourists brushed aside.

Gatting, a yeoman of the game, is often remembered as one of its more pathetic victims. From the distance of the former colonies, the comical rage of his on-field argument with Shakoor Rana to then being sacked as England captain on the risible charge of dallying with a barmaid, Gatting was the personification of an empire rendered impotent. But he earned the veteran cricket correspondent Colin Bryden's respect: "Although Gatting took a lot of flak I found him someone with great personal integrity. He kept stressing that he believed in freedom of speech and met the demonstrators, notably in

Pietermaritzburg where he received a memorandum on a makeshift stage."

The Englishmen no doubt thought they had landed themselves a deal that was more about money than it was about cricket. They had not figured the situation would trap them in the crossfire of a society that was ready to go to war with itself. They were disabused of that naivety in the chaos of their arrival. Protestors greeted the team, who were in turn met by police with guns and dogs. Violence

66 A month after coming they were chased home 99

followed and blood spilled. Television viewers saw police shoving Gatting out of the way. He looked as if he had avoided being mown down by colliding trains.

Those were strange days, indeed. There we were going along abnormally here in Apartheid South Africa; the next a planeload of exotic cricketers blinked in the harsh African sunlight, having been spirited into our midst unseen. In the South African media, much of it muzzled by restrictive laws and its own illiberal thinking, rebel tours were almost universally welcomed and reported on as if they were the real thing.

On the other side of the fence, where black cricket survived despite the 317 laws designed to afford whites a superior life and blacks a brutal one, there was nary a whimper at the undermining spectre of rebel tours, at least in public. But by the time Gatting's team touched down, push was ready to come to shove across all sectors of South African society. Seen in that light, there might have been some

sympathy for the tourists. There was not. A month after the smell of cordite marked their arrival they were chased home with several games cancelled.

White English-speakers dominated South African cricket and, for many, rebel tours made their mythical heroes flesh: imagine Zeus and Apollo landing in your back garden. So the awe was palpable when players like Gatting, Chris Broad and John Emburey stepped out of the mist of isolation.

Many black South Africans had shaped a different view of England. To them it was a fine, moral place that gave Basil D'Oliveira a stage on which to prove Apartheid wrong. They wore the sting of betrayal stoically when Graham Gooch toured. Gatting's team bore the full brunt.

Ah, yes: the cricket. In the only 'Test' played, at The Wanderers, the rebels batted exactly like the cricketers caught in the headlights of history they were. They were rattled out for 156 and 122 as the South Africans won by seven wickets. But the only real champions were the demonstrators. They were the true Invincibles. *The Wisden Cricketer, February 2010*

Telford Vice is a South African freelance writer

Not welcome: fans protest at Bloemfontein

Flawed genius of the county circuit

Domestic cricket was never better served than when Alan Gibson was writing about it. A new collection of his writings opens up a world of colour

LATE LAST year a group of county cricket correspondents met in a Derby pub. It was a bit of a crisis meeting – but more of a wake and a reunion. These were blokes who used to spend their summers together. Now that newspapers have lost interest in all non-international cricket, they rarely see each other. Bad as things are, the barman still said he had not heard so much laughter in ages.

The greatest county cricket writer of all time, even if he were still with us, would not have been present. He would not have been asked because he hardly knew his younger colleagues. Alan Gibson (1923-1997) rarely went into press boxes. This was a drawback because he sometimes failed to discover germane facts, like hat-tricks or world records. On the other hand, he might have been sucked into the boring rubbish about how-many-balls-for-his-fifty – although somehow I doubt that.

Instead Gibson wandered the ground meeting, and to some extent creating, his own cast of characters. Some were on the field, like the Shoreditch Sparrow (Robin Jackman) and the eponymous Demon (of Frome – Colin Dredge). Others were behind the bar, like Phyl at Edgbaston, and GRIP (Glorious Red-headed Imperturbable Pamela) at Bristol. Usually Gibson was close to the bar, the constant subtext of this wonderful, funny, sad collection: an elegy for a brilliant, tormented man and a way of life we are losing.

I remember once glimpsing Alan at Northampton, nursing a half of lager just before an 11am start. It took me a while to realise it was not lager but a huge scotch and water, cunningly disguised. But for two decades he gave

The Times the most talked-about cricket report in any paper, anywhere – maybe the only talked-about cricket report.

However, it was not a report, not normally – and when he did have to knuckle down and write one, it was not much cop. Mostly it was a variation, in the musical sense, on the day's theme. "I wrote about the cricket," as John Woodcock put it. "Alan wrote about a day at the cricket." Or about spending much of the day on the train getting to the cricket, hence the 'Didcot'.

Reading Gibson was like watching Gower bat: every bit as elegant, with a gentle method that concealed the art. Chesterfield, 1974: "The morning was commandingly but, as it turned out, deceptively attractive, like a fairy woman of the Hebrides or a call by Boycott." Lord's, also 1974: "Randall's fielding once again was outstanding. He does not look like a fielder. He seems to mooch about lopsidedly, his arms, which are rather too long for his body, hanging by his sides ... He does not produce an effect of athletic coordination. But just give him a smell of the ball and you see the tiger."

The book is presented chronologically (handsomely, too) with a section for each of his years on the county circuit, 1967-86. But each year also has a commentary, written by Alan's son Anthony, which provides a muffled drumbeat of impending doom.

Anthony gives an introduction telling the story of his father's gilded youth and fraught career. He was president of the Oxford Union, traditionally a route leading to the Cabinet. Nothing seemed to shake Alan Gibson's underlying sense of failure, hence the alcoholism which destroyed his career as a commentator, both his marriages and ultimately his career on *The Times*. In the end newspapers prefer plodders to geniuses – certainly if they habitually file late, erratically and pissed.

Watcher from the wings: cricket was blessed to attract a man like Alan Gibson below

In 1976, when Gibson's reports perhaps reached their highest pitch of imagination and flair, Anthony records stoically that his father refused to attend his wedding: "Had he turned up, he would undoubtedly have had too much to drink and there would have been a scene." Yet on the next page he explains how that year Alan founded the magnificently mad JJ Society (still extant), celebrating the feats of Gloucestershire's Jack Davey and his non-existent middle name. Beneath all the fun you hear this constant silent shriek of suppressed rage. How blessed cricket was to attract a man like Alan Gibson. How delightful that his son has celebrated him with his glorious memorial.

The Wisden Cricketer, February 2010

Matthew Engel is a *Financial Times* columnist and former editor of *Wisden*

ROB SMYTH REVIEWS Start the Car: The World According to Bumble

Bumble hits top gear

English cricket's everyman loses none of the wacko warmth in print

LIFE IS supposed to begin at 40 but for David Lloyd it hit top gear at 60. Although he had been round the block many times – as an England player, first-class umpire, *TMS* commentator, England coach – it is only since 2007 that Bumble has become the voice of Twenty20, discovered the joys of Twitter and his beloved Manchester band, The Fall. Now, as cricket's man of the people, a crackpot enthusiast that the cover of this book proudly describes as "one ball short of an over", he seems to have found his true calling.

Start the Car is the story of Lloyd's life covering all points east and west, from what makes a good pub ("good bar stools and good ale: the ideal tools for chewing the fat") to the pros of corporal punishment (Bumble felt the belt for, among other things, "climbing on to the backyard wall to see if I could get a glimpse of my cousin Kathleen in the bath"), the joys of *Slumdog Millionaire* and why Piers Morgan should shut his mouth. It has the quality of an all-day session in his local: an infectious, unapologetically laddish and very funny trip through his stream of consciousness. It could be a cure for misanthropy.

The diversions are a conceit that could have backfired but nothing feels forced or inappropriate. In any case all roads lead inevitably back to Lloyd's love of cricket. The pen portraits of his Sky colleagues, written with mischief and huge warmth, are exceptional. He does not skip over the flippin' murder incident in Zimbabwe ("I will always have to live that down") and the book contains strident opinions on video evidence, Twenty20 ("a form of entertainment using cricket equipment"), the primacy of Tests and the need for red and yellow cards.

Big dumb grin: David Lloyd at the mic below

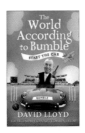

It is full of anecdotes. Some will be familiar, like the time Jeff Thomson broke Lloyd's box on a Perth flyer. But there are other lesser-known gems: Jack Simmons' farcical attempts to signal to his team-mates that he was about to bowl his faster ball, Tino Best whispering sweet nothings about Lloyd's wife into a stump mic and Allan Lamb locking Lloyd and his fellow umpire Ray Julian in their dressing room before shoving lit newspapers under the door.

This is the story of a life well lived, told with charm and style. At an age when others are gathering their free bus pass, Lloyd is still starting the car, speeding along in the fast lane with a big dumb grin on his face.

The Wisden Cricketer, July 2010

Rob Smyth is a freelance sports writer and author of *The Spirit of Cricket*

CRICKETERS are easier to fall in love with than any other sportsmen. It is to do with the amount of time they are on TV. While footballers and rugby players get only 90 minutes in front of the cameras, a Test series flushes out the characters, imperfections and nuances.

This is why we feel we already know Stuart Broad. It is a shame then that, as with most cricket autobiographies, the ghost-written *My Side of the Story: Bowled Over – An Ashes Celebration* offers as much insight as Ian Wright's football punditry. But what were we expecting from a book with three titles?

This is an autobiography by a man so young he pretended to be Matthew Hayden in his back garden. Broad's early life as a son of the Test cricketer Chris and his progression from batsman to bowler at Leicestershire is skimmed over to get to the real selling point: a Test-by-Test account of the Ashes. While the retelling offers little new, the reader does get the impression that Broad is frustrated by his changing roles.

The best thing in the book is a trip to the cinema. A few weeks after Chris Broad survived the Lahore attacks last year father and son sat in front of a cinema screen watching a shoot-out during an action film. "I turned to Dad and saw him shaking. His face was completely white." It is an insight into a cricketer's life at the end of the Noughties.

The Wisden Cricketer, February 2010

Daniel Brigham writes for *TWC*

Nothing to say: Stuart Broad

Literary lions

This year a *TWC* panel selected the best 50 cricket books. Here's the top 10 …

The books were voted for by a panel of distinguished friends of the magazine. The top four books all got the same number of first-choice votes. But when our panel's second and third choices were added in there emerged a clear – and unexpected – winner.

Each book is profiled by one of the panel who voted for it. And our No.1 is considered by the writer whose five nominated books won more votes in total than anyone else's. So here you are – our favourite authors on our favourite books. The Wisden Cricketer, July 2010

10 Mystery Spinner: The Story of Jack Iverson (2000) Gideon Haigh

JACK IVERSON, the unorthodox Australian spinner, was not one of the all-time greats of the game, yet his strange, compelling life inspired one of cricket's greatest biographies. Gideon Haigh's beautifully written narrative is like a classic legend, the tale of an ordinary man who conquers the world through the discovery of a unique skill but then falls because of the tragic flaws in his personality. Iverson had barely played any sort of cricket by his 30s. But he found that he could impart dramatic spin using his middle finger and thumb and in the 1950-51 season he won Australia the Ashes. By the age of 58, gripped by depression, he shot himself. Haigh's is a mesmerising book, mixing research with rich allusions to cricket history and literature. He is as good on bowling as he is on Iverson's character. It is a heart-rending but uplifting story.
Leo McKinstry

9 The Cricket Captains of England (1979) Alan Gibson

THE TITLE could not be simpler and the book does what it says on the sleeve. But the cover does scant justice to the rounded, gentle portraits of captains as real people not just cricketers. Gibson writes of Lionel Tennyson that "slow horses were his principal enemy". Mike Brearley "had the misfortune to be educated at Cambridge" while the trouble with Archie MacLaren "was that, if he disapproved of the choice of the selectors, he would tell not only them but his unfortunate team".
Richard Hobson

8 The Best Loved Game (1979) Geoffrey Moorhouse

A REGULAR cricket-writer or cricketer might arrive on a ground and notice something deeply obscure and technical about the state of the pitch; a Martian or an American might just notice a group of men standing around in white not doing very much. Somewhere between the two you get the perceptions of Moorhouse with a keen but sympathetic eye. He writes about 1978, one of the drabbest, wettest seasons in memory; in almost every chapter it is either raining or about to rain or has just rained. Good. It was the best of times for his purposes. If cricket could go on through the drizzle, then perhaps the game could survive anything.
Matthew Engel

7 Australia 55 (1955) Alan Ross

EACH paragraph brims with fresh delights. Seldom has Australia – the unlovely suburbs, the whisky-decked verandahs, the illusion that every man is equal – been sketched in such exquisitely rhythmic sentences. The swoops and glides of cricketers on the field of play never have. A softly struck Hutton off-drive resounds like "the plucking of banjo strings". Miller "barely bothers to shake the hair out of his eyes" before batting. These are memorable, near-faultless word-pictures of a man, ever alert to the unusual, lying with one hand behind his head on a Queensland beach; words written quickly and to deadline but never in haste.
Christian Ryan

6 Beyond a Boundary (1963) CLR James

BEYOND a Boundary's claims for everything are very large. It can be as bombastic as it is beautiful. And yet, though full of conclusions, its magic – I think, of structure – is that one can receive it as not a work of conclusions but something more slippery and singular, a work of thought and experience, of an individual in a sport, a sport in a society, a society in an individual. "We need not accept the analysis," James writes of an English art critic. "It is sufficient if it throws some light." This holds true of his book every time one returns to it.
Rahul Bhattacharya

5 Harold Gimblett (1982) David Foot

THE GREATEST sports books are not in essence about sport at all. They are always about the human condition. As its sub-title *Tormented Genius of Cricket* implicitly makes clear, the achingly tragic story which David Foot tells is much more than "runs and catches". Harold Gimblett's bright talent came darkly wrapped in depression. He committed suicide, aged 63, in 1978. Gimblett was Foot's boyhood hero, and he examines him with a beautiful, tender frankness. The Tormented Genius was fortunate in one respect; he got another genius to write about him. The book makes me regret terribly that I never saw one of Gimblett's carnival innings or met the man himself. But it makes me appreciate that Foot is one of the very best writers of his generation.
Duncan Hamilton

4 Pundits From Pakistan (2005) Rahul Bhattacharya

AMID all cricket's turmoils the search continues for illumination and warmth. *Pundits from Pakistan* provides both. Asked to cover a Test series between India and Pakistan, Rahul Bhattacharya visits the border and sees pomp and ceremony and frustrated humanity. He meets historians and philosophers, goes to see Shahid Afridi in his family home, talks to Danish Kaneria, the only Hindu in the Pakistan team, and watches a Test in Multan. The tale is told with wry intelligence. *Pundits* is a laughing, loving, lamenting book. The game is a starting point. The real journey is into the heart of the nation and the mind of man.
Peter Roebuck

3 It Never Rains (1984) Peter Roebuck

IF, during the rainy summer of 1982, Peter Roebuck had batted as well as he wrote he would have made his Somerset team-mate Viv Richards look like a ten-a-penny blocker. But he would have produced a lesser book. The heart of this funny, insightful, harrowing diary is Roebuck's civil war with doubt. After reading it, his team-mate Martin Crowe wondered why he played cricket at all. But there is light as well as shade. Compared with other books on the list, this matches Foot's *Tormented Genius* for emotional frankness, Brearley for insight, Gibson for erudition, Hughes for laughs and anything in the wonderful *Guardian Book of Cricket* for style. For me it is the greatest cricket book yet written.
Paul Coupar

2 The Art of Captaincy (1985) Mike Brearley

THE MORE I watch and play cricket, the less I feel I know about it – or rather, the more I realise I do not know about it. Maybe it is this great unknowability that compels us to seek out the wisdom of those who see the game clearly. Few see it as clearly as Mike Brearley. We guessed as much when he was captaining England in the late 1970s, the man with "a degree in people" in Rodney Hogg's memorable words, the man who grew a strategic beard on an Australian tour purely to wind up the crowd. *The Art of Captaincy* is an astonishingly wise and wide-ranging book. Its influence has been incalculable. Of all cricket books it is the one I have reread the most.
Marcus Berkmann

50 to 11

1 The Willow Wand: Some Cricket Myths Explored (1979) Derek Birley

The author who won most votes, **Gideon Haigh,** *on the myth-shattering 1979 book that topped the poll*

TACKLING cricket myths as a subject must have been like commencing a survey of Richard Nixon's lies – where to begin? But Derek Birley, the then Rector of Ulster Polytechnic, poured a lifetime's learning and enthusiasm into his survey and the effect was bracing and salutary. It could not have come at a less comfortable, or more timely, instant in cricket history, as its former grandees tried pretending they could return the genies of commercialisation and professionalism to the bottles from which Kerry Packer had released them. Birley's particular *bête noire* was the association of cricket with "not cricket": the game's self-legitimising claim to the occupation of a special, rarefied and inherently English moral universe. Almost every reputation precious to cricket's establishment came in for Birley's scrutiny: Lord Harris was a punitive reactionary, Lord Hawke a tiresome braggart, Sir Pelham Warner a brazen hypocrite. Many writers came off almost as badly, from CLR James in his guileless effusions about WG Grace to EW Swanton for his majestic condescension towards cricket north of Watford. How does it stand up today? Here and there the book has not worn well. But Birley was among the first to identify the implications of the game's infiltration by "the values of show business", noting its abiding tension: "The needs of cricket as a contest have always been to some extent at odds with the notion of providing entertainment."
Gideon Haigh is a writer based in Melbourne and author of four books in our top 50

The Modi operandum

Lalit Modi became the most influential man in cricket in the last five years but where did he come from and what is he like? Writing before his fall, **Sharda Ugra** explained

Let's get any compliments out of the way: Lalit Modi has created an event that will mark a tectonic shift in cricket. The Indian Premier League has altered what a valuation firm called cricket's "very eco-system". If Kerry Packer gave cricketers their first round of handsome wages, the IPL has spread the cash around even more and turned a cricket event from sporting contest into an entertainment spectacle that sends stabs of jealousy through the hearts even of World Wrestling.

Modi's IPL has claim to being the hottest sports league in the world with vast numbers flung around, thousands packed into stadiums every night for six weeks, tickets tough to come by, television ratings to match general entertainment channels in India and a half-million strong audience even in the UK.

Modi, 46, has never been this big, this successful, this contentious. He was one of the least successful sons of a famous Mumbai business family. As a student he fled Duke University in the US on a drug charge. As a businessman he dabbled in a media company that brought ESPN into India but eventually had only Fashion TV to make its biggest noise. Before 2005 his grandest title ever was executive director of the cigarette company Godfrey Phillips.

Now he is commissar, sorry commissioner, of the IPL. It has taken all of

five years for him to go from nobody to Indian cricket's big cheese. In all his early years as a businessman in the mid-1990s looking for leverage he had tried to sell an idea: an inter-city league in India.

The league was never meant to replicate the local loyalties of European football but rather business models of American sports with their commercially manufactured allegiances that impressed Modi in his student years. His business partners ESPN were meant to telecast the league, which signed up several big-name players, had a plan, created eight teams with marketable names like Calcutta Tigers, Bangalore Braves and Hyderabad Hawks. It would be called the Indian Cricket League – the name Modi registered and Zee TV stole to launch its event that lasted two years.

It was the TV rights issue over the planned ESPN broadcast of the inter-city league that ran into trouble with Jagmohan Dalmiya in power at the BCCI. The tussle gave Modi an enemy and it took him a decade to break into the Indian cricket board, working in alliance with its former president IS Bindra and the anti-Dalmiya brigade. The toppling of

66 He lives a charmed life. Every species of celebrity wants to be his friend 99

Dalmiya in 2005 was a monumental coup for Modi but what gave the IPL its ultimate cachet was what Bindra calls the "fortunate circumstance" of India winning the World Twenty20 in 2007. Until then both 50-overs and Twenty20 options were being mulled over. Once Misbah-ul-Haq had chipped one into the sky, there were no doubts left. What came into play after that was Modi's skill. "He can market apples as oranges and oranges as apples," an associate says. All fruits were put out in the basket to big business and Bollywood – two worlds already enraptured by Indian cricket and its superstar players.

As the IPL gathered strength Modi hit top form as businessman and powerbroker. A CEO of a national cricket board said dealing with Modi was like being in discussion with George Bush: "Either you are with him or you are against him." The IPL is not cricket's Afghanistan or Iraq, so everyone is with him. On the record, that is.

The closest anyone in office has come to speaking coolly is when the BCCI president, Shashank Manohar, said: "Mr Modi is a very good marketing person. In one line I've described him and that's all I would like to say." James Sutherland, Cricket Australia's CEO, who met to discuss the IPL with Modi in its early stages, said: "To grow in a cluttered entertainment market, cricket must provide a compelling proposition to its fans. Lalit has a remarkably clear view of this relationship between the sport and the public."

The public praise amuses many. "Lalit Modi is the most intensely disliked person in cricket," an IPL insider said. No one will say that on record, not even from the ICC, whose very structure the wrecking ball that is

the IPL could dismantle. Modi is on the ICC's finance and commercial affairs committee and arrives to meetings with homework done and numbers at hand. The ICC president, David Morgan, calls Modi "an interesting and bright person", saying that in committee "he is very good at looking at costs and seeking to reduce them. It is a welcome expertise." The idea that Modi and the IPL are dangerous is, to Morgan's mind, incorrect. "He's not sought a window [for the IPL]."

Lavish endorsement from peers would have satisfied most men. Modi, though, is made of a cloth that is a second skin to politicians and publicity-hungry pop stars. It is why he uses Twitter. It is why there is a "Modi speaks" link on the official IPL website with a smiling photo. It is why whenever he turns up at a match the TV production unit has one man assigned to what is called the "Modi-cam", which follows his every move. In South Africa during the IPL's second season India saw him walking down the 64 steps at Centurion shaking hands with the crowd. He has done a spot of commentary and shows up next to presenters during the pre-match rituals.

Modi's IPL, for all its carpet bombing of endorsements, is like an Orwellian politburo in which dissent is betrayal. Its lack of regulation reflects its commissar-chairman. A franchise executive said the IPL was "business first and cricket later", with team owners higher up the ladder than the average cricketer. One player calls the IPL a "gathering of Modi and friends who make the rules as they go along". Modi's brother-in-law Suresh Chellaram is a member of the Emerging Media consortium which owns the Rajasthan Royals. Gaurav Burman, who is married to Modi's step daughter, owns Global Cricket Ventures, the exclusive licensee of the IPL's digital, mobile and image rights.

But no criticism can bother the man who has the world eating out of his hands. Lalit Modi lives a charmed life. Players across countries, eras and skills, business tycoons, politicians, movie stars, advertisers and every species of celebrity want to be his friend. Even the Dalai Lama is turning up in the crowd. Cricket can only pray. ▲

The Wisden Cricketer, May 2010

Sharda Ugra is senior editor at Cricinfo.com

Locked out of Eden

Once the epitome of the Indian cricket experience, the 90,000-capacity Eden Gardens now stands empty more often than not. Daniel Brettig finds that politics is to blame

WHAT WOULD an Australian summer be like without the MCG? English summer without a Lord's Test? Yet in India over the past five years Kolkata's Eden Gardens – a capacity of 90,000, a riot of noise and scene of famous matches such as India's stunning win over Australia in 2001 – has been overlooked. Since the start of 2005 it has had only four international matches and between the end of 2007 and end of 2009 it has had none. A quartet of mostly minor fixtures is scheduled for the 2011 World Cup.

So why the cold shoulder? Indian cricket remains dominated by regional quarrels. The ground-scheduling system is far from straightforward and dictated by personalities and past sins. The great transgression of Eden Gardens is to be the home ground of Jagmohan Dalmiya, former president of the BCCI. His power created enemies in the current board.

According to Biswarup Dey, joint secretary of the Bengal Cricket Association and a member of the six-man BCCI tour-and-fixture committee, Eden Gardens ranks last among all Indian grounds. "The BCCI allots matches to different venues in India and, I don't know why, Eden Gardens is put in 22nd position on the list of grounds, which is the last," he says.

Most baffling of all is the denial of Tests to a ground that first held one in 1934, making 2009 the 75th anniversary. Kolkata's crowds have been known to misbehave but they have always turned out in vast numbers for Tests. The BCCI has ignored this while handing matches to venues like Nagpur, where there have been countless rows of empty seats.

"Every team – Australia, England – every team, including Pakistan, are keen to play here because of the crowd," says Biswarup. "In a Test only Kolkata will guarantee at least 70,000 present."

The Wisden Cricketer, January 2010

Daniel Brettig writes for the Australian Associated Press

Crowded out: Eden Gardens, 1996

Did I really do that?

How it happened in 2003

■ Weeks before the World Cup Andy Flower, the Zimbabwe captain, asks Olonga to meet him at a restaurant.

■ Flower explains that a friend, Nigel Hough, believes a stand should be taken against the Zimbabwe government.

■ Hough wants the team to boycott the World Cup and Olonga is asked to persuade the black players.

■ After further meetings Olonga tells Flower he doesn't believe that they could get the rest of the team on board.

■ Discussion continues about the best form of protest. There is concern that any action is not interpreted as the white majority in the team influencing the black minority.

■ Olonga and Flower meet David Coltart, a human-rights lawyer and opposition party (MDC) MP. Coltart suggests the black armbands.

■ At 9.30am on February 10, 2003, before Zimbabwe's opening World Cup match against Namibia, Flower and Olonga release a statement saying that they will each wear an armband as a way of "mourning the death of democracy in our beloved Zimbabwe".

■ Team-mates offer tacit support. Spectators offer more visible and audible backing.

■ Olonga is dropped from the team. He and Flower told not to wear black armbands again.

■ Before Zimbabwe's final group game against Pakistan, Olonga's father receives a message: "Tell your son to get out of Zimbabwe, now."

■ Before last WC game, Olonga and Flower announce their international retirements. Olonga is told by Ozias Bvute, of the ZCU, "You are on your own now" before being handed a plane ticket back to Zimbabwe.

■ But Olonga goes to Joburg to stay with friends instead before later to Britain where he settled.

Henry Olonga was the man who, alongside Andy Flower, risked everything standing up to Robert Mugabe at the 2003 World Cup. **Emma John** met him

For those of a nervous disposition Henry Olonga needs to carry a health warning. Within minutes he has demanded a life story, then peppers my faltering response with questions. Twenty minutes later, when I feel I have regained control of the situation and switch my recorder on, he looms over it and says, solemnly, "Why did the chicken cross the road ... ?" before leaning back in his chair, pleased with himself.

Perhaps I was expecting something more reserved, more statesmanlike. The image of Olonga that endures – will always endure – is that of the political protestor at the 2003 World Cup; the man who sacrificed his playing career, and his safety, to take a stand against Robert Mugabe's regime by wearing a black armband to mourn "the death of democracy" in Zimbabwe. Forced to flee his home and, seven years later, still living in exile, Olonga might be expected to be serious, resigned, haunted even – anything but this bundle of energy wired to a non-depleting power source.

He lives in south-west London and is publishing his autobiography. At a time when ghosted works are rushed to the shelves before the subject has even finished living the story, it is interesting that it has taken Olonga so many years to commit his to print – he has turned down approaches in the past, feeling that he was "still very raw" and unsure that he had lived enough to merit an entire book.

Olonga's father John and older brother Victor still live in Zimbabwe. Olonga says he misses "certain aspects – friends, the lifestyle, the climate, the friendliness of the people", but he does not say it as if he is desperate to go back any time soon. You wonder, of course, if he would be allowed to return – and what would happen to him if he did. "I can't answer that," he says, sounding serious for the first time. "I just don't know what would happen. It's possible there would be no problem. But while Robert Mugabe is still the premier it's wise for me to say I consider it unsafe."

"I came here with nothing," he says, "but in a short amount of time I was shown a tremendous amount of kindness. There were total strangers who wanted to help me settle down – some sent £50, or £100, saying 'Welcome to England'." David Folb, Lashings' gregarious impresario, welcomed him into his home for the first two years of his stay and signed him up to play for his roving all-stars.

Despite all that has happened to him since, Olonga says Zimbabwe was a great place to grow up. "The opportunities I

66 We were able to put our differences aside and stand up for the common good 99

had were extraordinary," he says, "for a young black man in a country that only 20 years earlier had had segregation." After his parents split up, he grew up with his father, a Kenyan doctor, on an acre in Bulawayo, a middle-class family.

He attended a state school that offered extra-curricular activities from Gilbert and Sullivan to a toast-making club. He "made the most of everything it offered", including its excellent sports coaching; in his teens he was running 100m in 10.6sec and reaching 7.35m in the long jump. Then he switched his attention to cricket, where his speed lent itself to seriously fast, if wild, bowling. By 17 he was being touted as a future Zimbabwean quick – and as the country's first black player.

In the end that title brought as much heartache as honour. As Olonga admits, he was a fairly average bowler and his eight years playing for Zimbabwe were made difficult through injury, inconsistent form and dressing-room tension over the cricket union's racial policies, including quotas.

He rarely sees Flower now. If you thought risking life and limb together was the basis of an undying friendship, you would be wrong. Olonga has said they used not to get on and their working relationship in the team was civil but cool. Then he changes tone. "He's a legend. I'm a guy who couldn't get in the side. I'm never going to be remembered for my cricket. We were able to put our differences aside to stand up for the common good and there's a lesson in that."

In the aftermath of the black armband affair Olonga was a vocal, and influential, supporter of the removal of sporting links with Zimbabwe, both in England and in New Zealand, where the Green Party flew him out to join their (ultimately successful) campaign to stop the Black Caps' 2005 tour. One wonders how much Olonga's life has become defined by that one gesture. How has it and its consequences changed him as a person? He refers me to the final chapter of his book: "The way it has played out, I find myself pinching myself, saying, 'Did I really do that?'" ◪ *The Wisden Cricketer, August 2010*

Emma John is a former deputy editor of *The Wisden Cricketer*

Big impact: bowling against England at Harare

In Auckland: protest at NZ's tour to Zimbabwe

THE YEAR

W henever an Ashes tour is on the horizon the preceding summer is stuffed with speculation about the make-up of the squad, every game is an indicator to 'that first morning in Brisbane' and each performance comes under extra scrutiny. Can he do that with a Kookaburra ball? Will he cope with the extra bounce? Finally, the talking is over, the squad is selected and, by the end of November, we will know how the next chapter in the wonderful Ashes story begins. England travel with more than hope – this is a real chance to beat an unsettled Australian side. But they thought that the last time round ...

But 2010-11 is not all about the Ashes. It is also a World Cup year in Bangladesh, India and Sri Lanka. The last World Cup in the Caribbean was a depressing shambles – low crowd numbers due to administrative stupidity and a dominant Australia made for a forgettable six weeks. As long as the ICC has learned its lesson (and the bloated schedule suggests not) this Asian World Cup could be an event to savour due to the passion of the locals and an England team that seems equipped to challenge for the trophy.

After a tough home summer – with too many off-field distractions – the winter's big events cannot come soon enough. **Ⰱ**

Edward Craig is deputy editor of *The Wisden Cricketer*

Contents

AHEAD

Ashes fixtures (Complete World Cup fixtures on pages 144-145)

Nov 5-7 **Western Aus v Eng XI** Perth	Nov 25-29 **1st Test** Brisbane	Jan 16 **1st ODI** ♀ Melbourne
Nov 11-13 **South Aus v Eng XI** Adelaide	Dec 3-7 **2nd Test** Adelaide	Jan 21 **2nd ODI** ♀ Hobart
Nov 17-20 **Aus A v Eng XI** Hobart	Dec 16-20 **3rd Test** Perth	Jan 23 **3rd ODI** ♀ Sydney
Dec 10-12 **Victoria v England XI** Melbourne	Dec 26-30 **4th Test** Melbourne	Jan 26 **4th ODI** ♀ Adelaide
Jan 10 **PM's XI v England XI** Canberra	Jan 3-7 **5th Test** Sydney	Jan 30 **5th ODI** ♀ Brisbane
	Jan 12 **1st T20I** ♀ Adelaide	Feb 2 **6th ODI** ♀ Sydney
	Jan 14 **2nd T20I** ♀ Melbourne	Feb 6 **7th ODI** ♀ Perth

I'M EXPERIMENTING WITH A RED SNOWBALL

January 2010: MCC tries out different coloured balls **above** The glorious winter ahead **left** England as Ashes winners and Australia the defending world champions

Case for the defence

Though the Ashes was six months away, *TWC* got together a panel of pundits to pick the side for the first Test at Brisbane. Hindsight is a cruel weapon ... but how did they get on?

England's side for the first Ashes Test in Brisbane is decided through the summer. Touring Australia requires a particular type of player, mentally and physically. Tall, fast bowlers do well, finger spinners less so. The crowds and press are fiercely partisan, the heat unforgiving. England have merely to draw the series to retain the Ashes but only once since Mike Gatting's victory in 1986-87 have they got within a single Test of Australia away from home. Their last 26 Tests on Australian soil make grisly reading: won three, lost 18. We asked 14 of the country's leading journalists and broadcasters to pick their XI for that first Test, the reasons for their selection and how they would see their choices affecting England's strategy over the summer's Tests. ⚡ *The Wisden Cricketer, June 2010*

Balance – Five bowlers or four?
Scyld Berry *Wisden* **editor. ASHES XI: Andrew Strauss, Alastair Cook, Kevin Pietersen, Paul Collingwood, Ian Bell, Matt Prior, Tim Bresnan, Graeme Swann, Stuart Broad, James Anderson, Steven Finn** England need five bowlers if they are to win two Tests in Australia, the minimum.

Andrew Miller UK editor, Cricinfo.com. ASHES XI: Strauss, Cook, Pietersen, Collingwood, Bell, Prior, Bresnan, Broad, Swann, Anderson, Finn Six batsmen is a risk against Australia but equally a statement – and there's little to fear about the post-Warne and McGrath attack.

Bob Willis 90 Tests for England, Sky Sports commentator. ASHES XI: Strauss, Cook, Pietersen, Collingwood, Bell, Prior, Bresnan, Swann, Broad, Anderson, Finn I believe we need five bowlers for balance, so no Jonathan Trott. The batting line-up picks itself having been well set for quite a while now.

Mike Selvey 3 Tests for England, *Guardian* cricket correspondent. ASHES XI: Strauss, Cook, Pietersen, Collingwood, Bell, Ravi Bopara, Prior, Broad, Swann, Graham Onions, Anderson I am happier with Prior at seven because he is not a Test match No.6, so just the four bowlers for Brisbane.

Steve James 2 Tests for England, *Sunday Telegraph* cricket writer. ASHES XI: Strauss, Cook, Bell, Pietersen, Collingwood, Eoin Morgan, Prior, Broad, Swann, Anderson, Onions The bowlers pick themselves: they are simply the best available.

Paul Newman *Daily Mail* cricket correspondent. ASHES XI: Strauss, Cook, Pietersen, Collingwood, Bell, Prior, Bresnan, Broad, Swann, Finn, Anderson We have to go with a five-man attack to have any chance of taking 20 Australian wickets.

Stephen Brenkley *Independent* cricket correspondent. ASHES XI: Strauss, Cook, Pietersen, Bell, Collingwood, Prior, Broad, Swann, Anderson, Onions, Finn If England think they can win with a four-man attack, they should think again. If there is a risk in batting Prior at six – and it should be Prior – then the alternative smacks of fear and would lead to defeat.

John Etheridge *The Sun* cricket correspondent. ASHES XI: Strauss, Cook, Bell, Pietersen, Collingwood, Prior, Bresnan, Swann, Broad, Anderson, Finn England used five bowlers in their Ashes triumphs of 2005 and 2009 and that is the way to go again, even though Flintoff has departed.

Vic Marks **6 Tests for England,** *Observer* cricket correspondent. ASHES XI: Strauss, Cook, Trott, Pietersen, Collingwood, Bell, Prior, Broad, Swann, Anderson, Finn No mucking about for the first Test of the Ashes series, no gung-ho, armchair selection of lots of bowlers. Give nothing.

Simon Wilde *Sunday Times* cricket correspondent, ASHES XI: Strauss, Cook, Bell, Pietersen, Collingwood, Morgan, Prior, Broad, Swann, Anderson, Finn As holders of the Ashes England should be looking to bat deep. Six specialist batsmen to begin with, though there may be occasions when five bowlers might be preferred.
The verdict 5-man 7 (out of 14) 4-man 7

Tim Bresnan – The coming man?
Willis: He performed very well on the flat tracks of Bangladesh and doesn't seem to have injury problems. He'd be in my team.

Berry: This summer Bresnan has to show he is capable of making a Test hundred, as he almost did in Dhaka.

Christopher Martin-Jenkins *Test Match Special* commentator. ASHES XI: Strauss, Cook, Trott, Pietersen, Collingwood, Bell, Prior, Bresnan, Swann, Broad, Anderson Whether Bresnan gets in ahead of Onions or Finn will depend on form in the three first-class games before Brisbane.

Selvey: I have been increasingly impressed with Bresnan's honest bowling, which is putting pressure on Broad.

Newman: I have been pleasantly surprised by his progress. He has to play in every Test this summer to gain experience.

Wilde: This is a big summer for Broad. He needs to develop with ball and especially bat. If not, then Bresnan, much under-rated, might demand inclusion. If Australia can pick Peter Siddle, England can pick Bresnan.
The verdict Bres Yes 6 Bres No 8

Batting – Is Trott yesterday's man?
Miller: Pietersen's promotion to No.3 is overdue, Collingwood scored his Adelaide double-hundred at No.4 and Bell's serenity in the middle order is now accepted fact.

CMJ: Trott and Bresnan are the two marginal choices but, if Trott recovers from his disappointing winter, there will be some psychological merit (both ways) to be gained from the hundred he scored in the last Test he played against Australia.

Selvey: I have real doubts about Trott, particularly the manner in which the South Africans destroyed him mentally. We could see the return of Ravi Bopara or even a call-up for young James Taylor.

James: I'm just not sure about Trott. Bell can cope at first drop and he does, after all, bat above Trott at Warwickshire. Eoin Morgan still has much to prove but surely the fearlessness and power demonstrated in the international one-day game can be transferred to Tests.

Newman: Pietersen should be at three as he is our best batsman and Bell has always been better at five or six.

Kevin Mitchell *TWC* columnist. ASHES XI: Strauss, Cook, Pietersen, Rob Key, Collingwood, Morgan, James Foster (wk), Swann, Broad, Anderson, Onions Key brings more smiles and nous than Trott.

Derek Pringle 30 Tests for England. ASHES XI: Strauss, Cook, Bopara, Pietersen, Collingwood, Bell, Prior, Swann, Broad, Anderson, Finn Bopara will be a better player by November. In 2009 he became overawed against the Australians and lost confidence. He won't be subjugated so easily this time.

Wilde: I would like to see Morgan continue to develop. I'm confident he can translate his talent into the longer form. If not him, then Bopara – ahead of Trott, who I fear will fade from view.
The verdict: Trott hot 2 Trott not 12

The bowlers – Finn it to win it?
Miller: His height is essential. Anderson's swing will have its unplayable moments.

Willis: I hope Finn's progress is swift this summer as he is the only thing resembling a fast bowler that we have.

Etheridge: It is not too late for a wild card like Harmison to state his case.

Wilde: Finn is unlikely to last five Tests in 44 days but he could hurt Australia in Brisbane with his bounce and accuracy.

David Lloyd 9 Tests for England, Sky Sports commentator. ASHES XI: Strauss, Cook, Pietersen, Collingwood, Bell, Prior, Andrew Flintoff, Swann, Broad, Anderson, Finn I have gone for romance with Andrew Flintoff. Everything will need to go 300% his way health wise but the opposition would not want to see a fit and firing Fred.
The verdict Finn Yes 10 Finn No 4

Unity: Anderson and Broad selected by all 14

How expert

is an expert?

Andrew Miller takes a look at *TWC*'s early-season selections and makes a few changes …

Punditry is a mug's game. Just ask Derek Pringle, the former England allrounder who might well have been bigger than Andrew Flintoff in every sense but for an lbw against Javed Miandad that went begging in the final of the 1992 World Cup. At the end of England's summer and during the one-day series against Pakistan he featured in a television discussion in which he was asked to name his squad for the 2011 event. With Darren Gough and Alec Stewart egging him on, Pringle controversially omitted the captain, Andrew Strauss, who – as fate would have it – embarked on a brilliant match-winning hundred in a one-dayer at Headingley minutes after the debate was aired.

It is not a good omen for the 14 wise men – Pringle included and myself as well – who were rounded up by *TWC* back in May and asked to predict their starting XI for the first Ashes Test at Brisbane in November. At the time England were basking in the glory of their World Twenty20 triumph; their home Test campaigns against Bangladesh and Pakistan had yet to take place. Australia in midwinter seemed a long way off.

Still, to give credit where it is due and to get the good news in at the top of the tale there was at least some consistency on display from the press-box selectors. The 14 pundits opted for 18 names between them (with a further four mentions in dispatches), which is only a handful more than Geoff Miller and his chums named in late September.

What is more, seven of the starting line-up were inked in as one, including four of the top five in Andrew Strauss, Alastair Cook, Kevin Pietersen and Paul Collingwood. However, such stunning

unanimity had less to do with great minds thinking alike and more to do with a meek acceptance of selectorial fact.

Being diligent professionals who would not have just scribbled down 11 random names on the back of a taxi receipt, the pundits would have known that times have moved on since the 1989 Ashes, when 29 players were served up in the course of six Tests by a band of blazer-wearers who really did choose their squads from the bottom of a gin bottle.

These days continuity is the watchword, which happens to take some of the fun out of the exercise, but never mind. At least *The Observer*'s Kevin Mitchell kept things interesting by plumping for James Foster and Rob Key. Perhaps, given how much time he spends ring-side, he would have been better off with James DeGale and Robert Guerrero. As for David 'Bumble' Lloyd, while his love of a Lancastrian is never to be under-estimated, he would have been better off calling up Lanky the Giraffe after his victory in the Twenty20 mascots race than the man he eventually chose as his wild card: Andrew Flintoff.

But I digress. Barring injury and pre-ordained rest periods, the four dead-cert batsmen have been near constant picks for England in 58 Tests dating back to May 2006*. Momentary hiatuses occurred when Strauss was dropped for the tour of Sri Lanka in 2007-08 and when Collingwood briefly made way at Headingley later that summer but that is the sum of the shuffling. Had the Pope declared, on arrival in Glasgow for his UK visit, that he was not a Catholic after all, it would surely have been less of a shock than the omission of any of that quartet.

Graeme Swann, England's greatest spin bowler since Peter Such, was also a 100% inclusion, as was Stuart Broad, whose heroics at The Oval last summer ensured the return of the urn. But perhaps a touch surprisingly Jimmy Anderson also picked up a full set of votes despite an average of 82.60 on the last trip to Australia and despite no end of navel-gazing about his lack of effectiveness when the ball does not swing.

Part of that faith in Anderson, one senses, comes down to the balance of the side – and it is in this respect that the pundits and professional selectors at last diverge. England's clear preference is for six out-and-out batsmen, a four-man attack and Matt Prior at No 7 to balance the books. But the lure of that extra bowler is too much for gamblers in the press. No fewer than five, myself included, believed you could balance the side with Tim Bresnan at No.7 – a fanciful notion in hindsight. Four wasted votes on the hapless Graham Onions. And as for Jonathan Trott, the man with a century in his solitary Ashes appearance and more than 1,000 runs in the 2010 international summer, his credentials at No.3 were trumpeted by a grand total of two.

So the final word belongs to Vic Marks of *The Observer*, the man whose chosen 11 is the envy of every man on the panel who wishes he could now start this progress from scratch. "No mucking about for the first Test of the Ashes series, no gung-ho, armchair selection of lots of bowlers. Give them nothing," he implored. Quite so. Too bad that at the end of the summer he was too busy weeping for Somerset's lost Championship to savour his moment of triumph. ◪

*Cook missed last Test in India March 2006; otherwise it is 61 Tests

Andrew Miller is UK editor of Cricinfo.com

World Cup countdown

Patrick Kidd looks ahead to 2011's big event and assesses each team's strengths and weaknesses

The World Cup returns to Asia a bloated and potentially broken tournament. In its 10th version 42 matches will be played to whittle down the field of 14 to eight, which will test the patience of most supporters but offer opportunities for bookmakers to cash in, and the final will be more than seven weeks after the opening game. It is a shame that the ICC has not learnt from the success of the World Twenty20 that short and sweet works. The relocation for security reasons of 14 matches due to be held in Pakistan will cast a pall over the troubled country.

But the two previous World Cups in Asia were successful and there is no reason why this one cannot work. An opening fixture in Dhaka between Bangladesh and India will be noisy and perhaps – just perhaps – could provide a thrilling start that gives energy to the whole tournament. ▟

Major minnows: left to right Canada's Bagai; Ireland's Stirling; Kenya's Obuya; Zimbabwe's Price

Australia

Strengths Vast, vast experience. They will be going for their fourth consecutive title.
Weaknesses Have struggled to keep bowlers fit and Asia is no place to be carrying niggles.
Star player Ryan Harris: he'll be 32, so he's no spring chicken, but he has pace, variety, strike-power and, perhaps most crucially, hunger.
Watch out for Will this be Ricky Ponting's farewell to international cricket?

Bangladesh

Strengths Fearlessness and the advantage of playing all their group matches at home.
Weaknesses A tendency to get carried away and lose matches with a few rash shots or indiscipline in the field.
Star player Tamim Iqbal: explosive batsman who can exploit the powerplays to put opponents on the back foot early.
Watch out for the crowd support if tickets are priced sensibly, unlike in the last World Cup.

Canada

Strengths Cruised through the qualifying tournament.

Weaknesses Infighting within the Canadian administration and the hint that the players have gone off the boil since qualifying.

Star player Ashish Bagai: the captain, wicketkeeper and leading batsman.

Watch out for whether John Davison, their 40-year-old Australian-born batsman who hit the fastest World Cup hundred in 2003, still has it.

England

Strengths The confidence that they gained from winning their first global title in the 2010 World Twenty20.

Weaknesses Do they have the upper-order firepower to get the best out of the powerplays?

Star player Kevin Pietersen: dropped in 2010, he will be motivated to prove his worth.

Watch out for Andrew Strauss proving his doubters wrong. Some say he should not be captaining England in one-day cricket but he was their best batsman in that format in 2010.

India

Strengths A batting line-up that is the envy of the rest of the tournament and the knowledge of how to score quickly in these conditions.

Weaknesses A tendency to self-destruct and an unhealthy fixation on Twenty20.

Star player Virender Sehwag: averages 45 over the past three years in ODIs, a real game-changer.

Watch out for the emergence of the next generation. Tendulkar, Sehwag and Dravid have to retire some time: are Virat Kohli, Suresh Raina and Rohit Sharma ready to step up?

Ireland

Strengths Lots of happy memories from the 2007 World Cup to draw on. They remain the most threatening of the minnows.

Weaknesses Not the fiercest bowling attack. Trent Johnston may again be the key wicket-taker with his accurate medium-pacers but he is now 36.

Star player Paul Stirling: just out of his teens and already turning heads.

Watch out for Johnston's "chicken dance", a celebration when he took wickets in 2007. Or does he have some new moves?

Kenya

Strengths Experience in World Cups, with a squad that includes a couple who even played in the 1996 tournament.

Weaknesses No form to speak of. They came last in the 2010 World Cricket League Div One.

Star player Collins Obuya: once a legspinning allrounder, he collapsed as a bowler but remains a reliable batsman and a very fine fielder.

Watch out for whether Maurice Odumbe returns at the age of 41. The man who helped to steer Kenya to the 2003 semi-finals was banned for five years for involvement with bookmakers but has been aggressively lobbying for a recall.

Netherlands

Strengths They know how to beat the big teams: England lost to them in the 2009 World Twenty20 and they beat Bangladesh in a rain-reduced ODI in 2010.

Weaknesses Fairly toothless attack in 50 overs and had the worst record in this summer's county 40-over competition.

Star player Ryan ten Doeschate: a genuinely world-class allrounder and fabulous fielder.

Watch out for Bas Zuiderent, who first appeared in the World Cup in 1996.

New Zealand

Strengths This is the form of the game they excel in, with a team full of bits-and-pieces players that offers lots of options.

Weaknesses Yet to go the distance in a World Cup. Do they *believe* they can win?

Star player Daniel Vettori: his batting has matured as he has got older (though he is still only 31) and he remains the key wicket-taker as well as a respected captain.

Watch out for Jesse Ryder: fans of the unpredictable (on and off the field) will be hoping he is selected.

Pakistan

Strengths Brilliantly, beautifully mercurial. When in the right mood they can snatch victories from nowhere. Sadly they can also snatch defeats.

Weaknesses With everything that happened to them in 2010, will they be mentally ready to play?

Star player Umar Gul: a master at reverse swing and capable of turning matches with one inspired spell.

Watch out for suspicious betting patterns and ludicrously overstepped no-balls.

South Africa

Strengths A 1st XI cluttered with class, especially among the batsmen, and experience of Indian conditions through the IPL.

Weaknesses Choking. Their failure to last the course is as bad as that of the New Zealand rugby team.

Star player AB de Villiers: the world's best one-day batsman.

Watch out for Wayne Parnell: a star of the 2009 World Twenty20 and Champions Trophy, he struggled with injury in 2010.

Sri Lanka

Strengths Twenty20 firebrands who are able to adapt to the longer game. Strong spin attack.

Weaknesses The majestic Lasith Malinga aside, their fast bowlers are unthreatening.

Star player Tillakaratne Dilshan: a creative genius, able to find places to score runs all round the ground.

Watch out for a possible farewell from international cricket for Muttiah Muralitharan.

West Indies

Strengths Ottis Gibson showed with England that he has the makings of a fine coach. Plenty of bowling attack options.

Weaknesses Uncertainty over their best XI and a tendency to be over-casual in the field.

Star player Chris Gayle: question marks over his captaincy but no one is a surer bet to make an ODI hundred in this team.

Watch out for Kieron Pollard: no Test cricketer but does he have the patience to turn his undeniable Twenty20 talent into a strength in the 50-over game?

Zimbabwe

Strengths Gradually developing a proper structure for discovering and developing talent.

Weaknesses This World Cup may be a couple of years early for the young squad to have fully matured.

Star player Ray Price: he's 34 and doesn't really spin the ball much but Price takes lots of wickets through guile and (not sure how) became the world No.3 bowler in 2010.

Watch out for Elton Chigumbura, the well-respected captain who could raise the international reputation of his country.

Patrick Kidd writes for *The Times*

WORLD CUP

Saturday February 19
GB | **India v Bangladesh** Dhaka ●

Sunday February 20
GA | **Kenya v New Zealand** Chennai
GA | **Sri Lanka v Canada** Hambanthota ●

Monday February 21
GA | **Australia v Zimbabwe** Ahmedabad ●

Tuesday February 22
GB | **England v Netherlands** Nagpur ●

Wednesday February 23
GA | **Kenya v Pakistan** Hambanthota ●

Thursday February 24
GB | **South Africa v West Indies** Delhi ●

Friday February 25
GB | **Bangladesh v Ireland** Dhaka
GA | **Australia v New Zealand** Nagpur ●

Saturday February 26
GA | **Sri Lanka v Pakistan** Colombo ●

Sunday February 27
GB | **India v England** Kolkata ●

Monday February 28
GA | **Canada v Zimbabwe** Nagpur
GB | **Netherlands v West Indies** Delhi ●

Tuesday March 1
GA | **Sri Lanka v Kenya** Colombo ●

Wednesday March 2
GB | **England v Ireland** Bangalore ●

Thursday March 3
GB | **Netherlands v South Africa** Mohali
GA | **Canada v Pakistan** Colombo ●

Friday March 4
GA | **New Zealand v Zimbabwe** Ah'bad
GB | **Bangladesh v West Indies** Dhaka ●

Saturday March 5
GA | **Sri Lanka v Australia** Colombo ●

Sunday March 6
GB | **England v South Africa** Chennai
GB | **India v Ireland** Bangalore ●

Monday March 7
GA | **Canada v Kenya** Delhi ●

Tuesday March 8
GA | **New Zealand v Pakistan** Kandy ●

Wednesday March 9
GB | **India v Netherlands** Delhi ●

Thursday March 10
GA | **Sri Lanka v Zimbabwe** Kandy ●

Friday March 11
GB | **Ireland v West Indies** Mohali
GB | **Bangladesh v England** Chittagong ●

Saturday March 12
GB | **India v South Africa** Nagpur ●

Sunday March 13
GA | **Canada v New Zealand** Mumbai
GA | **Australia v Kenya** Bangalore ●

Monday March 14
GB | **Bangladesh v Netherlands** Chit'g
GA | **Pakistan v Zimbabwe** Kandy ●

Tuesday March 15
GB | **Ireland v South Africa** Kolkata ●

Wednesday March 16
GA | **Australia v Canada** Bangalore ●

Thursday March 17
GB | **England v West Indies** Chennai ●

Friday March 18
GB | **Ireland v Netherlands** Kolkata
GA | **New Zealand v Sri Lanka** Mumbai ●

Saturday March 19
GB | **Bangladesh v South Africa** Dhaka
GA | **Australia v Pakistan** Colombo ●

Sunday March 20
GA | **Kenya v Zimbabwe** Kolkata
GB | **India v West Indies** Chennai ●

™

Wednesday March 23
Quarter-final – TBC v TBC Dhaka ●

Thursday March 24
Quarter-final – TBC v TBC Ah'bad ●

Friday March 25
Quarter-final – TBC v TBC Dhaka ●

Saturday March 26
Quarter-final – TBC v TBC Colombo ●

Tuesday March 29
Semi-final – TBC v TBC Colombo ●

Wednesday March 30
Semi-final – TBC v TBC Mohali ●

Saturday April 2
Final – TBC v TBC Mumbai ●

Group A	Group B
Australia	India
Pakistan	South Africa
New Zealand	England
Sri Lanka	West Indies
Zimbabwe	Bangladesh
Canada	Ireland
Kenya	Netherlands

Top trunks: Stumpy left and friend

Batting

Leading runscorer: **Sachin Tendulkar (I)**

1796 @ 57.93

Highest score: **Gary Kirsten (SA)** 188* v UAE at Rawalpindi, 1996 right

Most fifties: **Sachin Tendulkar**

13

Most centuries: **Sourav Ganguly (I) below, Mark Waugh (A), Tendulkar, Ponting (A)** 4

Lowest team total: **Canada, 36 v Sri Lanka** at Paarl, 2003

Highest team total: **India, 413 for 5 v Bermuda** at Trinidad, 2007

Bowling

Most wickets: **Glenn McGrath**

71 @ 18.19

Best bowling: **Glenn McGrath (A) 7 for 15 v Namibia** at P'stroom, 2003

Most five wickets in an innings: **Gary Gilmour (A), Vasbert Drakes (WI), Ashantha de Mel (SL), McGrath** 2

Most four wickets in an innings: **Shane Warne (A)**

4

Hat-tricks
Chetan Sharma (I) v NZ at Nagpur, 1987
Saqlain Mushtaq (P) v Zim at The Oval, 1999
Chaminda Vaas (SL) v Bang at Pie'burg, 2003
Brett Lee (A) v Ken at Durban, 2003
Lasith Malinga (SL) below v SA at G'town, '07

Keeping

Most dismissals: **Adam Gilchrist**

52

Most dismissals in an innings: 6, **Gilchrist** below v Namibia at Potchefstroom, 2003

Most dismissals in a tournament: 21, **Gilchrist (A)**, World Cup 2003

Fielding

Most catches: **Ricky Ponting**

25

Most catches in an innings: 4, **Mohammed Kaif (I)** v SL at J'burg, 2003

Most catches in a tournament: 11, **Ricky Ponting left**, World Cup 2003